WHAT'S *REALLY* WRONG WITH THE MIDDLE EAST

Brian Whitaker

What's *Really* Wrong with the Middle East

SAQI

ISBN 978-0-86356-624-0

First published by Saqi, 2009

A full CIP record for this book is available from the British Library.
A full CIP record for this book is available from the Library of Congress.

Printed and bound by CPI Mackays, Chatham, ME5 8TD

SAQI

26 Westbourne Grove, London W2 5RH
2398 Doswell Avenue, Saint Paul, Minnesota, 55108
Verdun, Beirut, Lebanon
www.saqibooks.com

Contents

Acknowledgments

My thanks, in alphabetical order, to those who found time to talk to me specifically for this book: Mahmoud Alhourani, Hossam Bahgat, Kholoud Bidak, Aida Saif al-Dawla, Khaled Diab, Gamal Eid, Kareem Elbayar, Magda Abu Fadil, Hossam el-Hamalawy, Nadim Houry, Ghada Kabesh, Amina Khairy, Jamal Khatib, Ghassan Makarem, Karim Makdisi, Nesrine Malik, Jehad al-Omari, Salam Pax, Basem Sakijha, Abdellah Taia and Nasr Abu Zayd.

For reading early drafts and making helpful comments, I am particulary grateful to Khaled Diab, Nesrine Malik, Ann Elizabeth Mayer, David Shariatmadari and Martin Woollacott – plus, of course, my patient editor at Saqi Books, Anna Wilson.

***

Since the main object of this book is to stimulate debate, readers can find further discussion on the relevant section of my website, www.al-bab.com/whatsreallywrong. The footnotes are also available there in an online version which provides easy access to web pages mentioned in the text.

Introduction

THE PROBLEMS OF the Middle East are always someone else's fault. While the west blames dictators and extremists, Arabs often turn the tables, blaming centuries of foreign interference. Both sides are right, up to a point, but they both also ignore a large part of the picture.

In a region dominated by autocratic regimes that cling to power for decades and whose tentative steps towards reform are directed mainly at self-preservation, dictators certainly have much to answer for and western governments have often taken on the task of removing them (or at least those among them that seemed to threaten their own interests). Among the more recent and dramatic cases, this resulted in the Iraq Liberation Act of 1998 which made "regime change" in Baghdad official US policy – a policy that culminated five years later in a military invasion. But we have only to look at the mess that followed Saddam Hussein's overthrow to see the folly of pinning too many hopes on toppling tyrants: change in the Middle East is a lot more complicated than that.

Governments are products of the societies they govern and in Arab countries it is often society, as much as the government itself, that stands in the way of progress. In Kuwait, for instance, it was not the hereditary Emir who resisted granting votes to women but reactionary elements in the elected parliament – and there are plenty of similar examples.

"Social discrimination is the greatest of all ailments facing Arab societies today," Hussein Shobokshi, a board member of the Mecca Chamber of Commerce, observed during a TV debate. "It creates government in its own image but it also poisons the mentality for reform and definitely for democracy ... While governments have been introducing little windows of opportunity to reform, there has been great popular resistance against equality based on gender and race from the people."[1]

Khaled Diab, an Egyptian-born journalist, summed up the problem more pithily when he told me: "Egypt has a million Mubaraks." In other words, the Mubarak way of doing things is not confined to the country's president; it is found throughout Egyptian society, in business and even within families.

In order to understand what is really wrong with the Middle East we have to look beyond the regimes to society as a whole – and this instantly shifts our perspective. The problem is no longer a simplistic one of good versus evil, or tyrants versus the rest. Instead, we see people who are not only oppressed and denied rights by their rulers but who also, to varying degrees, are participants in a system of oppression and denial of rights. Thus, the oppressed often become oppressors themselves, victims become victimisers too, and acknowledging that fact is the first step towards a solution.

It scarcely needs to be said that this situation did not develop in a vacuum. There are historical reasons – which brings us to what is sometimes called "the Arab malaise". Samir Kassir, the Lebanese journalist assassinated by a car bomb in 2005, described it thus:

> The Arab people are haunted by a sense of powerlessness; permanently inflamed, it is the badge of their malaise. Powerlessness to be what you think you should be. Powerlessness to act to affirm your existence, even merely theoretically, in the face of the Other who denies your right to exist, despises you and has once again reasserted his domination over you. Powerlessness to suppress the feeling that

you are no more than a lowly pawn on the global chessboard even as the game is being played in your backyard.[2]

There is no doubt that the Arabs' recent history, from the territorial carve-up after the first world war, through the *nakba* – "catastrophe"[3] – of 1948 and numerous wars involving foreign powers, either directly or by proxy, has left a deep mark. If positive change is to come, however, the overhanging cloud of fatalism and resignation needs to be blown away. To be aware of the past obviously has value when considering the present. But to analyse the past endlessly and blame the Other (often with good reason), as Arabs tend to do, merely reinforces the sense of powerlessness and adds to the malaise rather than addressing it. If Arabs are ever to take charge of their predicament they must stop asking "How did we get here?" and instead say: "This is where we are. How can we move forward?"

No one can deny that people in the Arab countries lack many basic rights and freedoms. Nor can anyone deny that democracy – to the limited extent that it is practised there – is seriously deficient, allowing autocratic regimes to survive without much risk of being removed by the people they govern. At the same time, though, it is a mistake to characterise the Middle East as some kind of latter-day Soviet Union (as the Bush administration tended to do), or to equate freedom with democracy (again, as President Bush often did, using the words almost interchangeably). Freedom and democracy are not unrelated, but nor are they one and the same.

Attractive as it may seem, removing autocratic regimes and holding free elections is not a panacea for the region's ills. This is not to suggest that democratisation is unimportant or that Arab countries should not be encouraged to hold elections and let people express their views freely whenever elections are held, but until the right conditions exist for democracy to take root and flourish we cannot expect democratisation to achieve much by itself. The fate of post-Saddam Iraq is evidence enough of that.

But if the Middle East is not the new Soviet Union, with Islam cast as the new Communism, and free elections are not the all-embracing cure, what exactly *is* the problem? The "freedom deficit", as it is sometimes known, would certainly loom large in any answer, though we also have to ask what sort of freedom. It is not just a matter of applying the "town square test" adopted by the former US Secretary of State, Condoleezza Rice:

> If a person cannot walk into the middle of the town square and express his or her views without fear of arrest, imprisonment, or physical harm, then that person is living in a fear society, not a free society.[4]

The town square test is meant to provide a simple yes-or-no way of distinguishing between "fear" societies and "free" societies but it is of limited usefulness: no Arab country today fits totally into either category. People are still imprisoned from time to time for expressing their views; there are still many taboos and red lines – and yet an increasingly wide range of opinions can be found in print, on television and on the internet. Focusing on freedom in this narrow sense also obscures other denials of liberty which may be less dramatic than dragging people off to jail and torturing them but are actually far more important in terms of the numbers affected and their ultimate consequences.

Put simply, the Arab "freedom deficit" results in a stultifying atmosphere where change, innovation, creativity, critical thinking, questioning, problem-solving, and virtually any kind of nonconformity are all discouraged if not necessarily punished. Along with that, there are systematic denials of rights that impinge on the lives of millions:

discrimination based on ethnicity, religion, gender, sexuality or family background; inequality of opportunity, impenetrable bureaucracies, arbitrary application of the law; and the lack of transparency in government – to mention just a few.

MY AIM IN writing this book is to contribute to two separate but related debates. One is the debate among Arabs themselves, about change – a debate that many in the west are still largely unaware of, and one which is still heavily circumscribed within the region by a variety of constraints and taboos. As an outsider, less troubled by those constraints, I hope to push it a little further by focusing on some issues that Arabs often feel uncomfortable about discussing.

The other debate concerns western policy towards the Middle East. At the time of writing, with a new president installed in the White House, many are hoping for a more constructive and less confrontational approach. That would certainly be welcome, but high expectations can also be dangerous. Just as foreign meddling has provided a reason – and sometimes an excuse – for Arabs not to take responsibility for their destiny, relying on Obama to deliver is no way to bolster their self-reliance.

It is not the purpose of this book to suggest what western policy should be, but to set out the "Middle East problem" in terms that go beyond common perceptions of the region. In doing so, I have sought to focus on actual concerns expressed by Arabs (patriarchy, tribalism, corruption, inequality, globalisation, etc) rather than the concerns of western governments. The conclusions that I draw about these are, obviously, my own but I have tried as far as possible to let Arabs provide the narrative – a narrative that comes partly from my encounters as a traveller interested in the Middle East and later as a journalist reporting on it for the *Guardian* newspaper; partly from written sources; and also from a series of lengthy interviews conducted specially for this book. For the interviews, I chose to avoid politicians and government officials as well as those among their critics who tend to be regular pit-stops for western journalists. I was looking for intelligent, independent-minded people who have formed their own opinion about what is wrong. They include writers, academics, bloggers, journalists, psychiatrists and various kinds of activists, from a range of Arab countries. Clearly, they are not a representative sample of Arab opinion as a whole, nor are they meant to be: quite the reverse, since they are all critical in some way of orthodoxy and the status quo. But by listening to their concerns we can see where Arab debate is heading.

Besides trying to avoid over-simplification and over-generalisation, one of the difficulties when writing a book such as this is keeping it to manageable proportions. As readers may have gathered by now, I have limited the discussion here to the Arab countries, which make up the vast bulk of the Middle East, though not the whole of it. Non-Arab Iran is similar in some ways to the Arab countries but there are also significant differences that would have made the project unwieldy. These considerations also apply to Israel. The Arab-Israeli conflict is a festering sore and, plainly, one of the region's major problems but, considering how much has been said and written about that already, I decided to set it to one side and concentrate on issues that deserve far more attention than they presently get. There is little doubt, however, that an equitable settlement of that conflict would transform the political atmosphere and greatly improve the prospects for progress and reform throughout the region.

One further note by way of introduction. My previous book, *Unspeakable Love,* investigated the problems faced by gay and lesbian people in the Middle East, and at first glance this book may suggest a rather startling change of direction. Despite the very different subject matter, I hope this will be regarded as a natural sequel. *Unspeakable Love* was not primarily a book about sex, nor even a "gay book" in the usual sense. As I pointed out at the time, it is impossible to address sexual rights in the Middle East in isolation, without also confronting a host of other issues relating to social, cultural, religious and political reform. Essentially, both books are about freedom and the obstacles to achieving it, and if the aim of *Unspeakable Love* was to look at one aspect of freedom through the lens of a microscope, the aim of this book is to present the bigger picture.

Brian Whitaker
February, 2009

1   Thinking inside the box

MOUNIR IS IN his second year studying law at Cairo University. Well, not exactly *at* the university. With 9,000 students in his class, there isn't room for them all. "The majority of students are basically like me – people who don't attend," he said. "We just show up for the exams and in four years we graduate. Then we get automatic membership of the Bar Association and become practising lawyers." Mounir doesn't bother much with textbooks, either. He explained:

> The textbook is usually a manuscript written by the professor teaching the class. There are photocopy shops outside the university and they commission former graduates of the law school to summarise the textbook. That's what I buy, 20–30 pages at a time.
>
> The summary is usually a question-and-answer sheet. When there is a matter of controversy it lists the various opinions and then summarises the author's view. Over the years this has become known as "*ra'i al-duktoor*" – the doctor's opinion. There's a big highlighted section in a box – so clear that you can't miss it – titled "*Ra'i al-Duktoor*". This is what you need to memorise because this has to be your opinion too.
>
> I memorise these and then I go for the exam. Basically, you analyse all the previous years' exams and identify the main questions. Typically, you need to write the doctor's opinion as the correct one after reviewing the literature.[1]

Unlike Mounir, Khaled Diab did attend classes while studying economics in Egypt, and one of the things he learned was not to ask too many questions:

> There was an emphasis on making profuse notes when you attended lectures. You tried to get the professor's [exact] wording because you would be expected to regurgitate that in the exam and the closer you came to how the professor put it, the higher the grade you were likely to get. That's partly a practical thing because often the exams are marked by assistants who are told to look for certain keywords and so on, but it's also an issue of prestige and authoritarianism in the sense that professors expect you to act like a disciple – what they say is gospel.
>
> I would often question the professor's thinking in lectures and exam papers, and that hurt my grades.[2]

Education may not be the most obvious of the Middle East's problems, and yet in many ways it is central. As in other parts of the world, school, college and university, together with upbringing in the home, are key factors that shape the mindset of each new generation. Through these mechanisms the ideas and attitudes of elders – the accumulated baggage of past and present – are carried forward into the future. The way a society rears and educates its young thus provides a window on the society as a whole – its strengths and weaknesses – as well as pointers to how the bonds of the past might be broken. In the Middle East, more specifically, the dominant styles of education and child-rearing help to explain why autocratic regimes have proved so resilient and why so many people in the region submit passively to restrictions on their rights and freedoms that others would reject as intolerable. It is all very well to talk about promoting freedom and democracy in the Middle East, as the United States did constantly under President George W Bush, but while mindsets remain unchanged such hopes are just a mirage. Change – if it is to be meaningful – must begin in people's heads.

Education in the Arab countries is where the paternalism of the traditional family structure, the authoritarianism of the state and the dogmatism of religion all meet, discouraging critical thought and analysis, stifling creativity and instilling submissiveness. These problems begin in the home, the 2004 Arab Human Development Report observed:

> Studies indicate that the most widespread style of child rearing in Arab families is the authoritarian mode accompanied by the overprotective. This reduces children's independence, self-confidence and social efficiency, and fosters passive attitudes and hesitant decision-making skills. Most of all, it affects how the child thinks by suppressing questioning, exploration and initiative.[3]

Schooling continues this process, and reinforces it:

> Communication in education is didactic, supported by set books containing indisputable texts in which knowledge is objectified so as to hold incontestable facts, and by an examination process that only tests memorisation and factual recall.[4]

Curricula, teaching and evaluation methods, the AHDR noted, "do not permit free dialogue and active, exploratory learning and consequently do not open the doors to freedom of thought and criticism. On the contrary, they weaken the capacity to hold opposing viewpoints and to think outside the box. Their societal role focuses on the reproduction of control in Arab societies."[5]

The main classroom activities, according to a World Bank report, are copying from the blackboard, writing, and listening to the teachers. "Group work, creative thinking, and proactive learning are rare. Frontal teaching – with a teacher addressing the whole class – is still a dominant feature ... The individual needs of the students are not commonly addressed in the classroom. Rather, teachers teach to the whole class, and there is little consideration of individual differences in the teaching-learning process."[6] One investigation into the quality of schooling in the Middle East found students were taught to memorise and retain answers to "fairly fixed questions" with "little or no meaningful context", and that the system mainly rewarded those who were skilled at being passive knowledge recipients.[7] Although that study was published in 1995, the World Bank's 2008 report concluded that many of its criticisms still applied thirteen years later: "Higher-order cognitive skills such as flexibility, problem-solving, and judgment remain inadequately rewarded in schools".[8] Moreover, the few Arab countries that have recognised this deficiency and tried to introduce such skills as an educational objective have generally failed to change the classroom practices. Egypt, for example, tried sending teachers to Europe to learn modern teaching methods but when they returned to Egypt they quickly reverted to the old ways. [9]

If this makes young Arabs well-equipped for anything at all, it is how to survive in an authoritarian system: just memorise the teacher's words, regurgitate them as your own, avoid asking questions – and you'll stay out of trouble. In the same way, the suppression of their critical faculties turns some of them into gullible recipients for religious ideas that would collapse under serious scrutiny. But it ill-equips them for roles as active citizens and contributors to their countries' development.

Moroccan writer Abdellah Taia sums up the result in one word: detachment. Detachment or disengagement, not just from power and politics, but from the realities of daily life. "It's as if the things you study in school, in university are not real – just things you study," he said. "Maybe you discuss them with friends, but it's only discussion. I think Moroccans – and Arabs in general – are very detached from things that really matter.

"In Morocco we have this idea that we have to be proud of our country, of our religion, of our family, of our king, and if foreigners ask we tell them it's good. But at the same time it seems as if *we* are not Moroccan society – that society is something abstract. We are in it but we don't see that society *is us*, and that we can influence it or change it." He continued:

There was a woman in Mohammedia, near Casablanca, who had three daughters and was pregnant again. Her husband obliged her to have a test and when they found the baby was another girl, he said: 'You are a woman who gives birth only to girls, and I want a boy.' So he forced her to give him permission to marry another woman. Later that day the wife took her three daughters and they jumped on the railway line together and were killed by a train. All of them.

When I heard this story I was shocked and I knew what people would say: that she wasn't a Muslim any more and would go directly to hell because of her suicide.

Here was this woman resisting with the last weapon she had got, which was her body. She was already condemned by her husband and even her last cry, her act of resistance (because that is what it was), was again misunderstood. What she did reflected the ignorance, the machismo of the men, the paternalism – everything.

If something like that happened in France or Britain there would be a huge debate. Everyone would be concerned, the country would be questioning itself and asking: Why? But in Morocco it's "OK, well, she's going to hell and it's not our affair, and anyway we don't talk about death in our house because it brings bad luck."

This is what I mean by detachment. There is no real thinking about anything, it's just like... It's like when you make bread and the dough sticks to your fingers. For me, this is the right image for a lot of things in Morocco and the Arab world. It's sticky and we are stuck in it. We can't go back and we can't go forward.[10]

MASS EDUCATION IN Arab state-run schools developed mainly in the latter half of the twentieth century and generally had two main objectives: to combat illiteracy and inculcate a sense of national identity. Starting from a very low base, Arab countries have made considerable progress in developing literacy and the biggest gains have been in female education: women's literacy rates have trebled since 1970 and school enrolment rates for females have more than doubled.[11] Taking into account the resistance to female education from traditionalists in some countries, this is a noteworthy achievement. In 1970, for example, Saudi Arabia had only 135,000 female students – 25 per cent of the total – but by the turn of the century the numbers were almost equal – 2,405,000 males and 2,369,000 females. According to the kingdom's education ministry, "Promoting the concept of equal educational opportunities for the sexes posed a problem but one that was ameliorated by Islam's insistence on the importance of learning in general (Muslims are exhorted 'to seek knowledge from the cradle to the grave') and the high status accorded to women within Islamic society in particular." The first Saudi government school for girls was built in 1964 and by the end of the 1990s there were girls' schools in every part of the kingdom. In line with the Saudi policy of keeping the sexes apart, female education was administered separately until

2003 when it was incorporated into the normal functions of the education ministry.[12]

Overall in the Arab countries, adult literacy increased from around 40 per cent in 1980 to 62 per cent in the early 2000s and school enrolment reached 60 per cent. This is certainly progress but it nevertheless means that 65 million Arabs remain illiterate and around ten million children aged 6–15 are not attending school. Adult literacy is still significantly below the world average of 79 per cent, school enrolment is slightly below and the average time spent at school is 5.2 years in Arab countries, compared with 6.7 years worldwide. As might be expected, those most disadvantaged educationally are females and the poor, especially in rural areas.[13]

Besides promoting literacy, Arab states – in the words of the World Bank – "placed a high premium on forging a common heritage and understanding of citizenship, and used a certain reading of history, the instruction in a particular language, and the inclusion of religion in the education curriculum as a way of enhancing national identity".[14] These principles were applied in different ways, depending on the preoccupations of the regime. In Syria education provided an opportunity for the Ba'ath party to indoctrinate the masses with its ideology through schools, and the party also established an "institute of political science" at Damascus University, providing compulsory classes in political orientation.[15] In Saudi Arabia, according to the Basic Law (constitution) of 1992, education aims at "instilling the Islamic faith in the younger generation, providing its members with knowledge and skills and preparing them to become useful members in the building of their society, members who love their homeland and are proud of its history."[16] Inevitably, these considerations have their impact on school curricula:

When it comes to the sciences, content is not usually a

controversial matter, save for some themes that are perceived to touch on religious beliefs such as the theory of evolution or on social taboos, such as sex education. But the humanities and social sciences that have a direct relevance to people's ideas and convictions are supervised or protected by the authorities in charge of designing curricula and issuing schoolbooks.

Consequently, such subjects usually laud past achievements and generally indulge in both self-praise and blame of others, with the aim of instilling loyalty, obedience and support for the regime in power. It is not unusual to find schoolbooks in many Arab countries with a picture of the ruler on the front page, even in the case of textbooks in neutral subjects such as science and mathematics.[17]

"Some researchers argue," the AHDR noted, "that the curricula taught in Arab countries seem to encourage submission, obedience, subordination and compliance, rather than free critical thinking." The same can be said of teachers who adhere slavishly to the official textbook, in some cases even when it is wrong or allows only one answer to a question when other answers are equally valid. One researcher visiting a Moroccan primary school found children being taught that $4 \times 3 = 11$ because of a misprint in the textbook. The teacher had previously taught that the answer was 12 but, since the new book was issued, he felt it best to follow the approved text.[18] That may be an extreme case but blogger/activist Hossam Hamalawy found similar rigidity at his school in Cairo: "In the chemistry exam a student wrote a formula that was right but he was crossed out because this was not what the government textbook said. You could get the same compound by two formulas."

"At school," Hamalawy continued, "you memorise everything, even literary critique. When you are given a piece of poetry, you study the points of strength and the points of weakness. You don't move your brain, you don't use anything – you just memorise what the government textbook tells you." [19]

Rote learning clearly has a place – for example, memorising vocabulary in a foreign language – but in Arab educational systems it dominates to the exclusion of understanding, analytical thought, problem-solving and so on. This approach reflects the authoritarian tendencies of Arab society, as well as the desire of the regimes not to be subjected to critical scrutiny. Historically, the attachment to memorising probably lies in the traditional religious education system that preceded state-run schooling, described here in connection with Saudi Arabia:

> Because the purpose of Islamic education was to ensure that the believer would understand God's laws and live his or her life in accordance with them, classes for reading and memorising the Qur'an along with selections from the *hadith* were sponsored in towns and villages throughout the peninsula. At the most elementary level, education took place in the *kuttab*, a class of Qur'an recitation for children usually attached to a mosque, or as a private tutorial held in the home under the direction of a male or female professional Qur'an reader, which was usually the case for girls.
>
> In the late nineteenth century, nonreligious subjects were also taught under Ottoman rule in the Hijaz and al-Ahsa province, where *kuttab* schools specialising in Qur'an memorisation sometimes included arithmetic, foreign language, and Arabic reading in the curriculum. Because the purpose of basic religious learning was to know the contents of holy scripture, the ability to read Arabic text was not a priority, and illiteracy remained widespread in the peninsula. [20]

This historical background also helps to explain the high proportion of the curriculum devoted to religion in Saudi Arabia and some Gulf countries. In Saudi elementary schools nine hours per week (out of 28–31 teaching hours) are devoted to Islamic studies. At intermediate level the total is eight hours out of 33, compared with only four hours for mathematics.[21] Religion is not necessarily confined to Islamic studies, however: other subjects such as Arabic language, history and social sciences can also contain large Islamic elements.

While governments tend to view education as a way of inculcating loyalty to the regime, Islamists have seized upon it as a way of influencing young minds in a religious direction. By the early 2000s the teaching profession in Kuwait had become heavily infiltrated by Islamists – an issue that came to the fore when one high school teacher, Sulaiman abu Ghaith, disappeared and then resurfaced in Afghanistan as a spokesman for al-Qa'ida.[22] Ahmad Bishara, a Kuwaiti parent, said the country had many teachers like Sulaiman abu Ghaith:

> The whole idea is to control the minds and influence the orientation of the students ... A teacher comes to the class and says: "Let's go to the mosque." Those who don't attend feel left out. Kids are asked if their parent goes to the mosque, prays at home, etc.
>
> One teacher asked my child in front of all the students whether his father takes him to the mosque on Fridays. It's embarrassing for the child and it alienates children from their parents.

Bishara complained. It was a private school and he was paying more than $7,000 a year for the privilege of having his religious credentials questioned.

"Teachers tend to come from the more conservative families – especially female teachers," Masoumah al-Mubarak, a professor of political science at Kuwait University said. "Among conservative families, teaching is one of the few approved professions for women. Most teachers, especially women, are conservative – salafi or ikhwan." In Kuwait, parents are very trusting of teachers, she said, but "if the family is not aware and alert they will lose that child":

> I had three kids in the American school (because we had lived in the US). I moved the third one when she was about eleven years old because the cost of the American school is very high and we wanted her to gain Arabic language [skills].
> After three months she said: "Mummy, I want to wear hijab." The teacher had told her that if she didn't [wear it] she would have her hair burnt on Judgment Day – she was really scared.

Dr Mubarak thought her daughter was too young for hijab and visited the school. She found two of the teachers dressed in the style of salafi women and most of the girls of her daughter's age were already wearing hijab. "I felt I was losing the battle," she said. "I didn't want my child to have a conflict with me or to feel I'm a bad mother."[23]

The teaching of religion in Syrian schools illustrates how the content of lessons can be shaped by politics, and also provides some insight into the ideological dilemmas faced by the authorities. The Syrian regime is founded on Ba'athism, a brand of nationalism that includes elements of socialism and pan-Arabism, and where religion plays a relatively minor role. Ba'athism began as a secular movement but soon discovered that in order to win support it had to reach an accommodation with religion – to the extent that it now claims the essential values and mission of Ba'athism are no different from those of Islam.[24] Although 74 per cent of Syria's inhabitants are Sunni Muslims, the regime itself is dominated (mainly for historical reasons) by members of the Alawite sect which is generally regarded as an offshoot of Shi'ism. Shi'i Muslims, including the Alawites and Ismailis, account for 13 per cent, various Christian groups 10 per cent, and Druze 3 per cent. Jewish communities have existed in Syria for centuries but today their number is extremely small – probably no more than a few dozen people.[25]

This forms a rather complex and difficult basis for constructing a course of "Islamic education" which not only accords with Ba'athist ideology but also satisfies the orthodox Sunni majority. There is also the additional problem of how to treat the various non-Sunni minorities. A study by Syria expert Joshua Landis shows how the regime tackles these problems in its "Islamic education" textbooks for schools.

The first issue to be resolved is the relationship between Islam and nationalism, between Muslim identity and Arab identity. The pre-Islamic period is known in Arabic as the *jahiliyya* (the "age of ignorance") – a time of barbarism, lawlessness and idolatry. In general, the more religious sentiment predominates over nationalist sentiment, the more unfavourably the pre-Islamic period is portrayed. The Syrian textbooks settle on a compromise which regards Islam as the main source of Arab greatness while also highlighting certain moral qualities that derive simply from being Arab. So, children are told that "the revelation of Islamic principles transformed the Arabs into a unified community (*umma*) possessing a high human civilisation which it spread to all people."[26] Pre-Islamic Arabs were divided and sinful but nevertheless displayed "bravery, manliness, generosity, patience, abstinence, and the honouring of agreements, love of freedom and hospitality" – qualities that "run in their veins with their blood".[27]

The overall message, Landis says, is that "to be an Arab is good, but to be a Muslim is better, and being both is the best." This solves one of the regime's ideological problems but creates another by implying that non-Muslims, even if they are Arabs, are not the best kind of Arabs. Landis continues: "By setting out a clear hierarchy of virtue among peoples, with Muslims at the top of the scale as God's preferred people and Christians, Jews, polytheists and atheists falling below them in descending order, Syria's Islamic [school] texts undercut the notion that Arabs or Syrian citizens are equal. Non-Muslims are defined as strangers to the Arabo-Islamic project who enjoy rights so long as they are 'under Muslim protection.'" Ba'athism's historic compromise with Islam therefore relegates almost two million Syrian Christians to the status of second-class Arabs, even though they were originally one of the main intellectual driving forces behind pan-Arabism. But the schoolbooks do offer one compensation: Christians will be allowed to join Muslims in heaven.[28] The same, however, does not apply to Jews. According to the tenth-grade textbook, "the tribe of Israel deserves God's tortures" because it "does not respect prophets". The ninth-grade textbook (written in 1969 and last revised in 1986) warns: "Our youth should ignore those traitors who encourage them to surrender to Israel. They should know that our conflict with our enemy is a conflict for existence, not for borders. Israel is an expansionist, colonialist enemy, which will not give up its colonialist plans unless forced to do so ..." [29] Landis comments:

> Clearly, the difference in the treatment between Christians and Jews is political. Because the Christian population of Syria has supported the state and is important in size ... it is favoured with entrance to heaven. The Jews are reviled and excluded from heaven in the Islamic textbooks because of Syria's bitter war with Israel.

Having reserved a place in heaven for Syria's Christians (even if they are not particularly good Arabs), the textbooks dispose of all the country's other religious minorities – including the Alawite elite – by sweeping them under the carpet. Religious education, like much else in the Syrian curriculum, has to be viewed in the context of the Ba'ath party's nation-building project which, as Landis notes, aims at "eliminating all sub-national differences among Syrians, whether they spring from regionalism, economic class, tribalism, or religion":

> Islamic instruction in Syrian schools serves this integralist agenda by inculcating a narrow brand of Sunni Islam on all Syrian Muslims regardless of sect ... No mention of the different sects of Islam is made in the textbooks. Not only are Alawites, Druze, and Isma'ilis not mentioned, but no mention is made of Shi'a Islam as a whole. Islam is presented as a monolithic religion and Sunni Islam is it.

IN AN AGE of technological revolution and globalisation, success and prosperity increasingly depend on knowledge in the shape of a workforce that possesses education, skills, information and know-how, plus the ability to acquire new knowledge and apply it for problem-solving and innovation. "For many developing countries, an abundant supply of low-wage, unskilled labour used to be a route to rapid growth and national prosperity, but this is no longer so," the World Bank noted. "In today's world, characterised by intense global competition and rapid technological change, the key to prosperity is a well-educated, technically skilled workforce producing high-value-added, knowledge-intensive goods and services; in addition, they must be employed in enterprises that have the managerial capacity to find, adapt, and adopt modern, up-to-date technology and sell sophisticated goods and services in local and global markets."[30] Vital though this is, the 2003 Arab Human Development Report found that Arab countries are steadily falling behind:

> Knowledge in Arab countries today appears to be on the retreat ... While knowledge in the region stumbles, the developed world is racing towards knowledge-intensive societies ...
>
> Based on their present performance, Arabs would remain in a marginal position in this next phase of human history. This position would be the logical consequence of a decline that has lasted for seven centuries, while much of the world made enormous progress in developing knowledge and human welfare. Continuing with this historic slide is an untenable course if the Arab people are to have a dignified, purposeful and productive existence in the third millennium.[31]

The nature and scale of this "knowledge deficit" was explored in some detail by the AHDR but a couple of examples illustrate the problem. The number of scientific research papers published in Arab countries (26 per million inhabitants in 1995) is far below the level found in developed countries such as France (840 per million), the Netherlands (1,252) and Switzerland (1,878). Although the number of Arab research papers has been increasing by about 10 per cent a year it is still very modest compared with the output of some developing countries such as South Korea and Brazil. In addition to that, Arab research activity "continues to be far from innovative", the AHDR noted. "Most of it is applied research and only a small portion is related to basic research. Research in advanced fields, such as information technology and molecular biology, is almost non-existent."[32]

At a more commercial level, one measure of innovative activity is the number of patents registered which, in the Arab countries, "lags far behind that of developed countries and other countries of the developing world". Innovative capabilities, the AHDR said, can also be gauged "by demonstrating the widespread presence of innovations in national and foreign markets that can be counted and evaluated. On that criterion, there are virtually no Arab innovations on the market."[33]

At the political level, innovative ideas in many countries come from think tanks. Think tanks are basically a half-way house between academia and politics: they carry out research and produce reports with the aim of influencing government policy. Their character, and the quality of their work, depends largely on their funding; while some have a high degree of independence, others seek to promote specific political or business interests. Regardless of their agenda, think tanks generate debate about alternative policy options and they can be seen as one indicator of the general levels of pluralism and freedom of expression. A study published in 2007 identified 5,080 think tanks worldwide, of which a mere 124 were located in Arab countries.[34] The total across the 22 Arab countries is somewhat less than in just one of the larger European countries, France, which has 162. Although Egypt is the Arab country with the highest individual total of think tanks (21), when population is taken into account this is only one-quarter of the level found in South Africa. In population terms the Palestinian territories have the highest number of think tanks – 6.5 per million inhabitants (presumably because of international interest and the consequent availability of funding). The other countries with more than one think tank per million population are Kuwait (3.08), Bahrain (2.86), Lebanon (2.75) and Jordan (1.48).[35]

Think tanks in Arab countries

Egypt	21	UAE	4
Palestine	17	Saudi Arabia	3
Iraq	14	Bahrain	2
Lebanon	11	Somalia	2
Jordan	9	Sudan	1
Morocco	9	Comoros	0
Kuwait	8	Djibouti	0
Tunisia	8	Libya	0
Yemen	7	Mauritania	0
Algeria	4	Oman	0
Syria	4	Qatar	0

Source: McGann, James: 'The global "go-to think tanks"'. Think Tanks and Civil Societies Programme, Foreign Policy Research Institute, Philadelphia, 2007. http://fpri.org/research/thinktanks/mcgann.globalgotothinktanks.pdf

Various factors have contributed to this lack of innovative research – some of them historical. Although universities have existed in the Arab countries for a thousand years or more, 75 per cent of them were established in the last quarter of the twentieth century – a relatively short time in which to consolidate themselves as research institutions[36] and to attract the kind of endowments that benefit prestigious universities in the west. The earliest Arab universities received *waqf* (Islamic charity) funding but those sources have declined over the years and government funding is often inadequate. Another problem is that many of the brightest Arabs leave their home country at the earliest opportunity. In 1995–96, for example, about 25 per cent of the 300,000 graduates from Arab universities migrated abroad. The only Arab Nobel laureate in science – Egyptian-born

Ahmed Zewail who won the prize for chemistry in 1999 – lives and works in California.

Research and development (R&D) is clearly not regarded as a national priority. Between 1990 and 1995 the Arab countries spent on average 0.2 per cent of their gross national product on R&D. Proportionally, Turkey and Mexico spent twice as much; Germany, France, Italy, Britain, Australia and Canada spent twelve times as much, while the United States, Japan and Sweden spent fifteen times as much. Historically, the oil-rich Gulf states in particular have tended to buy-in expertise from abroad rather than develop it themselves. Another notable feature of R&D spending in the Arab countries is that the meagre amounts of funding come overwhelmingly from government sources. Industry and the service sector contribute only three per cent in the Arab countries, compared with 50 per cent or more in developed countries.[37] One possible reason is that the largest Arab enterprises are often protected from competition, either through state ownership or political cronyism, and therefore have little incentive to innovate.

The underlying problem, though, is that "ingrained structural impediments" (as the AHDR put it) stand in the way of developing knowledge-based societies in the Arab countries. A knowledge-based society is essentially non-authoritarian and open to new ideas. It favours transparency and encourages a spirit of enquiry. It acknowledges unwelcome realities and addresses them. It is flexible and adapts quickly to changing circumstances. These are all traits that Arab societies, at home, at school or in the workplace, actively discourage – and the implications of this are far-reaching. The Arab countries cannot develop knowledge-based societies without radical social and political change. They can, if they choose, try to stay on the sidelines, but self-imposed backwardness is an expensive luxury. Ultimately, they will have no choice but to join the knowledge revolution, and social and political change is bound to accompany that.

A study in 2004 identified five categories of work-related skills which are usually needed in any productive process:

1. Expert thinking: solving problems for which there are no rule-based solutions;

2. Complex communication: interacting with others to acquire information, to explain it, or to persuade others of its implications for action;

3. Routine cognitive tasks: mental tasks that are well described by logical rules, eg maintaining expense reports;

4. Routine manual tasks: physical tasks that can be well described using rules, eg counting and packaging;

5. Non-routine manual tasks: tasks that are not based on clear rules but require optical recognition and fine muscle control.[38]

Not surprisingly, the need for the first two of these – expert thinking and complex communication – has been increasing, while the need to perform more routine – rule-based – tasks has been decreasing in most countries belonging to the Organisation for Economic Co-operation and Development.[39] It is easy to foresee this trend continuing, accelerating and spreading elsewhere as economies become more knowledge-based. Clearly, Arab countries need to reform their education systems and prepare themselves for the future. Reasonable as that may sound, however, in an Arab context it is not only problematic but profoundly subversive. "Expert thinking", which at times requires people to think the unthinkable or "think outside the box", is something that Arab societies and their regimes try hard to prevent. Similarly, "complex communication" involves explaining and persuading – not merely waiting for unquestionable instructions from on high. To encourage this kind of behaviour in education and to promote it as a virtue in the workplace invites the question: why not apply it in politics too, or in society more generally? At present, although cracks are certainly appearing, there are still too many taboos surrounding blue-skies thinking. Arabs who work with knowledge – at least, those whose natural curiosity has not been thoroughly eroded – sooner or later run into the question: "Can I go there?"

Almost half a century ago, a presidential decree in Egypt established the Central Agency for Public Mobilisation and Statistics (Capmas) as the country's "official source for the collection of data and statistical information, and its preparation, processing and dissemination".[40] Capmas is in charge of "providing all the state bodies, organisations, universities, research centres and indevelopment [sic] and evaluation processes with the information that can help them to make informed decisions".[41] In effect, this gives the Egyptian state a monopoly on statistics. Anyone wishing to compile data independently, through surveys or interviews, must first obtain a permit from Capmas's "General Department for Security". Where controversial issues are involved, the security department often delays permission indefinitely or refuses it outright, without giving reasons. Capmas may also delete certain questions from a survey or demand that they be re-worded.[42] Whether or not a permit is granted "depends on contacts and the sensitivity of topics", according to Reem Saad, an associate professor at the American University in Cairo, but "certain topics can't be researched".[43] Besides restricting academic work, this also affects opinion pollsters. Region-wide polling, which began in the early 2000s, has been hampered by some countries refusing permission for questions that they regarded as too sensitive. A Gallup poll in 2002, for example, included the question: "Do you believe news reports that Arabs carried out the September 11 attacks?" – which was forbidden in Morocco, Saudi Arabia and Jordan.[44]

Government restrictions are not the only obstacle, though; there is a more generalised aversion to knowledge and ideas that venture beyond the normal comfort zone. Jehad al-Omari, a specialist in cross-cultural management who advises western businesses on the intricacies of working in Arab countries, explained:

> When you ask the question whether our culture has anything to do with our level of backwardness or lack of progress or lack of democracy or lack of discipline, you are immediately barked at. You cannot say that, you cannot blame the culture, because it's almost sacrosanct. People don't accept that level of self-criticism.
>
> This idea of looking inwards and saying "Where did we go wrong?" is not there. Nobody is willing to blame tribalism or the culture or whatever you want to call it. That idea is not there yet. They will always blame the leadership. It's always externalising the problem, it never internalises the problem. It never says "How did *I* contribute to it?"
>
> The first time I read a book which was exposing the Arab culture I threw it away. It was a book by Hisham Sharabi and it was one of his first Arabic books, called *Introduction to the Study of Arab Society*.[45] It talked about Arab culture: laziness, dependence, etc. My first reading of it was immediate rejection. It wasn't until four or five years later that I re-looked at it and I read it. By that time I had been in Britain for five years and I thought "Hmm!". The idea of seeing yourself as others see you is revolutionary for most people, and it's an extremely difficult and painful process.[46]

Hisham Sharabi (1927–2005) was one of the first modern Arab

writers to develop a critique of his own society, drawing on the ideas of Marx and Freud, and his work is still banned in some countries. In most of the Arab world it was not until the 1960s and 1970s that social sciences emerged as fully fledged disciplines. "The emergence of specialised research and training in these fields," the Arab Human Development Report observed, "is tied to the rise of the modern nation-state, the national projects it proposed and the difficulties it faced in its early stages. From the outset, social sciences and human sciences dealing with 'national history' were subject to political and bureaucratic steering."[47] Even today, continuing preoccupation with the mirage of national unity and the myth of social harmony makes it difficult to explore many problems objectively, especially when they concern marginalised ethnic or religious groups. Merely raising such issues is often regarded as unpatriotic and an attempt to stir up *fitna* (discord).

Another problem is the belief in Arab "specificity" – the widely held notion among Arabs that their own societies are so uniquely distinctive and self-contained that research carried out elsewhere, into other societies, is of little relevance. While the Arab countries, in all their aspects, are much studied by universities and think tanks in other parts of the world, the AHDR noted that there is no comparable tradition in modern times of Arabs studying "the Other". "This tendency," it said, "has sometimes deprived Arab scholars of a comparative perspective and the capacity to link the particularities of their context to general structures and trends in the wider world."[48]

Possibly the reluctance to contemplate "the Other" with a view to learning from it stems from nationalist sentiment or a belief in the superiority of Islam. The latter was certainly the position adopted (at least until recently) by the Saudi interior ministry's Crime Prevention

Research Centre. In a report entitled "Security in the kingdom of Saudi Arabia following strict implementation of Islamic criminal legislation," it claimed that in comparison with other countries, the Saudi crime rate – 0.22 crimes per thousand population – was uniquely low. "The proof that security prevails in the kingdom," the report said, "is that a traveller may go anywhere in this vast country without being harassed by tribes, such as the Harb or Juhayna tribes who [previously] claimed dues from the people travelling across their territory." Following the strict implementation of Islamic law, "everybody started enjoying a sense of social peace and security," it continued. "People may carry any amount of money without fear of looters or highway robbers. Thus, security problems which were nightmares for the natives and pilgrims alike have ceased to exist ... Fear for life, honour or property is something of the past." Bizarrely, the interior ministry provided copies of this report at a news conference just days after simultaneous bomb attacks on housing compounds in the capital had killed 35 people and injured more than 160.[49]

Political constraints on freedom of thought usually have more impact in the human and social sciences than in natural science because of the subject matter, but natural science sometimes comes into conflict with religious belief. Historically, though, science has been less of a problem for Muslims than it has for Christians. Islam has had nothing comparable to the "Galileo moment" in 1633 when the Italian scientist, Galileo Galilei, was forced by the Vatican to recant his "absurd" and "heretical" belief that the earth revolves around the sun. Galileo's views were deemed absurd because they conflicted with a verse in Psalm 93 which says that the earth "cannot be moved", but he was not by any means the first to recognise that the earth does move. Muslim astronomers, such as Ibn al-Haytham, had reached a similar conclusion centuries earlier without retribution from their own religious authorities.

During the first century after the birth of Islam Muslim armies defeated the Persians and moved into what is now Iraq. Around 762 the Abbasid caliphs established their capital in the newly founded city of Baghdad, from where they ruled a vast Muslim empire for the next five centuries. This was the high point of Islamic civilisation, when scholars of various religions from around the world flocked to the *Bayt al-Hikma* (House of Wisdom), an unrivalled centre at the time for the study of humanities and for sciences, including mathematics, astronomy, medicine, chemistry, zoology and geography, as well as some more dubious subjects such as alchemy and astrology. Drawing on Persian, Indian and Greek texts – Aristotle, Plato, Hippocrates, Euclid, Pythagoras and others – the scholars accumulated the greatest collection of knowledge in the world, and built on it through their own discoveries. Probably the most famous mathematician at the House of Wisdom was al-Khawarizmi, known as the father of algebra. The English word "algebra" is derived from the title of his book, *Kitab al-Jabr*, and al-Khawarizmi's own name gave rise to the word "algorithm".

Several important figures are also associated with the southern city of Basra, another key centre of learning. Al-Jahiz, born in Basra in 776, seems to have come from an ordinary background and as a youth helped his father to sell fish. His most famous work was the seven-volume *Book of Animals* which included his observations on the social organisation of ants, communication between animals and the effects of diet and environment. Altogether, he wrote about 200 books on a wide range of topics, including *The Art of Keeping One's Mouth Shut* and *Against Civil Servants*. He died at the age of 92, allegedly when a pile of books in his personal library fell on top of him. A century later al-Mas'udi spent some time in Basra writing about his travels to India, China and East Africa. As with many scholars of his day, his interests were broad and his writing contained elements of history, geography, sociology and anthropology which, unusually for the time, he approached in an analytical way. He also explored problems in the earth sciences – such as the causes of earthquakes – and was the first writer to mention windmills, invented by Muslims in Sijistan. Ibn al-Haytham (also known as Alhazen) worked as a civil servant in tenth-century Basra before taking up science. Moving later to Egypt, he became head of a project to regulate the flow of the Nile but, on investigation, he decided it was impossible. This annoyed the Fatimid caliph in Cairo, and Ibn al-Haytham reputedly escaped punishment by pretending to be mad until the caliph died. Among the mathematical problems he explored was the squaring of the circle. He also wrote a seven-volume treatise on optics and the nature of light. This explored reflection from plane and curved surfaces, refraction, and the structure of the eye – though he failed to understand the importance of the lens.

Certainly at this point Islam did not seem to present an obstacle to cultural and scientific innovation but, on the contrary, provided the regional unity that enabled one of the world's greatest periods of enlightenment. One thousand years later the situation was rather different.

Charles Darwin's theory of evolution was given a mixed reception by Muslims: hostility in some quarters and equanimity in others. The first Muslim critique came in 1881 from Jamal al-Din Afghani who wrote (referring to Darwin's ideas about natural selection): "Is this wretch deaf to the fact that the Arabs and Jews for several thousand years have practised circumcision, and despite this until now not a single one of them has been born circumcised?"[50] On the other hand, Hussein al-Jisr, a Lebanese Shi'i scholar, saw room for an accommodation between evolution and scripture. "There is no evidence in the Qur'an," he wrote, "to suggest whether all species, each of which exists by the grace of God, were created all at once or gradually."[51] The latter view was echoed much more recently by the late Zaki Bedawi – for many years the foremost Muslim scholar in Britain – who said: "I don't see a contradiction between [the theory of evolution] and Islam."[52] Some go even further in reconciling evolution with Islam. A book published in 2005, *Evolution and/or Creation: An Islamic Perspective,* claims that Darwin's ideas about evolution and natural selection were partly derived from Muslim philosophers and scientists, including Ibn Sina (also known as Avicenna) who died in 1037.[53] Currently, according to Abdul Majid, a professor of zoology in Pakistan, there are three strands of Islamic thought about evolution: outright rejection, total acceptance and partial acceptance.[54] However, the popular Muslim website, IslamOnline,[55] espouses a strongly rejectionist view:

> It's a plain fact that what the Darwin theory wants to prove runs in sharp contrast to the divine teachings of Islam, and even to all the teachings of all heavenly revealed religion ... The claim that man has evolved from a non-human species is unbelief, even if we ascribe the process to Allah or to 'nature', because it negates the truth of Adam's special creation that Allah has revealed in the Qur'an.[56]

So far, there has been little orchestrated creationist activism by Muslims of the kind seen among Christians in the United States, though there have been a few isolated incidents. A science lecturer at Khartoum University was reportedly arrested and beaten up because of the content of his courses[57] and in 2006 Muslim medical students at the prestigious Guys Hospital in London distributed leaflets opposing Darwinism as a part of the activities for Islam Awareness Week. One member of the hospital's staff was quoted as saying he found it deeply worrying that Darwin was being dismissed by people who would soon be practising as doctors.[58]

Islamic creationism, as an organised movement, is relatively new and small, though well funded and apparently growing in influence. It is centred in Turkey and is based around the Foundation for Scientific Research (BAV), headed by Adnan Oktar, who has written dozens of books under the pen-name Harun Yahya. At first sight, BAV's activities seem to be part of an internal Turkish battle between Islamists and secularists – one which it claims to be winning. "Darwinism is dying in Turkey, thanks to us," BAV's director, Tarkan Yavas, says. But it also has bigger ambitions, looking ahead to Turkey's possible future membership of the EU. In Yavas's view: "Darwinism breeds immorality, and an immoral Turkey is of no use to the European Union at all."[59] In 2007 one of BAV's publications, the *Atlas of Creation*, was sent free of charge to scientists and schools in Britain, Scandinavia, France and Turkey. The books are also freely available on the internet[60] – which makes them a ready source of material for regurgitation in student essays anywhere in the world.[61] BAV has frequent contacts with American creationists and, although its books are superficially Islamic, their arguments have been shown to rely extensively on Christian material produced by the Institute for Creation Research in California.[62]

Islam's scientific heritage may be one reason why Muslims in general seem untroubled by modern science. There is also a popular belief that science tends to confirm, rather than contradict, what is written in the Qur'an. Many Muslims claim that their holy book contains scientific information which could not possibly have been known to the Prophet or anyone else in seventh-century Mecca – and this is cited as evidence that the Qur'an must have come directly from God.[63] One of the best-known examples is the claim that the Qur'an accurately describes various stages in the development of the foetus; another is that when the Qur'an talks about a "protection" against the sun it is referring to the ozone layer.[64] As far as evolution is concerned, the Qur'an provides less than the Bible for anti-Darwinists to get their teeth into. It portrays God as the creative force behind the universe but – unlike the *Book of Genesis* in the Bible – does not go into detail about the creation process. It says God made "every living thing" from water;[65] that He created humans from clay[66] and that He created them "in stages".[67] In the view of many Muslims, this clearly allows scope for evolutionary interpretations.

Farida Faouzia Charfi, a science professor at the University of Tunis, notes that even the most fervent religious believers can be enthusiastic about science. "In those countries where fundamentalism has taken hold among the youth in the universities, it is striking to observe that the fundamentalist students are in a majority in the scientific institutions," she writes – adding that "fundamentalists are even more numerous in the engineering than the science faculties".[68] This, Charfi says, often surprises westerners because they tend to assume "that a scientific mind is of necessity modern", but Islamists reject modernity only up to a point: they "want to govern society with ideas of the past and the technical means of modernity". One example she cites is an election rally in Algeria where Islamists used laser technology to project the words "Allahu akbar" ("God is greatest") on to a cloud in the sky. Al-Qa'ida's activities – its use of videos and the internet plus, of course, crashing airliners into buildings – provide numerous other examples.

Charfi, an expert in the optical and electronic properties of semiconductors and electromagnetism, suggests that despite this apparent enthusiasm Muslims are often selective in their acceptance of science and simply ignore or reject any parts of it that seem to conflict with their religious beliefs. Support for Charfi's argument about selectivity comes from a study of attitudes towards evolution among Muslim students (Turkish and Moroccan) in the Netherlands which found that their views were "much more one of negotiation" with Darwinism than downright rejection:

> Though a few students ... simply negated the whole of evolution theory on the basis of its perceived incongruence with the creation account in the Qur'an, the vast majority constructed types of *bridge models* in which some aspects of evolution were accepted and others rejected.
>
> The construction of these models does not imply that the students experienced the encounter of two different accounts of origin as very problematic or disconcerting. On the contrary, they hardly recognised the implicit presence of evolutionary assumptions underlying studies like medicine, chemistry, and bio-medical sciences. Students in these disciplines were of course aware that they were required to take some courses and exams related to evolution theory, but they considered this quite unproblematic as they felt that external reproduction [of Darwin's ideas in an exam] does not require internal acceptance.
>
> In the students' bridge models, microevolution and the concept of "the survival of the fittest" appeared on the accepted side of the equation. Students reasoned that it is impossible to deny the logic and empirical backing of these concepts. They also connected microevolution to theistic evolution, the idea that God has guided the adjustments in his creatures. Several students accepted the Big Bang and believed that the Qur'an contains references to both the Big Bang and evolution theory.
>
> For almost every student I talked with, macroevolution

was on the negated side in the bridge models. In contrast to microevolution, macroevolution was connected to atheist aspirations ... Likewise, no student accepted the idea that human beings have sprung from apes.

... In line with the acceptance of creation, it clearly stood out that the existence of God went unquestioned among the students. Atheism was strongly refuted. All students believed in angels, *djinns* and devils, to which they applied both supernaturalist and naturalist characteristics. Especially for medicine students, hesitations on the true origins of psychiatric ailments stood out – are they *djinns* or genes?[69]

The students in the Dutch study were all described as having "enlightened" political views (acceptance of democracy, equal gender rights, etc) – which suggests that the kind of selectivity noted by Charfi is not confined to Islamists and Muslim traditionalists. The author noted that along with partial acceptance of microevolution and theistic evolution, some students also produced a few explanations of their own: "A Moroccan female student approached evolution theory as a potential divine ordeal. In her view, bones that support evolution theory could possibly exist by God's will to test the faithfulness of his people: is their faith strong enough to believe in spite of the facts?"

In Charfi's view, this approach – rejecting or partially accepting some aspects of science on the basis of literal interpretations of religious texts – is completely unacceptable. Science comes as a total package and trying to cherry-pick, or using Qur'anic verses to re-calculate the speed of light (as some do),[70] makes a nonsense of it:

To partially accept fundamental laws of physics is to render the whole theory incoherent. The rational step is to propose another theory that is logically coherent; this requires an analysis of the principles that underlie theories and their relations and not a simple rejection of some of them. In order to undertake such work, an open mind that is free of all constraints is necessary.

To explore, understand, criticise, innovate, create without forbidding any question, without banning any field and giving the imagination free play – all this implies that one has freed oneself from all dogma. This is unfortunately not the case in the Islamic world where reference to the sacred is inevitable and where the most socially correct thing is to be in conformity with Islam ... It is in the name of this unavoidable reference to the sacred that scientific knowledge is mutilated.[71]

Arab societies have, in the past, negotiated between science and Islam very successfully. But many of Islam's contemporary manifestations are backward looking and anti-intellectual, while the high value placed on conformity in Arab societies is suffocating change. The ability to explore, understand, criticise, innovate and create that Charfi seeks does not apply to science alone: it is one of the keys to the Arabs' future. Without it, the prospects for positive change, for fighting tyranny and religious dogmatism, look slender. Without it too, the Arab countries will drift ever more helplessly, unable to play their rightful part, politically or economically, in an increasingly globalised world.

2 The gilded cage

POWER, ACCORDING TO Mao Zedong, the founder of modern China, comes from the barrel of a gun. As far as the Middle East is concerned he was only partly right: power also comes from a father's genes. Among the Arab countries, Bahrain, Jordan, Kuwait, Morocco, Oman, Qatar, Saudi Arabia and the United Arab Emirates – more than a third of the total – have hereditary rulers. Not only that. Syria is officially a socialist republic but when President Hafez al-Asad died in 2000 his son succeeded him, and there are signs that the republics of Egypt, Yemen and Libya may eventually follow a similar course. In Iraq, before the invasion, Saddam Hussein had also begun to share power with his sons, Udai and Qusay. Even Lebanon – one of the more democratic Arab countries – is a land of birthright politics where family dynasties pull many of the strings.

Arab countries may not be unique in this respect but it is impossible to understand the forces that shape them without considering the importance of blood, kinship and family life. "Arab society," Halim Barakat, the Syrian-born sociologist wrote, "is the family generalised or enlarged, and the family is society in miniature."[1] The same can be said of politics, with the Arab family as a microcosm of the Arab state, and the Arab state as a family writ large.

This has far-reaching implications for anyone seeking political change in the Middle East. It is not enough simply to point to the prevalence of authoritarian regimes and imagine that whoever cuts off the monster's head will be welcomed with flowers. The regimes – even the most unpopular ones – are products of the societies they govern and to grasp the nature of the problem we have to start by looking at society's building blocks. While presidents and kings hog the limelight, their style of government is replicated in countless other situations: in factories, offices, schools and homes. As journalist Khaled Diab said of his home country, "Egypt has a million Mubaraks".[2]

Aisha grew up in Sudan, in a family with four girls and no boys – and her father, a military attaché, was unhappy about that.[3] "He made it very clear that he felt unfulfilled and ashamed and scandalised that he had no sons," Aisha recalled.

> Because we were girls, we were pretty much imprisoned. We were never allowed to go out, we had no friends. We were only allowed to go to family members' houses. It was all very supervised. He spied on us, he kept tabs on us. He'd drop us off somewhere and pretend that he'd gone but would actually still be around. Or he would listen in on telephone conversations.
>
> We went to western schools and we learned English and we had quite a westernised lifestyle, but he expected us still to be good Arab girls and not internalise any of the education that we had.
>
> Once, he picked me up from school – I was about 14 – and he sent me out of the car to get something from a shop. He went through my bag while I was in the shop and he found some random boy's telephone number. He wouldn't let me go to school for two weeks. He said: 'That's it – you're not going to school any more.' That was a big crisis in my adolescent life. My mum begged and my grandma begged, and he finally let me go back, but on the condition that I'd cover [my head], because I wasn't covered then. He put conditions, that he would let me go back to school based on x, y and z.

The over-protective paternalism that Aisha experienced at the hands of her father has parallels in the Arab state. In much the same way, the state assumes the task of providing its citizens with moral guidance, in effect shielding them from those undesirable kids in the next street. So, in the most extreme case – Saudi Arabia – the adverts for whisky and pictures of inappropriately dressed women in imported newspapers are laboriously blotted out by hand,[4] while an elaborate system of internet censorship blocks access to websites showing pornography and sexually explicit material or sites deemed to encourage gambling, drug use or conversion to Christianity.[5] The unspoken assumption, of course, is that adult citizens are too child-like to be entrusted with making their own judgements about such things.

Despite insisting that his daughter must wear the hijab, Aisha's father was scarcely a traditional Muslim at the time. It was more a case of "Do as I say, not as I do":

> He was a real hedonist. He drank, he smoked and he was quite bohemian. He liked music and he used to play the 'oud and have parties. He wasn't devout at all, but I think there's an age that Arab men get to – forty-five, forty-six – when he suddenly started praying. He stopped drinking suddenly and became devout but in a very non-spiritual way – in a cultural way more than spiritual. I didn't feel it was about him finally returning to God. It was 'I can't get away with doing this any more – I'm an older guy and I have my reputation to maintain in society.' I'm being really, really cruel but I think that's why he did it.

Aisha's mother, a professor of English literature, received much the same treatment as the girls:

She used to teach at the university, and he would spy on her – he would go and ask if she had any doctoral students that were male. He made her resign because he thought she wasn't conducting herself in a professional manner, and then he made her withdraw her resignation. He was very controlling.

We reacted differently, my sisters and I. My eldest sister just clammed up. She's quite a subdued, demure character anyway, so she kind of went into her shell. She's thirty-five and unmarried – which for an Arab girl says a lot. She's kind of terrified of men.

I rebelled massively when I was fifteen, sixteen. Every single day was a struggle because I was so appalled by his behaviour. It didn't start as a personal thing – I was defending my mother against his treatment.

There was one time when they had a domestic fracas. He was a big, scary man – 6ft 5 and in the army – so he wasn't anybody you messed with. I physically got in his way and he slapped me black and blue. I just didn't care as long as he wasn't getting to my mother. After that I became absolutely dedicated to pissing him off and not letting him get away with anything, because of how he behaved. It took up a great deal of my teenage life, this campaign.

Aisha's story is not by any means unusual. In the traditional Arab family, Halim Barakat writes, the father sits at the top of a pyramid of authority and requires "respect and unquestioning compliance with his instructions".[6] The Arab Human Development Report of 2004 – compiled by Arabs under UN auspices – painted a similar picture, of families with a father "who often tends to be authoritarian, bestowing and withholding favours; a mother, usually tender-hearted, submissive, and resigned, who has no say in important matters except behind the scenes; and children who are the objects of the father's instructions and the mother's tenderness."[7] Though the father may often be an invisible presence, spending most of his time outside the home, he remains the figure of authority even in families where it is the mother who "actually exercises power over the children ... entrusted with raising and disciplining them" and sometimes using the father "to scare or threaten them".[8]

In families without a father, God can be assigned a similar role as the invisible presence who must not be angered. Ghada Kabesh, a divorced working mother in Cairo, recalled how her toddler son's nanny would say: "If you don't eat this, God will hate you" or "If you don't wear those socks, God will hate you." She continued: "Many things we were taught as kids, when I look at them now, I see them as completely stupid. There are so many tiny little things that we are told, they somehow accumulate and they make us who we are. This is why people get to be thirty-five but they don't have the guts to stay out at night without having the permission of their dads. I tell the nanny, 'Stop saying this bullshit.'"[9]

Of course, similar families can be found in other parts of the world and among more than 300 million people in the Arab countries themselves there are obviously variations. Nevertheless, this generalised picture of family structures is one that Arabs readily acknowledge as prevalent in their societies, even if it is changing in places. Thus, the family is not merely the basic unit of social and economic organisation but also, in a sense, the basic unit of government: it becomes the primary mechanism for social control – or, put another way, the point where liberty begins to be constrained.

The authoritarian and patriarchal attitudes observed at ground level in the family are replicated throughout society, right up to the top. "Rulers and political leaders," Barakat says, "are cast in the image of the father, while citizens are cast in the image of children. God, the father, and the ruler thus have many characteristics in common. They are the shepherds, and the people are the sheep: citizens of Arab countries are often referred to as *ra'iyyah* (the flock)."[10] A central feature in this type of society, Hisham Sharabi writes, whether it is conservative or progressive, "is the dominance of the father (patriarch), the centre around which the national as well as the natural family are organised. Thus between ruler and ruled, between father and child, there exist only vertical relations: in both settings the paternal will is the absolute will, mediated in both the society and the family by a forced consensus based on ritual and coercion."[11] In the words of another writer, "the family is a gilded cage – protection and prison, security and bondage."[12]

It sounds oppressive, and often it is. Escape is difficult but, much as individuals may complain about being trapped, they are usually more ambivalent when asked if they want to break free. Together with wider kinship ties (such as clans and tribes), the Arab family provides a sense of belonging and a collective safety net in times of trouble – support that in some countries would be provided by the state.

The Iraqi blogger known as Salam Pax described his own experiences, growing up in Baghdad:

> It's good to have the family structure we have. I know very well that if anything goes wrong I can always fall back on something. I've got that safety net under me all the time. That's the plus. But again, because I'm depending on the family so much, I need to constantly make sure that they approve of all my decisions.
>
> It doesn't matter where you are, the structure is there ... decisions are made at the top and have to be followed by everyone else, and every time you need to do something it has to be referred up before you can get approval. This

happens on a bigger scale, the tribal scale, and it happens within families as well. It's a sort of pyramid where you've got one person at the top.

Most governments in the Arab world function like that, too. There is this person who is the head of the family, the head of the tribe, the head of the state, who has final call on every single decision, and you *will* do what he says, otherwise there is always this fear of being cast outside the family, which is shameful. To be thrown out of the family is something that from a young age you should be worried about – it is not something that is proper.

You should always be within this structure, within the family, and if you do anything they don't approve of and you are outside it, then you lose connections, you lose approval from your society. Who do you belong to then? What's your tribe? You say it's tribe X, but tribe X tell me they have nothing to do with you, so you don't get married, you don't get jobs.

It's even more difficult for women because once their families don't want to be associated with them they are really, really in trouble.[13]

The strength of these ties varies from family to family and from place to place. "The more you are in the countryside," Salam Pax continued, "the more hold the family has on you ... the simplest decisions, whether it's building your own little house on the land, or getting married. Getting married is obviously the family's business – there's no question."

His own family ties were looser than many but he still found them restrictive: "You have to walk within the paths they give you." At university he studied architecture, a choice that was "very much a compromise", he said. "Medicine, engineering or finance – these are the sort of options that are approved by the family. Anything else is sort of unacceptable. Architecture ended up being something that I studied at an engineering university. It gave me a chance to have my own interests but still, at least within the Iraqi system, it was 'engineering'."

Young Arabs normally stay in the family home until they marry – and sometimes after they marry, too. "You get attached to the family and the family get attached to you," Salam Pax said. "You will be looking after your parents, probably your grandparents, maybe a sister that is not married, a distant cousin who might end up near you and you'll have to look after them as well. It's very complicated. You are never really making decisions for yourself if you are within that structure, and it can get a bit too much." Although the extended family can often provide a "leg up" into employment, situations such as this have the opposite effect, limiting mobility and opportunities to progress in a career:

> Your choices are always made thinking: 'I need to stay within a reasonable distance from my family.' One of my cousins will never be able to live in a house separate from his parents because they just want him there, and he *will* be there. His sister, she's practically a dependent, so he will look after her as well. He's married, he's got a kid, and he is the only person who is working in the house. This will not change, and all his decisions – whatever he is doing now, whatever he will do in the future – will always be influenced by that attachment.
>
> If they move, they have to move together. So, even getting out of Iraq when there was no way they could stay where they lived, was delayed because they had to make sure that this unit moved together. It puts him under great pressure because he's got a wife and a kid and he needs to know on which side he will focus, but it pulls him on both sides.

In Egypt Khaled Diab opted for independence at the age of twenty-four, renting a flat on his own in the Agouza district of Cairo, but neighbours found it odd that anyone would live alone through choice rather than force of circumstances:

> The way they look at you, people can't fathom the idea that someone would live alone unless they have a conflict with their family. When I first moved into my apartment I met one of my neighbours in the lift and he accosted me and started sort of being friendly but it was really an interview to find out who I was and what I was doing, whether I was a threat to their daughter, maybe, or whether I would bring down the tone of the building.

Like many young Arabs from relatively prosperous families, Sudanese Aisha broke free – after a fashion – by studying abroad. Following the death of her domineering father, her mother lacked the strength to prevent her leaving: "My mum let me go because she was tired of fighting. I said: 'Just one year. I'll do my masters and I'll come home.'" Five years later, Aisha has not only completed her masters degree and a doctorate but has embarked on what promises to be a high-powered career in financial services in London.

"When I left, I thought: 'Fantastic! I'm home free, this is it!'" she said. But increasingly, Aisha feels she is living on borrowed time – the victim of what she calls "an emotional kidnapping". Her mother wants her to return home and marry a Sudanese man – and has already put forward several potential husbands. To her mother, the fact that none of her daughters is married has become a burden, almost to the point of turning into a family scandal:

> The last time I was there she said: "That's it. You're taking the piss, you've done your masters, you've done your PhD – just

come home. You need to get married, you need to settle down."

It's her obsession. It's all she ever talks about. That's the thing to her: scandal and honour and what the family is going to say ... She recognises that it [arranged marriage] doesn't guarantee happiness but she just says: "Tough! This is your fate, this is what you were born into – you have to sort it out."

She's very dramatic and hysterical. If I tell her I'm not coming back, her left arm will go numb and she'll get palpitations and she'll go to the hospital. She does this all the time. I don't know how much of it is real, but it does affect me. Fundamentally, because we are close, we do have a bond because of my father and because of what we went through. Emotionally, it's very difficult for me to do that to her.

What her mother does not know, though, is that Aisha is already living with a man in London:

I have a long-term partner who is white and Catholic. We can't get married, we can't have children, because it's a secret relationship. It's not secret to his family – they are lapsed Catholics, very lapsed, but in my own head ... It's apocalyptic – the worst thing in the world as far as [my mother] is concerned.

But why is it so horrible? Why apocalyptic? My partner is not a murderer, he's much more of a gentleman than many of the candidates who have been proposed to me. What is it that makes it so difficult for a mother to say: "You obviously get on, I know how difficult to please you are, you've found somebody, he seems like a nice man – why don't you go for it?"

The system is so powerful that basically when she looks at us she won't see her daughter any more. She won't see me, she won't see the girl that she has brought up, she'll just see me as a scandal and she will see him as a demon. Number one, he's not Sudanese, number two he's not Muslim, number three, he's white – everything's just wrong about it. It would tear my family apart.

Even in my family there are girls who have married westerners and the treatment that they've got is just ... it's like something out of the crucible, it's appalling. They've been told: "You can't marry in Sudan, you can't bring him here." They let it be known that "if you do marry him you won't be welcome in any of our houses again". And fair play, most of them have said: "Fine!"

If I were a man it would be frowned upon but at the end of the day if a man wants to do it, he can do it. But for a girl to do something that is so against the establishment – not only do I go out and choose my own mate, but I go out and choose a totally different race – somebody who wasn't born a Muslim. She won't see – nobody will see, if I do present her with this person – her daughter's happiness.

In the meantime, Aisha feels the strains of her secret life:

What it does, which is very dangerous, is it pushes so much under ground and it stifles so much. It stifles creativity because when I have to think about where I travel, what I say, what I do, I'm always censoring in my own head in case something slips. I've had to give up job opportunities because it would involve my partner coming with me. He's had to give up promotions because it would involve him going to Switzerland or Milan or whatever, and I can't go with him because my cover will be blown. So not only has it infected me, it's kind of infected him as well.

There's a kind of sub-strata of Sudanese boys and girls who work in the UK now who have a totally schizophrenic lifestyle, and who I think are damaged by it because they can have a boyfriend for five or six years and live with them perfectly happily, and then they just think: "Oh my God, I can't do this any more" and they go back home and marry a Sudanese man and have a child in nine months. I've seen girls do that and it's a very scary thing. They just think: "My life is over as far as I am concerned."

I could very easily buckle and say, OK, I'll come home and quit my job and break my partner's heart, and convince myself that I'm doing it for the greater good because I don't want to dishonour my sisters and I don't want to hurt my mother and I don't want to blacken my father's name.

I never thought I would go back. I never thought it would be difficult for me to say I'm not coming back, but over the past four years there has just been this kind of slow emotional campaign that is very difficult for me to ignore. I can't just say: "Sod you, I don't care. I'm staying whether you like it or not." It's difficult.

I have a little sister who is very sensitive, I have a volatile mother who is almost sixty and the person who has kept her attention all her life has died, so she needs mothering as well. Sometimes I go out in London and think I'm having such a good time and my mum's probably sobbing and crying somewhere – she's been very clever, she knows what she's doing. There's a massive yoke of guilt around my neck and I don't know what's going to happen.

The family safety net thus becomes a snare. Some reject it outright and forfeit the security, the sense of belonging and of common purpose that it brings. Others reject it initially but are gradually drawn in and eventually succumb, sacrificing their individual freedom for the wishes of the group.

"To be alone and fighting with the whole of society is not easy,"

Moroccan writer Abdellah Taia said, "because society is so much stronger than the individual. If you want to do something guided completely by what you want, they don't let you." For some, this "giving up" process (as he calls it) leads to religion – "OK, I've lived, I've had enough pleasures in my life, now I'm going back to God, I will save some money to go to Mecca, it's time to become respectable" – but it also has a secular version where people suddenly plunge themselves into family life and forget all their previous interests:

> My brother is a lot older than me. When he was young he liked David Bowie ... Woodstock ... *The Brothers Karamazov* by Dostoevsky. Then one day, at the age of 35, he asked my mother to get him a wife, and he abandoned everything.
>
> I remember clearly one time he gave me a long lesson about how cinema died. He told me there are no good movies any more: the good ones were made in the 1960s and 1970s – Bertolucci, Scorsese, etc – and he said there will be no more.
>
> It was as if he had decided there was nothing left in life beyond money and marriage. He didn't see that I was still young and that [by saying these things] he was killing something inside of me. I was really sad, but years later I understood that he was the one who died at that time. It was not the cinema, it was not me. He had just become like everyone else.
>
> All these things about sex and marriage – it's just a way of controlling you. Everyone is controlling others. All the time there are people who will tell you what you are doing is not good. It's not only your family, it's almost a *systeme totalitaire*.[14]

At one level this reflects the natural affinities and sense of duty towards other family members that are found in all societies, but it also goes well beyond that: the balance between individual and collective interests is weighted very much in favour of the collective. This is one of the more important differences between Arab and western culture. While expressions of individuality, along with notions of personal autonomy and independence, are often regarded positively in the west, Arabs value them less highly. The idea that elderly parents might live alone or in residential care homes, as happens in many western countries, strikes many Arabs as callous.[15] Where westerners see individualism, Arabs tend to see selfishness – and frown upon it. Advising a Muslim mother about the upbringing of her child, the Egyptian-based website IslamOnline warns: "When it comes to individualism, there is a difference between allowing a person to develop and individualism. Individualism is totally selfish, seeking one's own needs first and last. There is no relation to a healthy social grouping and there is no sense of responsibility to others ..."[16] In several articles on the same website, individualism is mentioned disparagingly in conjunction with consumerism, capitalism and liberalism.[17] The Arabic word for "individuality" or "individualism" (*fardiya*) is derived from a root with a mixture of positive and negative connotations: uniqueness and rarity but also isolation, separation, withdrawal, loneliness – even oddity. When Arabs ask a stranger: "Are you alone?" the answer is usually obvious but it's an expression of concern and, usually, an offer to remedy the situation by providing company. It rarely occurs to them that someone might be alone through choice.

Arriving in the United States for the first time, Halim Barakat was struck by the way Americans behave "as independent individuals who constantly assert their apartness and privacy":

> One of the first things I observed was that Americans travel on their own, hardly relating to one another. This is in sharp

contrast to Arabs, who almost always travel in close company of two or more people, intimately and spontaneously engaged in lively conversation. Finding myself in the moving crowds of New York city, however, I realised I had to view the people around me in new ways. I realised that what I saw in America were crowds not groups. What you have is a mass of individuals who maintain their psychological distance in spite of their spatial closeness.[18]

Mark Allen, who spent many years in the Middle East with the British foreign service, saw it from the other side:

The Arab, from the moment of his birth, is utterly social. Arabs strongly dislike being alone and typing this I realise that I am unable to recall finding an Arab all alone. There is always somebody else about ... Our own ideas of the "social" imply the "other", leaving our own privacy and independence, our home, and going out into the world to be with others and others, if we are lucky, with whom we have chosen to be. The context of family diminishes from school onwards and we leave home shortly thereafter. The Arab individual's context is family all the way through. Social means family. A great many live close to other family members throughout their adult lives. Migration and mobility, the pressures to find work are, of course, eroding the validity of this generalisation, but anybody who has stood by the arrivals gate of a Middle Eastern airport and witnessed the ecstatic scenes as relations are reunited, will know the underlying truth of the matter.[19]

Another cultural difference is that the nuclear family – mother, father and children – is a more recent development in Arab countries than in many other parts of the world. Hisham Sharabi, writing in 1988, describes the nuclear family as slow to emerge and still "restricted in most cases to the upper and middle urban strata".[20] The wider kinship ties can be pictured as a series of concentric circles extending outwards. Beyond the immediate and extended family is the clan (*ashira*) comprising those who share a common ancestor or family name, and beyond that, the tribe (*qabila*). There can also be subtribes and tribal confederations.[21] In places where they matter, any of these multiple allegiances may come into play at different times, according to circumstances, as epitomised by the famous Bedouin proverb: "I against my brother, my brother and I against our cousin, my cousin and I against the neighbours, all of us against the stranger."

The protective power of such ties is not to be underestimated. Governments tread warily when confronted by them – though how warily depends on the status of the family or tribe, and other factors. Knowing that a man comes from a "big" (ie important) family can influence the way officials deal with him. In northern Yemen, where tribes are often heavily armed, the state crosses them at its peril; on occasions, tribes have defied the national army, and seen it off – though often the outcome of disputes is a compromise. Yemen is an extreme case but elsewhere, in more ordinary situations, there is strength in numbers. Ahmed, a West Bank Palestinian,[22] recalled a problem faced by his family in the 1990s. For several years they had been running a successful advertising business using street billboards. "We were working hard and we were working legally," he said. "We did it with the municipality of each city – we paid them money and they gave us the electricity [to light the signs] and the right to put the signs in the street."

All went well until shortly after the Oslo Accords brought the Palestinian Authority into being, and the family were approached by another company. "They wanted us to sell them some of the rights we had in the streets," Ahmed said. "We didn't like it, so our first reaction was to say: 'Sorry, it's not for sale.'" But the other company did not give up. "They came again and again and again – every time with a different approach. They were playing in a way that, if you were simple, maybe it would have worked. Then we started to have problems. For example, we started to have signs broken in Gaza – we didn't live there so we couldn't protect them – and we started to have people in the municipality refusing our business."

More worryingly, no one was in any doubt that the company trying to take them over had close connections with the Palestinian Authority. "It was obvious that if we were weak and knew nobody we would be crushed. It got really nasty but luckily we were also in politics in Palestine, and we knew a few people in the Authority who were fair and didn't like what happened."

Eventually the whole family was drawn in for a collective show of strength. "At one of the meetings, on purpose, we got all my brothers and all my relatives to sit in the office so they could see how many we were – and leave us alone." The ploy seemed to work and the family kept their business but others without those resources were less fortunate. "In Ramallah we heard of many 'accidents' – of buildings or land, small restaurants even, which were taken in this kind of style. Sometimes we would believe the story, sometimes we would think the person was exaggerating, but when it happened with us we knew they were not exaggerating. This stuff was happening."

Set against a picture of "selfish" western individualism, Arab commitment to family and kin – belonging, helping, sharing, caring – appears virtuous, even if its effects are sometimes suffocating. But suppression of individuality in this way is selfless only up to a point. It is one thing to say that children who have been raised by their parents should reciprocate eventually by caring for them in old age but to impose a lifelong duty of support and allegiance on more distant relations, simply because of a common ancestor in the past, is something else: it has no rational basis but it unlocks the doors to success and survival. "Connections will always help you," Salam Pax said.

> For me, it usually was my dad's position in his tribe, and the name of the tribe. I didn't really know much about my father's extended family – I was never really interested in this – but still, when I mentioned my full name, suddenly some stranger would say "Ah! My cousin, of course! Come over!" – and so I'd come to the front of the line or get some sort of extra help.
>
> These things sometimes strike you as totally unfair. But that name has helped me. This happens all the time, and you are expected to do the same in the same situation. People think: "I will need you one day and I will get back to you."
>
> My life would have been more difficult without it. It never felt wrong but I know it's unfair in a lot of situations because there's absolutely no reason why X should go to the front of the line just because his name is similar to the one of the clerk there.

Jumping the queue may be a fairly trivial matter but the obsession with kinship undermines the principles of meritocracy and equality of opportunity. Nepotism hampers economic development and places Arab countries at a disadvantage in relation to those parts of the world where such practices are less prevalent. The other side of the coin is that people without favourable kinship ties are placed at a disadvantage, and distinguishing between them according to the chance circumstances of their birth opens the way to discrimination not only based on family background but also on their religious and ethnic backgrounds too. This is not to suggest that Arabs are unaware of the negative effects; they are very obvious and newspapers regularly complain about them. "However, while most people condemn the practice in general terms, they make private exceptions for themselves and their families," Khaled Diab said. "In the official parlance, the rhetoric is one of a meritocracy (particularly in the republics, which rose to power with the mission of removing the nepotistic rot of the *ancien régime*). Few are openly appointed to jobs because they have the right connections – it is usually a backroom thing. However, this kind of backroom intrigue goes on a lot."

How much use people can make of these kinship ties depends on their status within the community; their accumulation of social capital. Social capital can be acquired in a variety of ways – through wealth, power or sheer numbers – but central to it all is the question of honour (*sharaf*). Honour is an old concept which bears some resemblance to modern notions of reputation, respectability and dignity. In the more traditional parts of the Arab world, any undeserved slight is liable to be treated as an affront to a person's honour. Mark Allen recalls one such incident, though it is an unusually dramatic example:

> I was sitting with a powerful shaikh [in a crowded room] and we were smoking cigarettes. I pulled out a box of matches to light one and the box was empty. The shaikh called across … to somebody to throw me a light. A box came through the air and I caught it. It was empty. The shaikh next to me looked at the man who threw it over, pulled out his revolver and aiming it at the head of the man, pulled back the hammer. It took me a moment to realise this was not in good part, running with the light and happy mood … Not so the Arabs. They were at once tense and all eyes on the gun.
>
> After a very long pause, an elderly and respected man rose to his feet and walked across … saying as he went that a lighthearted slip should not spoil a good evening. As he approached the possible line of fire, the shaikh put his gun

away and the man next to me on the other side produced a lighter. I was 22, insignificant among their number and a foreigner, but I was the shaikh's own guest. A jab at my ribs was a stab at his face and, to maintain his enormous honour, he chose to react asymmetrically.[23]

Honour can be gained or lost and, if lost, steps must be taken to restore it as quickly as possible. Honour can also, sometimes, be acquired in unusual ways when circumstances catapult someone to a higher status than would normally be expected according to the usual criteria of age, seniority and family. Twenty-four-year-old Hussein, from a refugee camp in Palestine, acquired it by spending nine months in an Israeli jail. Returning home after his release, he was immediately approached with requests to mediate in local disputes – a role normally reserved for highly respected older men in the community. His status within the family changed too, as anthropologist Julie Peteet observed:

> During visits to Hussein's family, I began to notice the deference paid him by his father, an unusual state of affairs in Arab family relations where sons are usually deferential to their fathers. Much about hierarchy and submission can be read in seemingly mundane, everyday gestures. Seating patterns in Arab culture are spatial statements of hierarchy. Those who stand or sit closest to the door are usually subordinate, younger males, while those farthest from the door and centrally positioned are older, respected men who are able to command obedience.
>
> The spatial arrangement of visitors and family members when congregating at Hussein's home did not conform to the traditional pattern. Indeed Hussein often was centrally positioned with his father clearly on the periphery. During conversations where his father was present, along with other

family members and friends, his father deferred to Hussein
in speech, allowing his son to interrupt him. Hussein's father
listened attentively as his son talked for lengthy periods of
time before interjecting himself. In short, he gave Hussein the
floor. When Hussein would describe his prolonged torture
at the hands of the interrogators, his father was quiet, only
occasionally to interject, "Prison is a school, a university" and
"Prison is for men".[24]

This usurpation of the father's role also occurs in families where the
son has far outperformed his father in political, professional or even
academic achievement. While some sons will continue to superficially
defer to their fathers, others will expect to be treated with the
"respect" their status deserves. In turn, if the family, including the
father, derives its prestige from a son who has become a successful
politician, professional, businessman, artist, etc, then the son becomes
the new patriarch.

Honour exists both individually and collectively. "Honourable"
or "dishonourable" conduct by one member of a kinship group is
deemed to affect its other members too. Thus the collective need to
preserve honour and avoid shame becomes an important mechanism
for imposing discipline and the penalties for misbehaviour can be
severe. In the most extreme cases a sexual transgression by one person
(almost always a woman) sullies the family's honour – which then
has to be "restored" by male relatives, usually her brothers, killing
her. Though "honour" killings, or at least those identified as such,
are comparatively rare, the publicity they attract in the west tends
to mask less dramatic aspects of the problem which do not result in
death: the huge amount of everyday anguish caused when people are
obliged to act against their will in order to satisfy family honour.

Honour is more about perceptions than actual behaviour – other people's perceptions or, in some cases, perceptions of people's perceptions. The same basic idea can be found almost anywhere in the world: "Whatever will the neighbours think?" But in some cultures it does not really matter what the neighbours think. They may not be interested or, even if they are shocked by someone's behaviour, the consequences will be minimal. In Arab culture, however, where so much hinges on reputation and coming from a "respectable family" is one of the main criteria when arranging marriages, the consequences can be serious. A loss of honour by one family member can affect all the others, to the extent that brothers and sisters may become ineligible for marriage.[25]

The crucial point here is reputation. Transgressions cause a loss of reputation only when they become public; those that remain private do not count. In practice, though, the dividing line between public and private is somewhat blurred. Perhaps because the consequences of a scandal are so grave, denial is often the preferred option. This can result in an emperor-with-no-clothes situation where errant behaviour is obvious to anyone who cares to look but nobody is obliged to react unless it is formally acknowledged. In an online discussion of homosexuality in Morocco, for example, one British resident in the country commented:

> There is no doubt that homosexuality is abhorrent to the majority of people here, but they "get around the problem" by simply refusing to admit it exists. So a Moroccan is likely to look very surprised if even the campest of people is described as a homosexual, and [will] refuse to entertain the idea if they like the person – though if they don't like the person it can become a (very real) reason for them not even to be in their company.[26]

Many young Arabs complain that these restrictions force them into a double life. In Egypt, Hossam Bahgat and Wesal Afifi write, "There is pressure to adhere to socio-religious norms, which entails obedience to parents and their expectations, but there is also the desire to enjoy freedom from these norms. The ability to enjoy these freedoms, however, is severely hampered by young people's guilt at transgressing social mores."[27]

The precise scale of the problem is difficult to judge. The reluctance to admit to breaking taboos makes surveys unreliable. Operations to "restore" female virginity through hymen reconstruction are one indicator, as are abortions. One Cairo gynaecologist told the BBC he was approached by two or three young women each week to enquire about hymen reconstruction (since virginity is expected when they marry).[28] Nor is this confined to urban areas. A doctor in Mansoura, a largely rural province of Lower Egypt, cited the case of a woman who had to save for four months before she could afford the operation (which costs around $175). In the meantime she feigned insanity to avoid having intercourse with her new husband.[29] Though opportunities for legal abortions are very limited in Egypt, another gynaecologist, who works with both poor and wealthy patients, said that approximately once a month she deals with a case of complications resulting from a backstreet termination.[30]

Another indicator in Egypt is the prevalence of *'urfi* ("customary") marriages which are not officially registered but in the eyes of the couple provide a veil of legitimacy for their sexual relationship. An article in *al-Ahram Weekly* explained:

> A young couple, in their first year at university, want to get married: Should they wait until they graduate? Even then, the young man may not be able to afford the expenses of marriage, buy an apartment or even find a job.
>
> For some, the alternative is to get two witnesses to sign a

paper that serves as the only evidence of their marriage. The relationship is usually kept secret, even from the couple's parents. Many young people are coming to believe that this form of marriage ... is the only legitimate alternative to premarital sex, which is condemned as sinful.[31]

Another use of *'urfi* marriages is by well-off married men seeking to provide "decency" for their extramarital affairs. For the male partner, these secret marriages involve none of the financial commitments that a normal marriage brings and, since he usually holds the only copy of the agreement, he is in a position to terminate it whenever he wishes. Women, on the other hand, often end up as the losers. Some idea of the prevalence of this practice can be gleaned from the number of paternity claims. In 1999, according to the Egyptian justice ministry, there were 12,000 paternity cases before the courts, of which 70–90 per cent were thought to be the result of *'urfi* marriages.[32] A study in 2005 put the number of cases somewhat higher, at 14,000–21,000.[33]

Despite all the hazards, Bahgat and Afifi suggest young Egyptians value *'urfi* marriages as a way of escaping the norms of parental and social control in order to "engage in consensual sexual relations that only a close circle of friends – if even that – are aware of". They continue:

> Although most young people admitted that *'urfi* marriages are not really religiously acceptable, or at least had doubts about its legitimacy, they nonetheless believed that any kind of framework for engaging in a sexual relationship was better than none at all, which was a view that young men in particular ascribed to ... The urge to keep *'urfi* marriages as discreet as possible was paramount among all those involved,

with most expressing fear of the responses of their families should they ever find out.

Young women expressed a further reason for becoming involved in an *'urfi* marriage that was not expressed by young men, and that was "to realise their dreams ... in making their own choices and decisions with regard to whom to marry and to live the illusion of escaping their parents' plans for them, without the need for any serious confrontation". These young women expressed exasperation at the contradictions between their mobility while pursuing a university education – a mobility that provided them with the opportunity to interact with men and to make their own decisions – and the restrictions on their mobility outside of this sphere, which essentially forced them to lead dual lives.[34]

It is this need for concealment, as much as anything, that troubles Sudanese Aisha. She fears it initiates young Arabs into a lifetime of deceit and duplicity. "Especially with men, what it does is create a kind of public persona and a private persona, and when the two run parallel for so long it's really unhealthy. They say: 'I've got away with all of this with impunity. What else can I do, what else can I get away with?'"

This irreconcilable gulf between pretence and reality is one factor that may eventually bring change, but the traditional concepts of the Arab family as a patriarchal institution and marriage as a social and economic alliance between two families are being challenged from other directions too. Later marriage, lower birth rates and increasing numbers of women who go out to work, all play a part.

In the past Arab women usually married in their teens or early twenties but nowadays many more are marrying in their late twenties or early thirties. The change, in some countries, has been dramatic. In the UAE, for example, the proportion of married women in the

15–19 age group dropped from 57 per cent in 1975 to just 8 per cent by 1995. In Kuwait and Libya the figures fell from around 40 per cent to 5 per cent and 1 per cent respectively.[35] Female education has undoubtedly contributed to this but men are also marrying later – a development that is often blamed on the high cost of marriage, the bulk of which is met by the groom's family. Besides the wedding celebration itself, which typically requires lavish displays of hospitality, other costs include the bride-price (thousands of dollars in some cases),[36] jewellery and furnishing the couple's new home. In Egypt the cost of a marriage for families living above the poverty line is eleven times their annual per capita household expenditure and as high as fifteen times among the rural poor.[37]

Needless to say, this arouses alarm among religious elements who favour early marriage as a way of keeping young people from sexual mischief. One Islamic website, for instance, blames the prevalence of masturbation (an indecent practice that has "crept into the youngsters of today") on the tendency to marry later – contrary to the advice of the Prophet – with the result that young people feel a need "to fulfil their carnal desires but ... cannot do so in the normal way".[38] In an effort to combat the trend, Islamic marriage-promotion charities have sprung up in several countries, sometimes organising group weddings where the costs are met through donations from businesses and individuals. At the first such wedding in Syria, in 2000, ten couples married; 350 guests attended the party and each couple received cash and gifts worth around $1,000.[39] The largest group wedding so far in an Arab country came in 2008, when more than 800 Saudi couples married under the sponsorship of a royal charity.[40] In Jordan, besides organising group weddings, a charity called al-Afaf (Chastity) also provides free match-making services and loans towards the cost of a wedding. The loans and marriagebroking facilities appear to be more popular than the collective weddings which some couples suspect will be used to draw them into religious organisations.

It seems likely, though, that these efforts will not reverse the trend towards later marriage and increasing numbers of young Arabs will either engage in illicit relationships which they try to keep secret or resort to technical ways of legitimising them. Besides the *'urfi* marriages prevalent in Egypt, *misyar* (visitor) marriages are especially popular among men in Saudi Arabia. Although recognised by some prominent Islamic legal authorities,[41] *misyar* is highly controversial because the female partner waives most of the rights associated with a normal marriage: the contract simply allows the "husband" to visit his "wife" from time to time for sex. In countries where pre-marital and extra-marital sex is not only stigmatised but also criminalised, this can become an attractive option for some women as well as men. According to Saudi officials, as many as seven out of ten marriage contracts in parts of the kingdom are of the *misyar* type. Most of the women who opt for *misyar* are divorced, widowed or beyond the normal age for marriage. Most of the men are already married and so, in effect, are taking on a mistress but *misyar* also has its appeal for unmarried men. "It's a great solution," a twenty-five-year-old unmarried medical student in Jeddah told Arab News. "I get to maintain all my rights, but I don't have to take care of her financially and don't even have to provide a house for her ... It costs less than having a girlfriend."[42]

Two other developments seem likely to challenge traditional stereotypes of the Arab family in the longer term. One is the increasing number of wives who are no less well educated than their husbands. A report by the Population Reference Bureau noted:

More couples in Arab societies now feature women with

similar or higher levels of education compared with their husbands. In countries such as Egypt, Jordan, and Lebanon as well as among the Palestinians, fewer than one-half of recent marriages fit the traditional pattern in which the husband is more educated than his wife. In these countries, between 20 per cent and 36 per cent of recent marriages have an educational gap in favour of women.[43]

The second development is that marriage, regarded as almost obligatory in traditional Arab societies, is becoming less universal. One indicator is the percentage of women aged thirty-five to thirty-nine who have never married, because those who reach the age of forty without marrying are unlikely ever to do so. Although the number of never-married women in this age group remains very low in Egypt, Mauritania, Oman, Saudi Arabia, the UAE and Yemen (4 per cent or less), the figures for other Arab countries range from 9 per cent (Bahrain) to 17 per cent in Algeria and 21 per cent in Lebanon.[44] In the more traditional areas failure to marry is still regarded as a personal and social catastrophe but elsewhere there also seems to be the beginnings of a recognition that women can achieve self-fulfilment in other ways.

THE ARAB FAMILY began as an extended tribal or clan-based unit. Though the trend today is more towards nuclear families (which often retain many of the old tribal characteristics and power structures), tribalism itself is far from dead. Clans and tribes may be disparaged by sophisticated urban Arabs but their continuing importance is undeniable:

> Tribal networks have not only endured but have taken on new and varied forms. Modern "socialist" or "nationalist" elites bent on "progress", or liberal monarchs with their eyes set on

modernisation, reinstated an already active tribal value system
and deployed tribal networks in mobilising allegiance or
restructuring modern political and social institutions. Tribes,
driven from nomadism to sedentary agriculture to urbanism
in less than a century, mutated in terms of forms, structures,
leadership patterns, environment and material or symbolic
capital. But tribes were not passive entities; they retained
their solidarity networks and value-systems ...[45]

Their importance today varies from place to place; they are most
relevant from Palestine eastwards to the Gulf, and in Sudan, but
they are also found in a more residual form in parts of rural Egypt
and the Maghreb countries (mainly among the Berber population).
Meanwhile Lebanon's multi-confessional faith-based politics also
has many of the hallmarks of a tribal system. Though absent from
some areas, tribalism has proved remarkably resilient in others. The
Marxists who ruled southern Yemen for more than twenty years
sought to eradicate it in the name of modernity – only to see it re-
emerge in the 1990s after their regime collapsed. Similarly, tribalism
began to re-surface in Iraq during the latter years of Saddam Hussein's
rule and has grown further in importance since his overthrow. In
the 1990s, following the Kuwait war, "Saddam suddenly started
encouraging tribal structures, encouraging tribes to come together,"
Salam Pax recalled.

[He] started wanting full lists of tribal shaikhs. There was a
tier system – first-grade shaikhs and second-grade shaikhs
– and he would give them gifts depending on how big the
tribe was and which tribes he was going to bring closer to
him, and which not.
  It became a bit of a business. People were trying to call
themselves shaikhs, because if I decide that I'm the shaikh of

the Pax tribe, then if people need mediation they will have to come and talk to me and I can demand money.

This also brought a revival of tribal courts:

Saddam's courts weren't delivering what people wanted, and then very slowly we started seeing more and more disputes being solved in tribal courts. I think it eased pressure off him, because ... the [official] courts were really, really inefficient. They wouldn't do anything and people just wanted to deal with problems more quickly. These were very quick.

Fasl ["judgment"] was when the heads of tribes would sit together and decide on compensation. It became so bad that you knew exactly how much money you were going to pay if you [accidentally] killed someone, how much you would pay if you ran someone over, if you stole certain things. If you killed a son of the shaikh, then you would probably be paying four times as much as for killing a normal person.

Some tribal shaikhs started charging a percentage out of their *fasl*, and that's when you realised the [official] courts didn't matter any more. If something went wrong, you wouldn't go to the police or the courts, you'd find out what tribe the person belonged to and deal with them.

Fasl was a term that Salam Pax, living in Baghdad, had not heard before the 1990s. These tribal ways had previously been associated with the Iraqi countryside but then they spread to the cities.

You had the middle class for decades and decades drifting away from that structure and not caring any more about their tribal roots. In come the 1990s and you have to know who you belong to. It became so silly. If you were a doctor in a hospital and a patient died, the family would demand *fasl*. You'd have to find out who was your tribal shaikh and get him to talk to the shaikh of the family, trying to explain: 'Look, this was an operation, he died by accident, blah, blah, blah ...' This whole tribal justice thing was big.

One doctor just quit his job because he couldn't afford how much they wanted. Someone died on the operating table. These things happen, and the tribe threatened they would kill him unless he paid *fasl*. It depends on the tribe, obviously, but when it's something as silly as this then you know exactly that the shaikh is going to get a cut – that's how it works.[46]

Under a tribal system people are not equal, said Jamal Khatib, a Jordanian psychiatrist. "The power and the value of each person stems not from himself – it stems from the tribe he belongs to. It does not stem from your work, it does not stem from your education, it does not stem from your goodwill, it stems from the tribe you belong to. The tribe you belong to provides you with the name, which is one of the strongest things in this area – your name, your family name. It provides you with the connections needed to get educated, to get employed, to get work, to get contracts. It protects you against others."

Beyond the protection they afford to their own members, though, the value of tribes is questionable. "They don't produce, they don't plan, they don't manufacture," Khatib said. Historically, they were nomadic and "if they needed something they would invade other tribes and take it. That's why, all through history before Islam, it was difficult to establish a state in the Arabian peninsula, because no tribe would accept to pay taxes to [benefit] another tribe." In seventh-century Madina, the Prophet Muhammad succeeded in halting tribal warfare by making the tribes subordinate to Islam and in turn made possible the creation of a state. "Without Islam this area would have been only tribes, there would be no nation," he said. This resulted in a triangle of forces – state, religion and tribe – which in Khatib's view has continued to shape the internal dynamics of Arab politics ever since: when the state is in trouble, Islam or tribalism fills the gap. Khatib, whose book, *'Ala Madhbah al-Hukm* (On the Altar of Governance), explores the roots of tyranny in the Middle East,[47] continued:

> In Iraq now, the real governors are either rival shaikhs or heads of religious factions. Take Somalia as an example. The driving power is either rival shaikhs or Muslim factions.
>
> Tribes follow the state as long as it gives. Once it starts to take, they consider that this is a violation of their tribe. The first war in Islam was because Abu Bakr al-Sadiq, the successor of the Prophet Muhammad, said tribes should pay *zakkat*, which they considered a tax. Tribes will follow authority as long as the authority gives them resources. Once the authority starts to take, they will fight it.
>
> After the Caliph Umar was assassinated then came Uthman who was from a rich faction of the Quraysh.[48] Tribes took over again and a lot of tribes were thinking of the state as a prize to win, not as an organisational system. I think this continues till now. It's the same – the same way they are looking at the state. If you go to Arab history, the second [Muslim] state was the Umayyad. The whole state was named after a tribe. Then the Abbasid – the whole state was named after a tribe. So tribes took over the state.
>
> You have the tribal system and the Islamic system – they are the lasting systems in this area for the last 1,000 years. But of course there are exceptions. If you come to the last century, Arab nationalism played its part during the 1950s, 1960s. The peak of that was the unity between Egypt and Syria in 1958, thanks to Nasser and his claimed victory in the Suez crisis.
>
> After the war of 1973 oil prices boomed so the weight of power in this area returned back to the Saudis and the tribal

system, with Islam, regained power over Arab nationalism. Fortunately for [the Saudis] the oil money made it easier. The tribe that rules has a lot of money so that they don't have to take taxes from the others – they can pay them. That's why there is no severe conflict [with tribes] except in poor places. Look at Iraq or look at Yemen: if a tribe is not taking its share, they are out of the system, they will fight the system. But in Saudi there is a lot of money that you can give to all tribes.[49]

At the centre of the tribal mentality is the concept of *'asabiyya* – solidarity. "Its positive aspects include a sense of belonging to a community," the Arab Human Development Report noted. "This can amount to a total dedication, or self-abnegation, for the sake of the community that bespeaks an impressive sense of common purpose, one often stronger than that found in some modern forms of societal organisation."[50] But *'asabiyya* – a word with connotations of tying and binding together – has strongly negative aspects too and is sometimes translated as "clannism":

> Clannism flourishes, and its negative impact on freedom and society becomes stronger, wherever civil or political institutions that protect rights and freedoms are weak or absent. Without institutional supports, individuals are driven to seek refuge in narrowly-based loyalties that provide security and protection, thus further aggravating the phenomenon. Tribal allegiances also develop when the judiciary is ineffective or the executive authority is reluctant to implement its rulings, circumstances that make citizens unsure of their ability to realise their rights without the allegiances of the clan.[51]

Clannism, the AHDR continued, "implants submission, parasitic dependence and compliance in return for protection and benefits ..."

The reproduction of this phenomenon across society turns it into an array of suffocating institutions that reward loyalty and discount performance. One is good so long as one's loyalty is guaranteed; it does not matter, naturally, if one's performance is poor; and woe betide clan members whose loyalty falters, however good their performance.

The worst effect of clannism is that it eats into the cohesive force of citizenship and its institutional manifestations ... it produces types of societal organisation that are modern in form but objectively backward ... In East Asia, for instance, traditional family capitalism is responsible for important modern achievements, but in the Arab environment it is associated with a rent-based economic model, with all that that suggests by way of exalting the values of obligation, favouritism, and inefficiency. Consequently, family capitalism in the Arab world has failed to realise the advances of "the Asian miracle".[52]

The simple fact is that Arabs cannot emerge into a new era of freedom, citizenship and good governance while their society continues to be dominated by the obligations of kinship, whether at a family or tribal level, and while kinship systems continue to provide the security and support that other societies manage to provide for all citizens, regardless of birthright or genes. This – and how to change it – is the central challenge that Arabs face today.

3   States without citizens

FOR A REGION that is considered among the most turbulent and volatile in the world, one of the more remarkable features of the Arab countries is the resilience of their regimes and the political longevity of their leaders. The late Syrian president, Hafez al-Asad, spent twenty-nine years in office, while Habib Bourguiba, the first president of Tunisia, outdid him – just – by completing thirty. Saddam Hussein ruled Iraq for almost twenty-four years, Yasser Arafat led the Palestinian struggle for forty-five and the late King Hussein of Jordan, who came to the throne at the age of sixteen, reigned for forty-six years.

Among those still alive at the time of writing, Colonel Muammar al-Gadafy of Libya is the doyen of Arab leaders, having come to power through a military coup in 1969. Not far behind in the longevity stakes is Sultan Qaboos who assumed the throne of Oman in 1970 after deposing his father. Ali Abdullah Salih of Yemen will have ruled for thirty-five years when his current presidential term expires in 2013 and Hosni Mubarak, who became president of Egypt in 1981, secured a fifth six-year term in 2005 which – if he survives – will take him up to the age of 83.

One country which has seen more frequent changes of leadership is Lebanon, but even there Karim Makdisi, Assistant Professor of Political Studies at the American University of Beirut, sees it as little more than a changing of the guard:

> In that sense it's a plus over Egypt and these places where there hasn't been any change of any guard at all since I was

born, basically. But what these guys [in Lebanon] represent, what they do, hasn't changed .... If you talk to taxi drivers or talk to anybody, they will all – regardless of sect – tell you exactly the same thing, which is that [our politicians] are a bunch of useless, corrupt people ... whose job is to make our lives difficult.

These might sound like the typical grumbles of taxi drivers all over the world but it is the degree of alienation in Arab countries that makes them remarkable. Makdisi (who had just spent the entire morning at a government office in Beirut for the annual renewal of his Lebanese passport) continued:

The state represents something which is almost always negative, and this is common throughout the Arab world. No one looks up to the state as something positive. You survive, and you live, and you get through, *in spite* of the state. That's the relationship.

In Egypt Hosni Mubarak is protected by the United States, and the Muslim Brotherhood are feeding on the fact that the vast majority have had it up to here – not so much with the fact that Hosni Mubarak has been around for [almost] thirty years but the fact that he doesn't provide them with jobs, he isn't providing them with what they need.

If he stayed for a hundred years but was providing them with something I'm not so sure there would be such mass demonstrations. But it's a combination of this kind of incredible corruption, the incredible sort of heavy-handed state enterprises with totally ineffective provision of services – and failure when it comes to the Arab-Israeli conflict, of course.[1]

Many ordinary Arabs complain of a huge and growing disconnect between governments and people. For Egyptian Khaled Diab the behaviour and attitudes of most Arab regimes are more akin to those of colonial rulers than a government which has genuine roots among the people. Given the history, this is not entirely surprising, he said:

> Egypt, for example, apart from a few isolated episodes, wasn't an independent country ruled by native rulers for nearly two-and-a-half thousand years. It was always the jewel in the crown of various empires. A lot of the empires were actually based there but it was often a foreign elite that ruled those empires.
>
> [After independence, Arab governments] took over a lot of the instruments of state that were left behind and didn't reform them, so the ruling elite became a kind of pseudo-colonial ruler. Rather than reform the system to make it reflective of the will of the people they also became a distant elite. People feel just as alienated from the native government today in a lot of Arab countries as they did towards their foreign rulers previously.[2]

To varying degrees Arab governments are facing what the 2004 Arab Human Development Report described as a "chronic crisis of legitimacy, often relying on inducement and intimidation in dealing with their citizens".[3] In countries where a government has been freely elected, its right to govern is not usually in doubt, but in the absence of free elections – or at least the sort when there can be a genuine contest for power – Arab governments must look for other grounds on which to base their claims to legitimacy.

Arab states emerged from the colonial era with two basic types of regime. One group were republics of a revolutionary/nationalist flavour while the others were monarchies which leaned heavily towards traditionalism. In concept, these monarchies reflected the patriarchal nature of Arab society, with rulers who regarded themselves not so much representatives of the people as their protectors or guardians.[4]

The monarchies based their claims to legitimacy on religious or tribal roots – claims that have no rational basis in a free society. The rulers of Kuwait, Qatar, Oman, Bahrain and the Emirates all came from old and prominent tribes and the "right" to rule was derived from their families' status. The Sabah family, for instance, was a clan of the Anizah tribe which had migrated from Nejd – the central plateau of Saudi Arabia – to Kuwait in the eighteenth century and had ruled locally ever since. The Khalifa family was another clan from the same tribe which had arrived in Bahrain about the same time. The Thani family which rules Qatar is a branch of the Bani Tameem tribe and also arrived from Nejd in the eighteenth century.

The Saudi royal family has tribal roots too, though its main claim to legitimacy today is religious – so much so that the king's religious title, Guardian of the Two Holy Shrines (Mecca and Medina, the two holiest sites in Islam) takes precedence over his royal title.[5] Similarly, the king of Jordan is official guardian of al-Aqsa mosque in Jerusalem, regarded as Islam's third holiest site. Jordan's current monarch, Abdullah II, also boasts of being a "forty-third generation direct descendant of the Prophet Muhammad".[6] Meanwhile the king of Morocco embodies both "spiritual and temporal authority" and is known as *Amir al-Mu'mineen* – the prince (or commander) of the believers.

Though monarchies in Egypt, Libya and Yemen were overthrown during the 1950s and 1960s, those that remain have so far proved surprisingly resilient. One reason, perhaps, is that safeguards built into the system can be used to prevent an "unsuitable" candidate from inheriting the throne. In Arab monarchies, although the royal family's right to rule is assumed, succession is not necessarily determined by order of birth (as it is with the British monarchy). The Saudi basic law, for example, merely states that rule passes to "the most upright" among the founding king's sons and their children's children.[7] On coming to power, a new ruler nominates his successor, usually by appointing him crown prince. The crown prince is chosen after informal consultations with senior members of the royal family or, in more contentious situations, through a formal meeting of a "family council".[8] A variant of this can be found in Oman, where the succession is to be decided by a meeting of the Ruling Family Council within three days after the sultan's death. However, Sultan Qaboos – who is childless – has also provided a sealed letter nominating his preferred successor, which is held by the Defence Council. If the Ruling Family Council fails to agree, the letter will be opened and whoever has been named will take over.[9]

Once nominated, a crown prince can also be removed and replaced by someone else. This happened in Jordan during the last days of King Hussein's reign, when he unexpectedly disinherited his brother, Hassan, who had been crown prince for many years, and instead nominated his own eldest son, Abdullah. The king's reasons were set out in a letter to Prince Hassan which was published in Jordanian newspapers.[10] In Morocco there is similar potential for a change of heir: the succession passes in direct male line and by order of primogeniture, *unless the King should, during his lifetime, designate a successor among his sons apart from the eldest one.*[11] These succession arrangements give Arab monarchies a flexibility that others in Europe have often lacked, and may well have contributed to their survival.

Technically speaking, Arab monarchs also rule by consent from their subjects, which again strengthens their claim to legitimacy, even if consent is little more than a formality and those giving the consent are a tiny section of the public. For a new ruler to formally take office he must receive the *bay'a* – pledge of allegiance – from leading personalities. In Saudi Arabia "citizens are to pay allegiance to the king in accordance with the holy Qur'an and the tradition of the Prophet, in submission and obedience, in times of ease and difficulty, fortune and adversity."[12] The "citizens" in this case are, in order of precedence, other members of the Saudi royal family, the *ulema* (religious scholars), the council of ministers and the consultative council (*majlis al-shura*).[13] In Kuwait a *bay'a* is required from parliament. Any individual or small group of individuals who refused to give the *bay'a* would, of course, immediately put themselves on a collision course with the new ruler but – unlikely as that may be – it is still a consideration in the selection process. Michael Herb writes:

> The need for a *bay'a* of citizens outside the ruling family does put a constraint on dynastic choices, for should a *majlis al-shura*, or the *ulema* in Saudi Arabia, refuse, as a group, to give the *bay'a* to a new ruler, it would cause a crisis of a severe sort ...
>
> In a more general sense, it appears that the ruling families, when they choose heirs apparent, do consider the popularity of different candidates and the reaction their succession to the rulership would evince. The ruling families have a valuable franchise and do not want to unnecessarily expose it to threats, among them the difficulties that might accompany the elevation of a truly unpopular king or emir.[14]

Although rejection of a new ruler may seem a remote possibility, it actually happened in 2006 when the emir of Kuwait died and his crown prince, Shaikh Sa'ad, was named as the new ruler. The late emir had been in poor health for several years, as had the 76-year-old crown prince – with the result that the prime minister, Shaikh Sabah, had been deputising for both of them. Initially, it was expected that Shaikh Sabah would continue to deputise following the accession of the crown prince.[15]

Five days after the emir's death, however, a group of royal family members made an unusual move. Instead of giving the *bay'a* to the crown prince, they visited the prime minister and "reaffirmed the trust bestowed upon him by the late emir", according to a statement from Kuna, the official news agency. On the same day a leading Kuwaiti newspaper, *al-Qabas*, took another unprecedented step by politely urging the crown prince to step aside. In a front page article, it said national burdens had exhausted Shaikh Sa'ad and urged him to make one further sacrifice by "leaving it to who is able among the sons of the honourable ruling family".[16]

In the meantime, Shaikh Sa'ad had not uttered a single word in public. He attended the late emir's funeral in a wheelchair, and in TV pictures he showed little reaction when Kuwaiti citizens offered condolences on the emir's death. The exact nature of Sa'ad's illness, and the extent of his incapacity, had not been officially disclosed but according to the pan-Arab daily, *al-Quds al-Arabi,* he was unable to concentrate or identify people and was possibly suffering from Alzheimer's disease.[17]

This presented two constitutional problems. One was that Kuwait's law of succession required a new emir to "be of sound mind" upon taking office – and it appeared that Shaikh Sa'ad might not be. The other problem was that under the constitution a new emir must take the oath of office at a special sitting of parliament "before assuming his powers".[18] The oath consisted of a single sentence – "I swear by Almighty God to respect the constitution and the laws of the state, to defend the liberties, interests, and properties of the people, and to safeguard the independence and territorial integrity of the country" – but there were fears that reciting the necessary words was beyond Shaikh Sa'ad's capability. The speaker of parliament was said to have been asked to shorten the oath – which he reportedly refused.[19]

After a good deal of backroom discussion during the week following the emir's death, there were reports that Shaikh Sa'ad had agreed to abdicate. Parliament, though, was becoming impatient. In the absence of a formal resignation letter, it met to consider medical reports on Shaikh Sa'ad's condition and then unanimously declared him unfit for office. A few minutes after the vote Shaikh Sa'ad's abdication letter arrived at the parliament building, conveniently blurring the question of whether he had jumped or been pushed.[20] Shaikh Sabah, the prime minister, was then sworn in as the new emir.

The Gulf monarchies, of course, are especially fortunate in that vast amounts of oil, coupled with small populations, have allowed them to minimise discontent and, in effect, buy legitimacy by providing for their subjects in ways that the poorer Arab states have been less able to do. Even so, the credentials of the religious-based monarchies have begun to be questioned. The extravagant lifestyle of numerous Saudi princes, including the late King Fahd himself, plus the regime's close relationship with the United States, strikes many Saudis as inherently un-Islamic – a theme that Osama bin Laden was able to capitalise on. In a tape issued in 2004 al-Qa'ida's leader condemned the Saudi regime for "violating God's rules", and for devout Muslims the truth of his allegations was all too obvious: "The sins the regime committed are great ... it practised injustices against the people, violating their rights, humiliating their pride," he said, blaming the royal family for wasting public money while "millions of people are suffering from poverty and deprivation".[21] In Morocco, too, the divine right of the king has also been publicly questioned – most notably by the Jamaa al-Adl wal-Ihsane (Justice and Spirituality Association), a technically banned organisation which seeks to impose Islamic law and establish a caliphate.[22]

Such challenges may not be an immediate threat to the regimes' existence but they do illustrate the hazards of depending on religious credentials. This is most apparent in Saudi Arabia because the ultra-conservative version of Islam that prevails there severely limits the regime's freedom to manoeuvre. It faces conflicting pressures from Islamists and traditionalists on one side, and on the other from a highly educated liberal elite, but is unable to satisfy either. While broadly recognising a need to reform and modernise, its solution is to proceed at a snail's pace for fear of alienating the traditionalists. However, it cannot proceed very far without confronting some of the basic tenets of Wahhabi religious teaching – for example, on the rights of women – which would inevitably damage its legitimacy in the eyes of the traditionalists. As a western diplomat in Riyadh put it: "There's an elite that's quietly trying to reform society but it feels constrained and unwilling to challenge the religious principles at the core of its claim to power." [23]

One example of tiptoeing around the edges was the king's decision in 2009 to replace the head of the unpopular religious police – a move intended to give the force a more humane face but which failed to address the underlying issue of whether the kingdom should be employing religious police at all.

So far, it is the legitimacy of the tribal-based monarchies that seems least vulnerable. While the traditional values of their societies remain strong (which may not be for ever) they are likely to remain secure, and that could give them enough time to evolve from absolutism to democracy under a titular European-style monarch. Among the Gulf states, Kuwait has probably gone furthest down this road, with an assertive but often reactionary parliament which is not afraid, on occasions, to battle with the emir.

It is the legitimacy of the Arab republics, meanwhile, that appears to be most immediately in doubt. Alongside the monarchies, a number of revolutionary regimes emerged in the twentieth century whose credentials were based primarily on nationalism: Algeria, Egypt, Iraq, Libya, Syria, Tunisia, the separate states of North and South Yemen – plus the Palestinian liberation movement which, though lacking a state of its own, fitted a similar mould. Typically, these revolutionary regimes pursued populist or socialist strategies – nationalisation, land reform and so on – which held out the promise of a better future for the masses. At the same time they presented themselves as defenders of the nation's independence, resisting the corrupting, exploitative effects of western imperialism and in particular generating unfulfillable popular expectations regarding the conflict with Israel.

In the wake of successive defeats by Israel, and amid high unemployment, poverty and rampant corruption, it has become all too obvious that they have failed to deliver. Some of the republican regimes have also begun to resemble monarchies, calling into question their stated purpose. This has left them scrabbling around for other reasons to justify their existence. As the Arab Human Development Report put it in 2004:

> Most regimes, nowadays, bolster their legitimacy by adopting a simplified and efficient formula to justify their continuation in power. They style themselves as the lesser of two evils, or the last line of defence against fundamentalist tyranny or, even more dramatically, against chaos and the collapse

of the state ...To a certain extent, it can be considered an implicit admission of the bankruptcy of the claims of positive legitimacy on which official propaganda still insists, with growing despair. Sometimes this political blackmail is pitched in idealistic terms as in claims that modernisation stands up to fundamentalism or terrorism, or that a strong state counters a passive course of drift and resignation.

The predominant approach can be described as pragmatic, characterised by its flexibility in selecting bases of legitimacy that fit the moment. Many a regime has converted from socialism to capitalism, or from secularism to Islamic discourse and vice versa, whenever such a move seemed likely to protect its survival.[24]

The report also noted: "Sometimes the mere preservation of the state entity in the face of external threats is considered an achievement sufficient to confer legitimacy." The one route to legitimacy that seems not to have occurred to any of them is that of governing well.

CONSIDERING THE WIDESPREAD public disenchantment with Arab regimes, the key question is: how do they survive? One view is that they maintain power through coercion and repression – that Arab societies, in the phrase adopted by the Bush administration, are "fear societies" where those who oppose the regime are ruthlessly crushed. Certainly there are elements of that but it over-simplifies the picture. As Timur Kuran puts it, "states rely on violence insofar as they cannot accomplish their objectives through persuasion and economic incentives".[25] No dictator can coerce a whole nation single-handed; he needs a critical mass of allies in order to survive. Wholesale repression risks creating too many enemies; it is far better to have a populace which is docile, submissive, acquiescent or even resigned rather than one which is angry and recalcitrant. So the goal, most of the time, is to secure people's cooperation or even their indifference but not, on the whole, to deliberately antagonise them. There is nothing particularly magical about the way this works. Whoever controls the state has access to state funds which can be used to buy support or to weaken opponents. Whoever controls the state also has the power to forbid or permit – again, in exchange for support. To some extent these are levers that governments use everywhere as an aid to survival but in non-democratic systems there are fewer constraints on their use.

The typical Arab regime is both authoritarian and autocratic – authoritarian because it demands obedience and discourages questioning; autocratic because power is highly centralised and concentrated around the head of state.[26] The head of state himself is modelled on the traditional Arab father figure: in concept, if not reality, he is wise and benevolent, commands respect, dispenses largesse and arbitrates between the conflicting demands of his sometimes bickering children. He may not be liked but he may nevertheless be admired for his *rujula* – "manly" qualities such as strength and toughness.[27] The typical regime is also highly personalised: appointments depend more on who people are and their relationships with others than on ability. This in turn leads to high levels of incompetence, which is one reason why chains of command are kept short, with little delegation of responsibility. There is also a lot of discretion in the exercise of power: laws and regulations may be enforced selectively or waived according to circumstances and the people affected by them. There is minimal transparency and almost no accountability. Taken together, the personalisation of government, the discretionary use of power and the lack of transparency and accountability lead to widespread corruption, cronyism and nepotism.

One way to describe this is as a "patrimonial" or "neopatrimonial" system – a politicised form of patriarchy derived from the word "patrimony" ("property inherited from one's father or ancestors").[28] The term "patrimonial" was first used by Max Weber, the German sociologist, in connection with a style of government found in early-modern Europe. Essentially, it is a system where "the mechanics of the household are the model for political administration".[29] For "household" in this context, picture a rather grand ancestral home with plenty of land, servants, gardeners, gamekeepers, etc; imagine how the lord of the household would have run it – then apply that to the running of a country. Patrimonial government has several distinctive characteristics. It is not based on hard-and-fast rules and is built around personal relationships. In a patrimonial bureaucracy "the line between persons and offices [is] notional"[30] and the holder of the office is more important than the office itself. How this works in practice can be seen from the following snapshot (taken early in 2009) showing distribution of senior government posts in the Gulf states:

In Qatar, ruled by Hamad bin Khalifa al-Thani, twelve of the twenty-six government ministers had the family name "al-Thani". These included the key posts of prime minister, defence minister, interior minister and foreign minister.

In Bahrain, ruled by Hamad bin Isa al-Khalifa, fifteen of the twenty-six ministers had the name "al-Khalifa". These included the prime minister, two deputy prime ministers, the interior minister, the finance minister and the foreign minister.

In Kuwait, ruled by Sabah al-Ahmad al-Jabir al-Sabah, nine of the twenty-five ministers had the name "al-Sabah", including the prime minister, two deputy prime ministers and the ministers of defence, foreign affairs, oil and interior.

In the United Arab Emirates (president: Khalifa bin Zayid Al Nuhayyan; vice-president: Muhammad bin Rashid Al Maktum), seven of the twenty-five ministers had the name "Al Nuhayyan" and three had the name "Al Maktum".

In Saudi Arabia, seven of the twenty-eight ministers, including the prime minister, deputy prime minister, defence minister, foreign minister and interior minister bore the family name "Al Saud".[31]

The point to note here is not just the number of family members involved but the positions they or close allies hold:

> Spheres that are strategically important for the survival of the regime such as internal affairs, security, oil and gas or defence are the exclusive preserve of the core elite. Ministries such as those for the environment, for water or for education, on the other hand, are usually headed by clients of the core elite rather than its own members. Those in charge of the economy or of religious affairs may be borderline cases, while the foreign ministry normally serves as a mouthpiece of the head of state.[32]

Personalisation of government can be applied in various ways, according to the needs of the situation. In Yemen, for instance, where national unity is an important issue, government posts are allocated to ensure that key tribal and regional elements from around the country are represented. However, a look at the higher levels of the military (whose main function is to protect the regime) shows several members of the president's family, plus others from his home village and tribe, in crucial positions. The most prominent – and feared – of these is the president's half-brother, Brigadier General Ali Muhsin al-Ahmar, commander of the first tank division and commander of the north western military zone.[33] The president's eldest son, Colonel Ahmed Ali Abdullah Salih, was given a key post as commander of the

Republican Guards and the Special Forces after failing to complete his training at Britain's elite military college, Sandhurst.

Similar structures are found lower down the chain, resulting in large numbers of people, chosen because of who they are or who they are connected with, whose fortunes are tied to those of the regime. Weber contrasted this with "rational-legal" systems where there is a much clearer separation between government and the state bureaucracy. In a rational-legal system the machinery of the state – the civil service, the security forces, the judiciary, etc – implements laws made by the government of the day but its loyalty is to the state. Governments come and go but the machinery of state carries on functioning, regardless of politics. Rational-legal systems operate much more like a machine; they are not only more impersonal but individuals are also replaceable: "Rational-legal bureaucracies ... boast clear-cut spheres of competence, ordered hierarchies of personnel and procedures, and an institutional separation of the 'private' and the 'official.'"[34]

Providing large numbers of government jobs is one of the chief mechanisms by which Arab regimes maintain control and establish their hegemony (at election time in Egypt, for example, state employees are bussed *en masse* to the polling stations). According to Acram al-Bouni, a former Communist who spent a total of seventeen years in Syrian jails, more than 1.5 million people are employed by the Syrian government. Assuming that each supports several family members, Bouni estimates that as much as half of the country's 19 million inhabitants may depend to some extent on government pay cheques, and consequently they fear change.[35] The trade-off, of course, is that by buying loyalty in this way the regimes sacrifice competence and efficiency in the bureaucracy. Another hallmark of patrimonial systems is that "the ruler does not distinguish between personal and public patrimony and treats matters and resources of state as his personal affair."[36] Willie Morris, a departing British ambassador in Saudi Arabia noted this in a confidential missive to his diplomatic colleagues in 1972 which later became public. Of the royal family, he wrote:

> They are a family which includes many of considerable ability, strong personality, and even their own kind of charm: but I doubt if there are any among them, not even King Faisal himself, who have seriously questioned the inherent right of the Saud family to regard Saudi Arabia as a family business, or to regard the promotion of the interests of the family business as taking priority over everything else.[37]

Little has changed since then. Holding the reins of power allows Arab regimes to grant business privileges to themselves or to others in exchange for support, or to restrict the business activities of those who are out of favour. "If you want to start a new company in Syria you've got to meet Rami," the wife of a Syrian official said. "There's a new private university starting up, but if I wanted to open a private school myself I would never get permission, even if I had the best teachers." This is one of the main barriers to reform, she said – reform is a threat to those who have got rich through political connections.[38] The "Rami" who every budding entrepreneur in Syria must meet is Rami Makhlouf, a cousin of President Bashar, whose business interests include SyriaTel (the main mobile phone company), all the duty-free shops, various hotels, the Dunkin' Donuts franchise and lots more besides. In 2008 the United States imposed sanctions on him on the grounds that he "improperly benefits from and aids the public corruption of Syrian regime officials". A statement issued by the US Treasury said:

Rami Makhlouf is a powerful Syrian businessman who amassed his commercial empire by exploiting his relationships with Syrian regime members. Makhlouf has manipulated the Syrian judicial system and used Syrian intelligence officials to intimidate his business rivals. He employed these techniques when trying to acquire exclusive licences to represent foreign companies in Syria and to obtain contract awards ... Makhlouf has become a focal point of Syria's telecommunications, commercial, oil, gas and banking sectors. Despite President Asad's highly publicised anti-corruption campaigns, Makhlouf remains one of the primary centres of corruption in Syria.

Makhlouf's influence with certain Syrian government officials has led to his being able to control the issuance of certain types of profitable commodities contracts. His close business associations with some Syrian cabinet ministers have enabled him to gain access to lucrative oil exploration and power plant projects. Makhlouf's preferential access to Syrian economic sectors has led to complaints about him from members of the Syrian business community.[39]

Benefiting from preferential access and using government contacts to intimidate rivals is not at all unusual among business figures associated with Arab regimes. Makhlouf's misfortune was to be associated with a regime that happened to be targeted by the United States.

In Egypt, "the regime *is* businessmen", Aida Saif al-Dawla, a political activist and professor of psychiatry, complained:

This is a time where you look at the political bureau of the ruling party and you look in the parliament, and if I asked you to divide them into politicians and businessmen, you wouldn't be able to do it ...

Some of them became rich businessmen because of their association, some of them became associated because they are rich businessmen. If you are an Egyptian and you absolutely believe in private enterprise and free markets, and if you are not going to enter a territory which already has its tycoon, you will be more than welcome to join, and you will be invited to join the political bureau of the ruling party.[40]

One of the more blatant examples of legislation passed specifically to further the business interests of one individual was the Lebanese law of 1995 requiring all vehicles to be equipped with a mini fire extinguisher as a safety precaution:

> That many vehicles were barely roadworthy, lacked lights, possessed faulty brakes and were driven with ruthless abandon by young men or with supreme indifference to other road users by middle-aged housewives apparently was of no consequence to the supporters of the fire extinguisher law. Unusually, the law was enforced with spot checks by Internal Security Forces policemen manning checkpoints along Beirut's streets, with transgressors receiving fines. Yet there was nothing altruistic in the sudden government interest in preventing motorists from burning to death in their vehicles. A cabinet minister had received an import licence for mini fire extinguishers and had used his influence to push through legislation requiring that at least one be carried in every vehicle. After a few months, the enforcement of the law dried up, presumably after the fortunate minister had sold his entire stock of fire extinguishers.[41]

"They come in, they take over states and they use the states for making money," Makdisi said. "They make money on a big scale and they distribute services on smaller scales, and buy support through the provision of services. To an extent all politicians do that but the difference here is that there's no alternative to it. In America, congressmen get elected – of course they're going to lobby for their own supporters ... but they are competing against all sorts of people. Someone else will run against the congressman and say 'This guy's stolen $10 million and I won't steal $10 million.' So [in the US] you have an interest to expose the person in power, whereas here [in Lebanon] the unwritten rule is that you don't expose anybody else. The unwritten rule is you cannot bring up any kind of indiscretions, whether it's criminal, corruption, administrative – anything. The agreement is that they all will protect each other's backs."

In the case of Rafik Hariri, the larger-than-life billionaire who became known as "Mr Lebanon", it was impossible to distinguish between Hariri the businessman and Hariri the prime minister. "There just was no line," Makdisi said. As prime minister, Hariri was widely blamed for cultivating a climate of rampant corruption and cronyism. Lebanese-based journalist Nicholas Blanford writes:

> His policy of appointing former employees into key positions in the government and civil service provided ample ammunition for his enemies. There were repeated allegations of Hariri using his vast fortune to bribe politicians and officials into approving his projects. The most notorious example was the allegation that some 40 MPs in 1991 (before Hariri was prime minister) were bribed with cash sums of $50,000 to $100,000 or interest-free loans of up to a million dollars from Hariri's banks to approve the law establishing Solidere.[42]

Nowadays, the central district of Beirut is known to everyone as Solidere, but Solidere was originally the name of the Hariri-led company that rebuilt it after the civil war – an acronym of *SOciété LIbanaise pour le DEveloppement et la REconstruction*. The idea of handing over reconstruction of the devastated city centre to a private developer did have some merit – it cut through the bureaucratic inertia – but it led to politicians, in effect, negotiating on behalf of the government with themselves.

> To counter the potentially intractable problems of having one company renovate properties owned by hundreds of different people and institutions, Solidere came up with an innovative plan to involve owners in the project by offering them shares in the company matching the value of their respective properties. A heavily oversubscribed share offering in early 1994 raised $650 million of which Hariri bought $125 million, becoming Solidere's largest shareholder with a 6.5 per cent stake in the company. While Hariri's supporters argued that the prime minister was putting his money where his mouth was, Solidere's many critics complained of a serious conflict of interest.[43]

The numerous allegations of foul play included claims that judges were bribed to grossly undervalue properties (and thus the value of shares received by their owners). Politicians and judges were also accused of insider trading – receiving tip-offs to sell their shares when the company was floated on the stockmarket. Besides being granted a more-or-less *carte blanche* by the government to redevelop more than 1.2 million square metres of land in the city centre, Solidere was also given permission to create a further 608 thousand square metres of prime real estate by reclaiming land from the sea. This lucrative arrangement, which according to one estimate will eventually yield between $3 billion and $5 billion in profits, was secured by Solidere agreeing to provide infrastructure such as sewage systems, which would normally have been the responsibility of the government.[44]

Among the many questions raised by Solidere's dubious exploits is that of government accountability. "People talk about it, but not officially," Makdisi said. "There has not been one real investigation.

There are some things sitting in courts that haven't been touched in decades now." If such things do not cause a public outcry in Lebanon, where people are able to speak their minds with relative freedom, the picture in other parts of the Arab world is bleaker still. Control of the media and the general sense of powerlessness among the public are obvious factors behind the lack of pressure for accountability, but low levels of taxation also play a part.

It was the cry of "no taxation without representation" that spurred the American revolution in the eighteenth century, and a quarrel between King Charles I and his parliament over tax that helped to trigger the English revolution in the seventeenth century. Charles had managed to rule for eleven years without parliament, generally making himself unpopular, but eventually, mainly as a result of military adventures, he ran into a financial crisis and was forced to seek parliament's approval for taxes. Seizing its opportunity, parliament set about restricting the king's powers and the ensuing civil war ended in 1649 with Charles having his head chopped off. It is interesting to consider, though, that English history might have taken a different course if Charles, like many Arab rulers today, had been able to draw on other financial resources, such as oil. He might well have stayed in power, regardless of his unpopularity, and continued to rule without recourse to parliament.

Taxes are never popular, and the higher the taxes are the more likely it is that people will demand a say in how the money is spent. High taxes, therefore, can act as a spur towards democracy and accountable government. Conversely, where taxes are low the pressure for democracy and accountability is likely to be less.

The Arab countries have notably low-tax economies. Among the Arab oil producers taxation accounted for only 5 per cent of gross domestic product in 2002, rising to 17 per cent in the non-oil countries – which is still very low compared with Germany (39 per cent), Italy (41 per cent) and Britain (37 per cent).[45] Taking the Arab countries as a whole, oil provides most of the government revenue – though the figure fluctuates with oil prices. In 2001 oil provided 59 per cent of Arab governments' revenue, rising to 73 per cent in 2006. Other non-tax revenue such as foreign aid and investment income accounted for a further 9 per cent in 2006, with the result that only 18 per cent of the governments' revenue came from taxes.[46] However, even this is deceptive because Arab governments rely heavily on indirect taxes – goods, services and customs duties – which are less likely than direct taxes to result in demands for accountability. Across the Arab countries, direct taxes provided just under 6 per cent of revenue in 2006.[47] As the Arab Human Development Report noted:

> This type of tax structure also minimises the opportunity for citizens to protest against their government. Direct taxes, in particular income tax, are viewed as the category of tax that gives citizens most proof that they are contributing to the public purse. In Arab countries, the majority of tax receipts are derived from indirect sales and customs taxes hidden in the price ... These types of tax typically conceal the direct link between tax payments and funding of the public purse, thus weakening public pressure for accountability. At the same time, income tax revenue is negligible and tax evasion is on the rise, particularly among influential social groups, which, in principle, should shoulder the greatest burden in funding the public purse, if only as fair return for their greater share of power and wealth. Moreover, in Arab countries, the share of direct taxes appears to have dropped over time, as a result of increasing resort to indirect taxes.[48]

These financial arrangements can assist regime self-preservation in two ways. While low taxes help to relieve pressure for government accountability, high revenues from other sources (mostly oil) provide authoritarian regimes with the means to buy support. Having tasted the benefits of oil, Arabs have become increasingly aware of its negative effects. In 2005, in one of the Doha debates organised by the Qatar Foundation,[49] a motion that "This house believes that oil has been more of a curse than a blessing for the Middle East" was carried by a large majority (63 per cent to 37 per cent).[50] Speaking in favour of the motion, Hossein Askari (an Iranian-born professor at George Washington University and a former energy adviser to the Saudi government) told the audience:

> Oil has been used as a crutch in this part of the world to avoid the reforms that are needed to create a vibrant private sector which would give jobs, productive jobs, and generate revenues for the government. Instead, oil has been used to create less productive government jobs and to give subsidies which are wasteful in order to buy loyalty amongst the peoples of the region.
>
> Oil has also been used to buy very expensive and sophisticated weaponry, which has been used both internally and externally in the region ... And of course in all of this, the western world has meddled ... The western world has supported all manners of dictators in this part of the world – and it's not because of your wonderful good looks – but it's because of oil ... Oil should have been and could have been a blessing. You don't need a PhD to know that the more resources you have, you're better off, but this oil has been mismanaged by the leaders and the governments of this part of the world, and the western world has also interfered and they also created problems. So on balance, what could have been has not been, and on balance, ladies and gentlemen, oil has been a curse.

To a greater or lesser degree, most Arab countries can be described as rentier states because of their dependence on revenue from rents. "Rent" in this context means income from abroad which accrues mainly to the government and involves little productive work. Oil is the classic example but there are others: Egypt benefits in a similar way from the Suez canal and several of the poorer Arab countries receive substantial rent in the form of foreign aid.

Rents allow governments to shower largesse on the populace. This not only helps to keep them docile but simultaneously enhances the regime's legitimacy and reinforces the image of the head of state as a father-provider to whom the public should show due gratitude. In oil-rich states the regime's "generosity" can go to remarkable lengths: in Qatar, for example, it extends to providing university education abroad for any citizen who wants it, and providing local phone calls free of charge. In the poorer Arab countries government hand-outs have traditionally focused on subsidising basic goods such as bread, sugar and fuel and the provision of non-essential government jobs – a practice that helps to keep down unemployment (another potential source of unrest) but also makes the employees and their families financially dependent on the regime. In addition, favours are often bestowed on groups that are important to the regime's survival – for example, the upper ranks of the military, who might pose a threat. Obviously, in a system where government hand-outs are partly discretionary, there is also scope to discipline groups that are out of favour by withholding largesse.[51]

In 2004 an extensive study of 107 developing countries through almost four decades found that "oil wealth is robustly associated with increased regime durability" and that "oil-rich states also have lower levels of social protest and suffer fewer civil wars than other developing countries".[52] The view that revenue from rents can help to perpetuate authoritarian regimes and thus impede progress towards democracy has widespread support among economists and political scientists.[53] However, this does not necessarily mean there is a direct causal connection between the two – otherwise periods of low oil prices would be catastrophic for the regimes that depend on oil. The 2004 study found that low oil prices did increase levels of social unrest, but not enough to seriously jeopardise the regimes – suggesting that "these regimes may have had robust social coalitions that went much deeper than the simple purchase of legitimacy" and that "they may have built institutions that could provide non-repressive responses to organised opposition".[54] In other words rents, in themselves, are not the only factor and their political value probably depends on how skilfully regimes make use of them. It remains to be seen whether the most recent dramatic fall in oil prices, coupled with the banking crisis and global recession that took hold in 2008, will have a more serious effect, especially in the light of predictions that it could become the deepest recession in several generations.

Regime survival also has an international dimension, though one that is often full of paradoxes and contradictions. Western interest in maintaining stability and the status quo results in the propping-up of autocratic regimes despite the declared policy of promoting freedom and democracy. On the Arab side, while adopting a generally anti-imperialism stance and zealously talking about national sovereignty, most regimes view alliances or cooperation with the west, and the United States in particular, as a practical necessity – either as a route to modernity or as a way to escape the west's wrath. This can be a tricky game to play, however. The benefits of a visibly warm relationship with the US have to be balanced against the possibility of negative domestic consequences that would damage the regime's legitimacy. The Egyptian government, for example, tries to play down its embarrassingly heavy dependence on American economic aid. In Saudi Arabia, the American military presence on the kingdom's "holy" soil – especially the Prince Sultan airbase near Riyadh – became a particularly sensitive issue which forced the Saudi government to impose stringent conditions on its use during the invasion of Iraq. In August 2003 the US formally handed the base back to the Saudis, though a small American presence remained, allegedly for "training" purposes.[55] Qatar, on the other hand, cheerfully played host to Centcom for the invasion of Iraq while, just a few miles away from the airbase, al-Jazeera television broadcast what the Bush administration denounced as lies, lies and more lies about the war. Some regimes adopt a contrary view, using defiance (or at least apparent defiance) of the United States to mobilise domestic support and thus enhance their survival prospects. But this can be a dangerous game too, as Saddam Hussein learned to his cost.

IN RECENT YEARS almost all Arab regimes have espoused some kind of political reform, while usually insisting, on grounds of cultural differences, that they must be allowed to do it in their own way and – crucially – at their own pace. By 2005 even ultra-conservative Saudi Arabia had taken its first very tentative steps towards democracy with local government elections – elections in which women were barred from voting and 50 per cent of the seats were still to be allocated by royal appointment.[56] Starting in 2003 Crown Prince Abdullah (later to become King Abdullah) also organised a series of wide-ranging discussions that brought together a variety of different elements from across the kingdom.[57]

Elsewhere in the region the year 2004 brought numerous reform initiatives, among them the Alexandria Declaration,[58] the Sana'a Declaration,[59] the Doha Declaration,[60] the Arab Business Council Initiative[61] – even one from the Egyptian Muslim Brotherhood.[62] Although these were mostly non-governmental in their origins, the Alexandria, Sana'a and Doha conferences had government backing. President Hosni Mubarak opened the Alexandria conference with a speech that made suitably encouraging noises:

> We have embarked on our own path towards political reform in Egypt some years back with the aim of continuing, developing and strengthening political practice. We have given special care to establish the fundamental basis for the institutional structure of the state, to create a democratic atmosphere that places citizenship, equal opportunity and freedom of expression, regardless of gender or religion, as fundamental rights that augment both public participation and the role of the civil society.[63]

A couple of months later, the Arab League's summit meeting in Tunis vowed "to pursue reform and modernisation in our countries, and to keep pace with the rapid world changes, by consolidating the democratic practice, by enlarging participation in political and public life, by fostering the role of all components of the civil society, including NGOs, in conceiving of the guidelines of the society of tomorrow, by widening women's participation in the political, economic, social, cultural and educational fields and reinforcing their rights and status in society, and by pursuing the promotion of the family and the protection of Arab youth". Ahead of the summit, fifty-two Arab NGOs from thirteen countries issued a rather stronger communiqué on reform from Beirut (since they were banned from meeting in Tunis).[64]

"All Arab reform initiatives share key common demands," Mona

Yacoubian writes. "These include calls for free and fair elections; constitutional reforms that feature a diminishing of executive power and a commensurate increase in legislative and judicial powers; the repeal of emergency laws and the abolishment of exceptional courts; an end to the practice of torture; and the lifting of restrictions on civil society, NGOs, and the media."[65] But Yacoubian, an adviser to the Muslim World Initiative at the US Institute for Peace, notes that all such initiatives – whether from governments or activists – tend to suffer from the same problem: they make grand statements of intent but have little or nothing to say about how these goals might be accomplished.

It was also no coincidence that all the declarations mentioned above were issued in 2004. The overthrow of Saddam Hussein in 2003, together with President Bush's speech announcing his "forward strategy of freedom" later that year,[66] certainly stimulated much Arab debate about democracy and reform, but it was not entirely new. In 1999, for instance, a government-backed "Emerging Democracies Forum"[67] was held in Yemen – a country which had adopted a multi-party system in 1990 following the unification of north and south, and had held the Arabian pensinsula's first competitive elections under universal suffrage in 1993 (all of it with very little support or encouragement from outside).

Actual reform, as opposed to mere talk of it, has been far more limited and those reforms that have occurred have usually been initiated from on high rather than as a result of pressure from below. During the Iraqi occupation of Kuwait, for example, the emir promised to restore parliamentary government once his country had been liberated. This was almost certainly aimed at pleasing the Americans, so they could say they were fighting for democracy, but the reinstated parliament turned out to be far less of a rubber stamp than most Arab parliaments and in 2006, after years of opposition from traditionalists, women took part in elections for the first time (though none won any seats). These were real steps forward, if only modest ones.

Nevertheless, it is difficult to avoid the conclusion that much of what passes for reform is just window-dressing for the sake of international respectability. "Few governments want to be seen as undemocratic," Kenneth Roth, the director of Human Rights Watch wrote, "Yet the credentials of the claimants have not kept pace with democracy's growing popularity." He continued:

> Even overt dictators aspire to the status conferred by the democracy label. Determined not to let mere facts stand in the way, these rulers have mastered the art of democratic rhetoric that bears little relationship to their practice of governing ...
>
> It is not that pseudo-democratic leaders gain much legitimacy at home. The local population knows all too bitterly what a farce the elections really are. At best, these leaders gain the benefit of feigned compliance with local laws requiring elections. Rather, a good part of the motivation today behind this democratic veneer stems from the international legitimacy that an electoral exercise, however empty, can win for even the most hardened dictator. Because of other interests – energy, commerce, counterterrorism – the world's more established democracies too often find it convenient to appear credulous of these sham democrats.[68]

Though willing to concede a vague desire for reform, they are fearful of letting it go too far lest, in the words of Timur Kuran, "the generated frustrations and hopes spark a revolutionary prairie fire". Like all nondemocratic rulers, those of the Arab world sense that the public declarations of support they receive vastly exaggerate their actual support and that "if reformist movements ever gather momentum, public discourse could turn against them and threaten their own survival".[69]

The ideal survival strategy, therefore, is to acquire permanent status as an "emerging democracy" without the need to ever fully emerge. Regimes in Egypt, Yemen and elsewhere have adapted to electoral politics (mainly by manipulating them to their own advantage) and are probably stronger, not weaker, as a result. One way of achieving this is through "parties of power" which depend on the state rather than genuine popular support and lack any coherent ideology:

> Parties of power develop from a ruling elite's drive to maintain control over the state ... Being created from above, these parties are not meant to become autonomous political forces in their own right, but are utilised by the ruling elites as instruments of co-optation, sometimes even coercion and political hegemony. To begin with, they simply serve the regime to sustain a network of patronage relationships with the major sociopolitical, economic and administrative actors of the country.
>
> By using the patronage networks, in fact, the regime seeks to ensure its very survival by granting these actors access to the spoils system of the state in return for their complacency concerning the existing order. What is more, such ruling parties also serve to provide regime-supportive majorities in the major elected institutions of the state ...
>
> A truly competitive multiparty system cannot emerge within a system of parties of power, which unbalances the electoral game in favour of a single party or a set of political parties that thrive on the spoils of the state.[70]

An intriguing question in all this is why – apart from Egypt where there are frequent strikes and demonstrations – public expressions of discontent are not greater than they are. One explanation is that Arab regimes have largely succeeded in making the masses docile and acquiescent. To some extent the prevailing sense of hopelessness helps too: what is the point of complaining if you know it will achieve nothing? For those who are tied to the regime through employment by the state, it is foolish to rock the boat, and where the state bureaucracy operates through discretion and favours rather than strict rules it is advisable not to be known as a troublemaker. Besides that, authoritarian rule is perhaps less shocking in a society accustomed to authoritarianism more generally.

This does not mean there is little discontent: Kuran suggests there is much concealment of grievances and "preference falsification" where "individuals unhappy about prevailing conditions routinely keep quiet, even feign contentment, simply to escape the punishments imposed on critics." He continues:

> Such preference falsifiers need not be hiding identical grievances. Some might resent the wealth disparities among Arab states, others the vested interests that keep key economic sectors closed to competition, and still others the un-Islamic decadence of their rulers.
>
> Whatever their motivational differences, individuals who misrepresent their political preferences under real or perceived social pressures help sustain an equilibrium whereby the prevailing autocracies survive indefinitely, along with their protectionist and dirigiste economic policies ... Insofar as Arab citizens hide, shade, or distort their misgivings about prevailing policies, Arab public discourse on the relative merits of political alternatives gets truncated and corrupted.[71]

The one major exception to this generalised picture of submerged Arab dissent is, as Kuran notes, the Islamist opposition:

If there is any public forum that an Arab government cannot close down, it is the mosque. Although it might arrest clerics for subversion and regulate the content of religious education, its ability to control organisations that claim an Islamic identity is still limited. Consequently, to dissatisfied people of all walks of life Islamism offers the safest forum for venting frustrations and exploring solutions on matters ranging from constitutional rules to making a living.

"These authoritarian regimes," Makdisi said, "essentially made it their business to take out any kind of social movements that were oppositional. They succeeded in essentially wiping out the leftists and the nationalists but they have failed decisively in taking care of the religious ones, because the religious ones found a mechanism, they have found alternative means – they are not just challenging the state because they want to take over the state."

Mass movements such as Hizbullah, Hamas and the Muslim Brotherhood, he said, "have understood what people want and they're channelling their efforts – at least part of their efforts anyway – into understanding and complying with what people want, in order to get this popular support, because their whole strategy rests on popular support". This is very different from capturing the state in the old-fashioned way that most of the existing regimes have done, or as insurgents might wish to do – and it is a difference that the regimes seem not to have grasped. Hizbullah, Hamas and the Brotherhood, are not simply about religion. They feed on discontent about corruption – a major factor in Hamas's election victory in 2006 – and they step in (often very efficiently) to provide social services that the regimes fail to provide.

The regimes, Makdisi said, simply don't care, and people know it. "If you're not someone who has to worry about the electricity because you and your family are going to get it all for free anyway, it's not of concern to you – you don't even think about it." Unless the regimes are challenged by mature, active citizens, they will probably continue to get away with it: "They have a direct interest to ensure that they do not develop a class of citizens – citizens as opposed to clients or subjects." But while the regimes may appear more and more aloof and disconnected from the people, the Islamist mass movements have established popular roots: their feet are firmly on the ground, even if they also have their eyes set on heaven.

4   The politics of God

KHOLOUD'S YOUNGER BROTHER was a typical nineteen-year-old, keen on heavy metal bands and studying at a university in Cairo, when suddenly he went missing. Three days later he reappeared without explanation but his family's relief at knowing he was safe quickly turned to alarm when they realised how completely he had changed.

"He used to have all these posters on his bedroom wall, Metallica and Scorpions and stuff like that," Kholoud recalls. "He tore them down, got rid of all his music tapes, and he said: 'I'm throwing them away and I'll start to know God again.'"

> We were all scared – mainly my mum. He started wearing a *gallabiya* to go to the university. He started to refuse every type of food. He was criticising every single detail in our daily life – such as saying cucumber is *haram* [forbidden] because of its shape.
>
> He was against everything except milk and dates – the "food of the Prophet". Thank God he wasn't talking about the camel urine. You can walk in the street in certain areas near here and find signs that say: "We sell camel urine that used to be used by the Prophet Muhammad." It makes no sense, what these people waste their time and energy talking about.[1]

Transformations of this kind are not unusual in Egypt. "In every four or five families you will probably find two or three cases," Kholoud said. "After two years my brother got back to normal gradually. He changed his way of clothing again and came back to having his usual long hair. We've never talked about why he gave it up. I'm sure he saw a lot of negatives and stupid, unbelievable things but it's not every time that the boy gets back to a normal level of thinking and dealing with others."

The experience of Kholoud's family was just a tiny ripple in the tide of religious fervour that has swept across the Middle East during the last thirty or forty years. The change may have been gradual but the outward signs are everywhere, from the increased numbers of young women who now wear hijab, to the bookshops stocked with religious titles and the popularity of websites such as Islamway, Islamweb and IslamOnline.[2]

Mahmoud Alhourani, a West Bank Palestinian, witnessed the change in neighbouring Gaza. "I remember Gaza before its intifadas," he said. "I used to go there for holidays from Hebron, and really Gaza was a lovely and happy place in the summer. We'd go and we'd eat ice cream in the street ... three cinemas were open ... there were little gaming machines in the streets, people selling things. Later, after the first intifada [1987–93] I had a chance to go again for a wedding. You could see how people had become more religious, Gaza was losing its charm. The whole city was going in this direction because people were desperate, people became more closed."[3]

Though not religious himself, Alhourani found this perfectly understandable. "I think religion fills a psychological need for people in general all over the world," he said,

> But sometimes this need can disappear in countries where they are comfortable, where they are secure. In the Middle East, apart from the politics part of it, religion has found big doors in people's spirit to enter and live there, because they are less confident about everything, less comfortable. I see it like a weak body which things from outside can attack and

make ill. I hope I'm not being too harsh on religion in this but ... when people have difficult times they go to religion – it's security and answers.

Once, when I was feeling a bit down about work and life, I went to a barbecue. This guy was sitting there with his wife and talking about religion – how religion was making him comfortable and how his life was good. He looked so confident when he was speaking, and he looked happy. I thought: 'I wish I could think like him'. But I know I don't think like him. Maybe he had even more problems than me but religion had made him numb – it's the best drug in the world. Imagine you have that kind of relationship with this superpower, Allah. Even if He kills half your children you will still be smiling because you think He is doing this for a good reason – it's part of His plan.

Religion is one response to what has become known as the "Arab malaise". For millions of believers, religion provides a comfort zone of certainty and hope in a world of doubt and despair. Khaled Diab, a secular Egyptian, explained:

There's a psychological comfort when things are going up in smoke around you, when a lot of your neighbouring countries are in conflicts, when there are threats – either real or perceived – all around you. Although living standards have improved for millions of Arabs, the relative gap between the Arab world and the west has grown.

People draw comfort from religion but then the rigidity that it imposes on their way of thinking sets them back further – they become less willing to think out of the box, less willing to question traditions and belief, and so on. The rigid prescriptions of religion are woefully inadequate for the modern age. The region is trapped in a cycle of religion holding back development, which leads to people embracing religion more, as a comforter.[4]

According to Diab – and it is a view he holds along with many others – the lurch towards religion began with the Arabs' overwhelming defeat at the hands of Israel in 1967:

> The result was a big, big push by the Islamists because they were able to use that to discredit the secularists. They said look, it's because you deviated from the proper path that we got this crushing defeat. And the Iranian revolution [1979], even though it was Shi'i, inspired a lot of Sunni Muslims to think: 'OK, if the Shi'i can have an Islamic republic, why can't we Sunnis also manage one?' There's a fair amount of admiration for Iran's balls, if you like, among hard-core Islamists in the Arab world.

More recent events have given further impetus to this trend. The success of the *mujahideen* in driving out Soviet forces from Afghanistan at the end of the 1980s bolstered the idea that devout Muslims, with God on their side, are invincible on the battlefield. Israel's unilateral withdrawal from southern Lebanon in 2000 after twenty-two years of occupation was another key event, allowing the local Shi'i resistance movement, Hizbullah, to claim victory and gain kudos in Lebanon and beyond, across sectarian divides. Six years later, Hizbullah also survived a heavy month-long bombing campaign by Israel which allowed it to claim another victory. Whether these were truly victories is less important than their psychological effect – the fact that so many Arabs regarded them as such. Most immediately, Hizbullah's celebrations in Lebanon during the early summer of 2000 were almost certainly a factor in the outbreak of the second Palestinian intifada just a few months later. More important, though, was the perception that military success is achievable when inspired by religion, and this held out the prospect of an end to the Arab malaise.

While some have turned to militancy, many more regard the Islamic revival as a call to piety and moral renewal, as exemplified by the preaching of Amr Khaled who, modelling himself on American televangelists, has established a huge popular following among women and the young. Central to this kind of revivalism is a Qur'anic verse, often quoted by Amr Khaled, which says: "Allah changeth not the condition of a folk until they [first] change that which is in their hearts."[5] That idea, in the opinion of Aida Saif al-Dawla, an Egyptian political activist and professor of psychiatry, postpones any need for real change and poses no threat to the establishment:

> Even the official media project this message that the world is not changed by changing systems, or by a coup or whatever – the world changes by every single person working on him or her self, changing him or her self, and eventually, when we are all good and changed, then corruption will go away, poverty will go away because nobody is going to be able to tolerate the fact that a neighbour is sleeping hungry while they have enough – this kind of charity talk.[6]

Abdellah Taia was a teenager in Morocco when the "return to God" movement arrived there and more women began wearing the veil:

> My teacher of Arabic literature was elegant, she used to look after her hair and have nice colourful clothes and shoes with high heels. Suddenly – boof! – in the middle of the year she appeared in a veil and gave us a whole class about this ... how what she had been doing was *haram* (forbidden) and now she had got back to God. I remember some girls in the class

went "ulululul" [to celebrate]. She was proud and happy and told us we should be one day like her. It was in 1990, just the beginning of this movement.

At the time I didn't understand that as a message coming from a teacher this is dangerous, but now in Moroccan schools and high schools the women teachers are obliged [to wear the veil] because the Islamists are among them and they put warning notes in their pigeonholes, saying things like "Go back to God, or otherwise ..." Even my sister, who is a teacher – now she's put on the veil. It's a huge phenomenon in Morocco.

Around the same time in my neighbourhood people used to come to us and invite us to join us to join them for couscous and religious discussion after the Friday prayer. I didn't go because I was not interested in that, but a lot did.

Taia, whose childhood dream was to become a film director, says Islamists also targeted the entertainment industry, encouraging stars to publicly declare their "return to God". It started in Egypt, the hub of Arab film production, with producers and others coming from Saudi Arabia to finance films and soap operas, he said. In that way they could reach – and influence – the Arab masses. The first star to declare her faith and retire was Shadia (Fatima Ahmad Kamal), in the 1980s:

Shadia was like Joan Crawford for Arabs, and suddenly she said: "I'm coming back to God." The good thing with her is that she didn't say her art was haram – she didn't renounce what she had done, and her films are still shown. But the others who came after her did.

The first male actor to do that was Mohsen Mohieddin. He was the favourite actor of Youssef Chahine [regarded as the greatest Egyptian director] and had starred in several of his films. He just ended his career. His wife, Nisrine, was an actress too. So beautiful. They both "went back to God".

It's dangerous because these people have so much influence in the Arab world and when they do that they get a lot of coverage in magazines.[7]

For thirty-five-year-old Taia, who now lives and writes in a tiny apartment in Paris, these are a cause of deep despair. "It seems that religion has become more and more strong since I was a child," he said. "I don't know how the Arab world will escape from this growing power of religion. No one in the Arab world has the strength to separate state and religion. No one has the courage to do it. There is no real secular opposition. In Morocco King Hassan II killed off the left. The real power is the king and he is also the official representative of Islam – *Amir al-Mu'mineen*."

IN THE ARAB countries religion is not only a source of personal comfort, but collective comfort too. It provides a sense of identity, belonging and solidarity in the face of threats from outside. No one, of course has a single, all-embracing identity. Besides religion, many factors – nationality, class, profession, politics, gender, sexuality and so on – all contribute to people's sense of who they are, and the priorities vary according to circumstances. But there is no denying the importance of religion in the way Arabs perceive themselves. In 2004 a poll by Zogby International asked people in six Arab countries which they considered to be their primary identity: as a citizen of their country, as an Arab, as a Muslim, or as a citizen of the world. In four of the six "Muslim" was the preferred identity – the exceptions being Lebanon and Egypt.[8] The poll's findings become particularly striking when compared with western countries, where national identity generally takes precedence over religion by a wide margin.

Primary identity in six Arab countries[9]

	Jordan	Morocco	Lebanon	Saudi	UAE	Egypt
Citizen	26	38	77	34	19	59
Arab	29	6	12	10	11	20
Muslim	33	48	3	56	66	17
Citizen of the world	6	8	8	<1	1	NA
Not sure	3	0	0	0	3	5

All figures are in percentages

For religion to be effectively linked to identity it needs to be expressed visibly and publicly. At an individual level this is most obvious in styles of dress – hijab for women and various kinds of beards for men – but it is also expressed communally through efforts to create a visible Islamic ethos in the public sphere, either through peer pressure or direct enforcement as seen in Saudi Arabia where the *mutawa* (religious police) enforce dress codes and the closure of shops at prayer times. The purpose is to maintain a public image of Islamic virtue, regardless of what people may actually do in private. The closure of cinemas in Saudi Arabia was one example of constructing this public facade. Though never formally banned, cinemas disappeared gradually during the 1970s and 1980s in the face of religious opposition. Mai Yamani, a Saudi-born writer and academic, recalls watching films in the kingdom during the early

1970s, in mixed audiences where women had their faces unveiled. But there was a backlash after the assassination of King Faisal in 1975. "He was too much of a moderniser for the clerics. He had introduced TV," she said. According to Ferej Alowedi, chargé d'affaires at the Saudi embassy in London, the problem was that many of the films in circulation at the time were "very offensive to our conservative society". While closing cinemas helped to keep up the appearance of a "pure" Islamic society, it came at a time when video cassettes and satellite TV were beginning to make the "offensive" films available for private viewing.[10]

Treating religion as a badge of identity leads to a heightened emphasis on its outward, physical aspects at the expense of spirituality and ethics. Codes of "correct" Islamic behaviour are prescribed, often down to the minutest detail, and often on the slenderest of scriptural evidence. This phenomenon is not confined to Arab Muslims of course – it occurs wherever people feel the need to assert a religious identity. Muttaqun Online, a website "for those who fear Allah" (registered, incidentally, in Florida), suggests that God does not recognise *sadaqa* (charity) from men who wear "unlawful" clothing. Men's clothes, it says, should cover the whole body but not reach below the ankles, and must not be tight-fitting. White and green are good colours to wear but red is bad unless mixed with another colour, and you must not tuck your shirt inside your trousers.[11] Beards are obligatory and must not be trimmed (though the moustache part should be cut). Vague scientific claims are sometimes invoked too in support of these practices. "Medical reports," Muttaqun says, "reveal that the beard protects the tonsils from sunstroke."[12] There are warnings on other websites against men wearing gold jewellery, silk or "feminine" attire. "Feminine" dress includes neck-chains, bracelets and earrings worn by men, according to IslamOnline.[13]

Among Muslims who regard such things as important, an extraordinary amount of effort goes into discussing the rules. In 2006, as Malaysia prepared to send a man into space, a two-day conference of 150 "astronauts, scholars, academicians and professionals" was summoned "to discuss the question of living in space for Muslim astronauts".[14] Since Muslims are required to pray five times a day, one of the issues they considered was how often to pray on a space station which passes through sixteen days and nights every twenty-four hours. They also discussed how to ascertain the direction of Mecca and how to perform ablutions and prostrations in weightless conditions. The result was an eighteen-page set of guidelines, available in Arabic, English and Russian.[15]

Emphasising the minutiae also leads to a kind of holier-than-thou competitiveness. The more detailed – and strict – the rules become, the more those who observe them can believe they are behaving as a "good" Muslim should. Some horrifying examples were reported at the height of the factional conflict in Iraq, when people were killed for the most trivial of "sins" – among them barbers who gave customers "un-Islamic" haircuts.[16] This reached a peak of absurdity when al-Qa'ida elements in Iraq sought to impose "gender" segregation of vegetables. Claiming that tomatoes are feminine and cucumbers masculine, they argued that greengrocers should not place them next to each other, and that women should not buy or handle cucumbers.[17]

As the religious tide swept across the Middle East, more extreme versions of Islam gained in prominence: more rigid in their interpretations of the scripture and less tolerant of alternative views. Supported by new wealth that oil had brought, religious ideas from the Gulf countries, which tended to be of the ultra-conservative kind or, in some cases, ultra-radical, spread their influence far and wide.

The shift towards extreme versions of Islam also brought growing intolerance. Independent-minded Muslims came under pressure to adopt "correct" views and practices (usually as defined by the most vociferous elements), and the attacks on various nonconformist thinkers in Egypt during the 1990s were one example. Farag Fouda was an outspoken secularist who ruthlessly mocked many of the leading Islamists. In 1992 a group of teachers at al-Azhar, Cairo's ancient religious university, who had set up a committee to confront the "helpers of evil", accused him of blasphemy. Five days later, Fouda was shot dead in his office by two members of the militant group al-Gama'a al-Islamiyya. The Muslim Brotherhood publicly welcomed his killing and during the trial of his assassins a scholar at al-Azhar who was also a former Brotherhood member argued in court that their action was justified because the authorities had failed to punish Fouda for his apostasy.[18]

Two years later, Naguib Mahfouz, the only Arab ever to win a Nobel prize for literature, was stabbed in the neck outside his home. Mahfouz, who was eighty-two at the time, survived the assassination attempt but with his right arm partly paralysed. Curiously, the motivation behind this attack was a novel he had published thirty-five years earlier – *Awlad Haratna* (Children of Our Alley), an allegorical tale of a Cairo backstreet in which God, Adam, Jesus and the Prophet Muhammad appear as thinly disguised characters. In 1959 the novel was sufficiently acceptable to be serialised in the semi-official daily, *al-Ahram*, though the religious authorities at al-Azhar succeeded in blocking its publication in book form and eventually it was published in Lebanon.[19] The book remained officially unavailable in Egypt but controversy was revived after Mahfouz won the Nobel prize in 1988 and various death threats ensued, including one from Shaikh Omar Abdul-Rahman of al-Gama'a al-Islamiyya, who was later sentenced to life imprisonment in the United States for his role in the 1993 bombings of the World Trade Center. Mahfouz's work was always controversial to some extent but in the changing religious climate it has tended to become more controversial, rather than less, with the passage of time. A similar situation developed around a novel by the Syrian writer Haydar Haydar, *Walima li Aa'shab al-Bahr* (A Banquet for Seaweed) which had been published in 1983 to literary acclaim. However, when the Egyptian ministry of culture decided to reprint it in 2000 students at al-Azhar rioted, claiming it was offensive to Islam.[20]

Another high-profile case was that of Nasr Abu Zayd who taught Arabic literature at Cairo University. In 1992 he applied for a professorial post and the Standing Committee of Academic Tenure and Promotion considered three reports on his work. Two were favourable but the third, prepared by the Islamist Dr Abdel-Sabour Shahin, questioned the orthodoxy of Abu Zayd's religious beliefs and claimed that his research contained "clear affronts to the Islamic faith". The committee then rejected his promotion by seven votes to six.[21] Not content with that, Shahin later wrote an article for an opposition newspaper accusing Abu Zayd of apostasy.[22] This in turn inspired a group of Islamist lawyers to file a lawsuit at the end of 1993, seeking to divorce him from his wife, on the grounds that a Muslim woman cannot be married to an apostate.[23] In 1994 a court in Giza threw out the case but in 1995 the Cairo appeals court reversed its decision, declaring the marriage null and void.

"After the verdict was handed down, I was accompanied by a police guard at every step," Abu Zayd told *al-Ahram Weekly*.[24] "My last visit to Cairo University after that was to take part in debating a PhD dissertation in the Faculty of Arts, Islamic Studies branch. The university was turned into a military fortress to protect me. The question was, 'Will the university be able to take these measures every time I go there to teach?' It was impossible to teach like this and, at the same time, I could not imagine not teaching. On the way home, I told [my wife], 'This is not going to work out.' She nodded ... When some of our neighbours asked our guards why they were with us, they responded, 'because of the *kafir* [the infidel]'."

In July 1995 Abu Zayd and his wife flew to Madrid for a conference and decided not to return to a life under siege in Egypt. They settled in the Netherlands, where he took up a professorial post at the University of Leiden. Today, Abu Zayd suggests that the Islamist campaign against him also had some backing from the Egyptian government: "It's very hard to make the distinction. It was not from the government as an official body, but the Islamist who made the case was part of the ruling party ... The entire affair came out of the university, and the university is a government institution."²⁵ His alleged "affronts to the Islamic faith" were not the whole story, he said. There was a political dimension too because he had been analysing the way presidents made use of religion:

> Sadat [president of Egypt from 1970 to 1981] wanted to have his own legacy. He wanted to fight against Nasserism and to fight against socialism and communism. It's well known he had to make a pact with Islamism. His discourse – if you saw how Sadat liked to look – with *gallabiyya*, with the *sebha* [prayer beads] most of the time ... He was a man of everything but he presented himself as "the believing president" (*al-ra'is al-mu'min*). It's very very important, this kind of symbolism. Nasser was just Nasser, the president, and when Sadat presented himself as the *mu'min* [believer] it meant Nasser was not *mu'min*. It was a game.
>
> My real crime in Egypt was that most of the time I was busy analysing this discourse. In analysing religious discourse I

did not mean the people who are in al-Azhar, I meant religious discourse in politics: the speeches of the president and how the president started his speeches by quoting the Qur'an, ended his speeches by quoting the Qur'an, presenting himself as something like the Mahdi, the imam. Whether he was a good Muslim or not, this was the discourse.

THE HARASSMENT EXPERIENCED by Abu Zayd and others who challenge the prevailing orthodoxy is often blamed on fundamentalists and/or Islamists. Though there are certainly Muslims who fit the general description of religious fundamentalism – a literalist reading of scripture, a rejection of other interpretations, an aspiration to "return" to the roots of their faith, and so on – that in itself does not make them troublesome politically. Those who focus in this way on a life of piety and devotion to God might be better described as "traditionalists"[26] since they may or may not be Islamists. The defining characteristic of Islamists is that they view religion as inseparable from politics but within that broad definition there are various kinds of Islamist thought, ranging from the traditionalist to the radical and even some that have been described as liberal. Islamists also differ among themselves over the means for achieving their goals, with some favouring armed struggle and others more lawful means.

Distinguishing between "violent" and "non-violent" Islamists, between "terrorists" and "non-terrorists", is an obvious concern of governments and security forces but it can easily give the impression that Islamists who engage peacefully in electoral politics are not a problem. While this may be true from a security point of view, the preoccupation with combating terrorism tends to obscure a much bigger issue at the core of Islamist ideology: the relationship between religion and the state.

One of the basic requirements for freedom in politics is that sovereignty belongs to the people. Power may be delegated to representatives but the people should remain the ultimate arbiters. Islamists, no matter how they try to dress up their ideology, do not accept this key point. Islamism, by definition, seeks to apply "Islamic" principles to the state – hence the slogans of the Muslim Brotherhood, "Islam is the solution" and "The Qur'an is our constitution." Some Islamists directly counter the idea of popular sovereignty with another slogan: *"La hukma illa lil-Lah"* ("Sovereignty belongs to God alone") and this leads to the claim that secular Muslims who question God's sovereignty in worldly politics are guilty of apostasy. According to the Egyptian theologian, Muhammad al-Ghazali, secularism in the form of a separation between religion and state is "unadulterated *kufr*" (unbelief), while according to the Saudi Directorate of *Ifta'* (Preaching and Guidance) whoever believes there is a guidance more perfect than that of the Prophet, or that someone else's rule is better than his ... is a *kafir* (unbeliever).[27]

The precise relationship between religion and the state is a matter of debate among Islamists. Some aspire to a full-blooded theocracy while others envisage a degree of popular decision-making – at least up to the point where it conflicts with the "principles of Islam" (which of course begs the question of how the principles of Islam are to be determined, and by whom). Although some visions of an Islamic state do allow more space for freedom and democracy than others, the underlying problem is still the same: an anti-libertarian assumption that linking the state with religion is both legitimate and necessary. Not only that, but religion claims the right, at least in some circumstances, to over-ride the will of the people.

While such ideas have become the hallmark of Islamist opposition movements, and it is generally the opposition movements that most actively propagate them, they are not necessarily rejected by Arabs in the Muslim mainstream. The number of out-and-out secularists in the Arab countries – certainly those who publicly identify themselves as secularists – is extremely small and some degree of linkage between religion and the state is accepted in virtually every Arab country, even those with relatively secular regimes such as Syria. The argument between governments and Islamists is usually about how much linkage there should be and what form it should take – not whether there should be any at all.

Saudi Arabia is the most extreme case among the Arab countries of binding religion and state together, as can be seen from its Basic Law which was promulgated by a royal decree in 1992:

> Article 1: The Kingdom of Saudi Arabia is a sovereign Arab Islamic state with Islam as its religion; God's Book and the Sunnah of His Prophet (God's prayers and peace be upon him) are its constitution ...
>
> Article 6: Citizens are to pay allegiance to the King in accordance with the Holy Qur'an and the tradition of the Prophet, in submission and obedience ...
>
> Article 7: Government in Saudi Arabia derives power from the Holy Qur'an and the Prophet's tradition.
>
> Article 8: Government in the Kingdom of Saudi Arabia is based on the premise of justice, consultation, and equality in accordance with the Islamic Shari'a.
>
> Article 9: The family is the kernel of Saudi society, and its members shall be brought up on the basis of the Islamic faith ...
>
> Article 11: Saudi society will be based on the principle of adherence to God's command ...
>
> Article 13: Education will aim at instilling the Islamic faith in the younger generation ...

Article 23: The state protects Islam; it implements its Shari'a;
it orders people to do right and shun evil; it fulfils the duty
regarding God's call.[28]

Among the other members of the Arab League, Islam is "the religion
of the state" in Algeria, Bahrain, Egypt, Iraq, Jordan, Kuwait, Libya,
Mauritania, Morocco, Oman, Qatar, Tunisia and Yemen. In Algeria
and Morocco, the official status of Islam is specified as an element of
the constitution that cannot be amended.[29] In the draft Palestinian
constitution (approved in 1993), Islam is the "official" religion but
"Christianity and all other monotheistic religions shall be equally
revered and respected"[30] and the tiny Arab state of Comoros seeks "to
draw on Islam for continuous inspiration for the principles and rules
governing the Union".[31] Lebanon, with its complex mix of Christians,
Sunnis, Shi'is and Druzes, has no state religion and officially aspires
towards a non-confessional system but, in the meantime, aims to
achieve a balance between the different religious groups through the
state and government structure. Syria, likewise, has no state religion
and "guarantees the freedom to hold any religious rites, provided
they do not disturb the public order".[32] Islam is not specified as
the official religion in the constitutions of Djibouti or the United
Arab Emirates and both promise equality without distinction on
religious grounds.[33] Sudan, also, has no official religion as such. Its
constitution merely says that "Islam is the religion of the majority
of the population" (70 per cent Sunni Muslims with a minority of
Christians and indigenous beliefs.)[34] However, the Sudanese state
does have a constitutional role in policing moral/religious standards:
"The state will seek by laws and directive policies to purge society
from corruption, crime, delinquency and the consumption of alcohol
by Muslims."[35] Article 18 adds:

> Those working for the state and those in public life should worship God in their daily lives, for Muslims this is through observing the Holy Qur'an and the ways of the Prophet, and all people shall preserve the principles of religion and reflect this in their planning, laws, policies, and official work or duties in the fields of politics, economics, and social and cultural activities; with the end of striving towards the societal aim of justice and righteousness, and towards achieving the salvation of the kingdom of God.

Article 65 also specifies "the Islamic Shari'a" as the source of law, along with "national consent through voting, the Constitution and custom", and goes on to say that "no law shall be enacted contrary to these sources".

In Yemen, Shari'a law is "the source of all legislation"; it is "the principal source of legislation" in Egypt and "the basis of legislation" in Oman.[36] In Bahrain, Kuwait, Syria and Qatar shari'a is "*a* main source of legislation".[37] The draft Palestinian constitution says "the principles of Islamic Shari'a are a major source for legislation" but it goes on to say: "Civil and religious matters of the followers of monotheistic religions shall be organised in accordance with their religious teachings and denominations within the framework of law, while preserving the unity and independence of the Palestinian people."

The Iraqi constitution, approved by a referendum in 2005, specifies Islam as "a fundamental source of legislation" and says that "no law that contradicts the established provisions of Islam may be established." It also, rather confusingly, says that no law must contradict "the principles of democracy" or "the rights and basic freedoms stipulated in this constitution".[38] These potentially contradictory stipulations reflect conflicting political pressures at the time of drafting and it is unclear how they might be reconciled in practice.

One further linkage between the state and religion concerns heads of state. Among the Arab republics, the constitutions of Algeria, Mauritania, Syria,[39] Tunisia and Yemen specify that the president must be a Muslim (a *practising* Muslim in the case of Yemen)[40] – thus enshrining the principle of religious discrimination in law. Among the monarchies, the accession of a Muslim ruler might be assumed but Jordan, Kuwait, Oman and Qatar specify it in the constitutions too.[41]

If the purpose of religion is to serve the spiritual and moral needs of people, it is reasonable to ask what purpose is served by states having a religion. It seems unlikely that much thought was given to this question when Arab constitutions were written. Possibly the drafters just assumed, in the light of Islamic history and other constitutions saying similar things, that it was a good idea. However, making Islam the official religion does have some practical effects: it can strengthen the state's claims to legitimacy (as a "defender" of the faith) and establish a legal pretext for the government to interfere in religious affairs – for example, by controlling what may be said in sermons and employing clerics and scholars who are amenable towards the regime. More negatively, it also provides a basis for the state to become embroiled in issues of personal "morality" that many would regard as private matters, such as sexual behaviour.

When most Arab constitutions were originally drafted, of course, governments did not have to contend with well-organised Islamist opposition movements. If their intention in adopting Islam as the official religion was to enhance legitimacy and influence the way it was practised locally, they have since been proved mistaken. Presenting themselves as defenders of Islam established a yardstick by which their performance could be judged – unfavourably – by Islamists and it is now the Islamists who tend to influence governments' religious policies, rather than vice versa. Once Islam is established as the official religion it requires only a few small steps of logic to argue, firstly, that the state should do nothing that conflicts with "Islamic principles" and, secondly, that it has a duty to enforce "correct" Islamic behaviour among its citizens. Thus, states which may have set out with the hope of controlling religion find themselves instead falling under its control.

One of the more ludicrous consequences of states espousing religion can be seen in Saudi Arabia where state resources are diverted to combat witchcraft – in effect giving official recognition to the power of magic.[42] In 2007 Mustapha Ibrahim, an Egyptian living in Saudi Arabia, was executed in Riyadh after being convicted of sorcery. "Ibrahim had been accused by another foreign resident of practising magic in order to separate him from his wife and ... evidence had been found in his home, including books on black magic, a candle with an incantation 'to summon devils' and 'foul-smelling herbs,'" the official Saudi News agency reported. For good measure, he had also confessed to adultery with a woman and desecrating the Qur'an by placing it in the bathroom, the agency added.[43] A few years earlier, communal violence in Najran province involving the Shi'i Ismaili sect, which reportedly left more than forty dead, was officially blamed on a "sorcerer".[44]

Superstition is strong in Saudi Arabia but the kingdom is not unique in that respect, nor in the harsh measures it takes against suspected witches: nineteen were hanged in colonial Massachusetts in the 1690s as a result of the famous Salem witch trials. The sensible way to deal with witchcraft, though, is to discourage superstition and protect the gullible from being conned by those who claim magical powers. Treating sorcery itself as a crime (and a capital one at that) rather than as a case of fraud gives it undeserved credibility and reinforces popular belief in its power. This was an issue that British legislators grappled with several centuries ago and eventually resolved through the Witchcraft Act of 1735 which repealed all previous laws but made it illegal to "pretend to exercise or use any kind of witchcraft, sorcery, inchantment, or conjuration, or undertake to tell fortunes ..." The key word here was "pretend". It signalled an important change because the law no longer recognised the existence of magical powers. Instead, the law's concern – as the act put it – was to prevent and punish "any *pretences* to such arts or powers as are before mentioned, whereby ignorant persons are frequently deluded and defrauded".[45]

Instead of challenging popular belief in magic, however, the Saudi authorities play along with it – apparently for theological reasons – arguing that the correct way to fight it is through the power of the Qur'an. Dealing with witches is one of the responsibilities of the Commission for Promotion of Virtue and Prevention of Vice (the religious police). In 2006 the commission set up a special department in the city of Taif and a year later was said to have arrested twenty-five people suspected of witchcraft (twenty-four of whom were described as non-Saudis).[46] In an interview with Arab News, Shaikh Ibrahim al-Ghaith, head of the religious police, revealed that the commission was working with divers to retrieve magical spells that had been cast and then thrown into the sea (presumably so that no one could reach them and undo them). "We cooperate with divers in this aspect," he said. "After the spells are found, they are then broken using recitations of the Holy Qur'an. We do not use magic to break magic spells, as this is against the teachings of Islam as mentioned by the Supreme Ulema. But we use the Qur'an as did the Prophet Muhammad (peace be upon him)."[47]

According to the IslamOnline website, "black magic is an undeniable fact":

> As for the Islamic legal status on practising black magic, it is forbidden ... Magic can be dispelled through magicians themselves or sorcerers or through applying their methods. However, it is forbidden to go to a magician or a soothsayer or the like to dispel the magic as stated in the hadiths of the Prophet. Magic can also be dispelled by the power of the Glorious Qur'an ... Surat al-Baqarah [the second sura of the Qur'an] is known to have the power of driving away evil spirits and dispelling magic.[48]

BATTLES BETWEEN SPIRITUAL and temporal power raged for centuries in Europe before being decisively (though not totally) resolved with the triumph of secularism. In the long term this is the likely outcome in Arab countries too – and certainly the only outcome that can provide real freedom – but at present the genuinely secularist voices are few and recent trends have been mostly in the opposite direction. Though the basic arguments about state and religion are very similar to those heard in Europe in the past, they are complicated by other issues. Objections to secularism also reflect the anxiety that many Arabs (and indeed Muslims more generally) feel about their relationship with the rest of the world, and especially the secularised west. Fauzi Najjar writes:

> The intellectual crisis agitating Muslim minds today centres on the relationship between modern Muslims and their past. For the last two centuries, Muslims have found themselves caught up between authenticity (attachment to their values

and culture) and modernity. They view most western ideas, ideologies and institutions as a threat to Islamic law, values and culture. Among these foreign imports, secularism seems to represent the greatest danger.[49]

Critiques of the west figured strongly in the work of Abu al-A'la al-Mawdudi (1903–1979) and Sayyid Qutb (1906–1966), two of the most prominent Islamist ideologues. Qutb, an Egyptian, was the leading figure in the Muslim Brotherhood from the mid-1950s until his execution in 1966. His political discourse contrasted the "realm of Islam" with the "realm of *jahiliyya*" (ignorance, decadence) which in his view had not only infected the west but much of the Muslim world too:

> Qutb seems to have been completely opposed to any reconciliation with democracy. In the beginning, he was opposed to the idea of calling Islam democratic and even campaigned for a just dictatorship that would grant political liberties to the virtuous alone. In his *tafsir* (interpretation) of *Sura al-Shura* (Chapter 42 of the Qur'an) he said: "Democracy is, as a form of government, already bankrupt in the west; why should it be imported to the Middle East?"[50]

Mawdudi, who founded the Jamaat-e-Islami in Pakistan, was also a fierce critic of western civilisation – arguing (among other things) that western democracy culminates in the tyranny of the majority and that secularism leads to the repudiation of God's universal lordship.[51]

To many ordinary Muslims, "secularism" ('*almaniyya* in Arabic)[52] has acquired deeply negative connotations, implying not just the separation of religion and state but hostility towards religion in general and Islam in particular. This has not always been the case.

Egyptian Copts have long used the term *'almaniyyun* to distinguish lay members from the clergy, and it had not yet become a dirty word in 1919 when the Egyptian Wafd Party was formed. The Wafd was originally known as the Secular Party – a name which indicated, according to Najjar, that the party "was based on social, political and national identities, with no reference to religion. Its slogan was *'al-din lil-Lah wa al-watan lil-jami'* ('Religion belongs to God, the homeland belongs to all'). The party was not opposed to religion; it simply rejected any ecclesiastical order in Islam, as well as the king's attempt to use religion to buttress his authority."[53]

Najjar attributes the increasingly negative perceptions of secularism in Egypt to the Islamists' smearing of Muslim secularists with charges of apostasy. More generally, Herman De Ley suggests it is a result of the imperial/colonial experience; while Europeans have tended to associate secularism with freedom, Muslims associated it with foreign domination:

> The dismissal nowadays of secularism, at least on the level of dominant Muslim discourse, has its historical roots in western colonialism and imperialism in the nineteenth and twentieth centuries: Muslims at that time were confronted with a political secularisation that was imposed by western powers. In the European countries themselves secularisation and laïcisation had clear emancipatory effects (liberating society and man's mind from the ideological and institutional shackles of the Church). In the colonies or protectorates, on the contrary, secularisation was enforced as an ideological weapon – against Islam, that is – in order to suppress national or political aspirations of Muslim communities. Even today in the Maghreb ... the word *laïkiyya*, being transcribed from the French word, *laïcité*, is used as an insult, in order to attack or weaken one's political opponents.[54]

Muslim attitudes were also negatively influenced by Ataturk's secularist/modernist revolution in Turkey, which abolished the Ottoman Caliphate in 1924 and, through a series of sometimes harshly authoritarian measures, sought to eradicate the influence of religion and tradition. Although by the 1920s the caliphate had become, in Ataturk's words, "no more than an historic relic", its abolition sent shockwaves through the Muslim world, prompting moves to re-establish it outside Turkey:

> There ensued a restrained but determined competition among a number of Arab rulers to appropriate the title or, alternatively, to prevent its appropriation by anyone ... King Fuad of Egypt was especially interested in gaining the title of caliph, and he was able to use the monarch's well-established leverage over al-Azhar to further his cause.[55]

It was against this political background that in 1925 Shaikh Ali 'Abd al-Raziq, a relatively obscure Egyptian shari'a judge and scholar of al-Azhar, published a provocative book entitled *Al-Islam wa usul al-hukm* (Islam and the roots of governance), advocating a clear separation between religion and the state. The Prophet Muhammad, he contended, was basically a spiritual leader and not the founder of a state, nor was he a king or the head of a state. 'Abd al-Raziq also argued that the caliphate established after the Prophet's death had no religious justification; it had often been corrupt and at cross-purposes with the Prophet's mission. Thus, it was up to the people, exercising their temporal sovereignty, to establish whatever form of government they saw fit. Not surprisingly, 'Abd al-Raziq was accused of promoting atheism. He was formally censured by al-Azhar's committee of *'ulama* (Islamic scholars), deprived of his title as a *shaikh* and removed from his post as a religious judge.

Following his condemnation by al-Azhar, he told an interviewer from the *Bourse Egyptienne:*

> The main point of the book ... is that Islam did not determine a specific regime, nor did it impose on Muslims a particular system according to the requirements of which they must be governed; rather it has allowed us absolute freedom to organise the state in accordance with the intellectual, social and economic conditions in which we are found, taking into consideration our social development and the requirements of the times.[56]

At one level, 'Abd al-Raziq's book – and especially its condemnation of the caliphate – can be read as a subtle attempt to frustrate the Egyptian king's ambitions: without committing himself on the sensitive question of whether King Fuad was fit to be caliph, he argued instead that the caliphate was unfit to serve Islam.[57] However, 'Abd al-Raziq's case for secularism is still pertinent today (the book is variously described as "a classic of modern Egyptian liberal thought"[58] and "among the most controversial works in modern Islamic history"[59]).

Much of the Islamism-versus-secularism debate – at least on the Islamist side – centres on the nature of Muslim rule established in the city of Madina during the seventh century under the Prophet's leadership. The importance that Islamists attach to this as a model also reflects their generally ahistorical view of religion as providing a set of rules established for all time that cannot be revised in the light of changing circumstances. Secularists, on the other hand, maintain that political institutions (among other things) do not need to be confined by traditions of the past or literalist interpretations of scripture.

Challenging popular views of Muslim rule in Madina, 'Abd

al-Raziq asserted that the Prophet "was never a king, and he never tried to establish a government or a state; he was a messenger sent by Allah, and he was not a political leader"[60] – and in this he somewhat overstated his case. While few would claim that the Prophet was actually a king, it is difficult to deny that his role extended beyond spiritual matters into politics. Islamists, meanwhile, tend to inflate their claims about seventh-century Madina in the opposite direction, typically arguing that it was a complete state with a constitution,[61] that Muhammad was the head of state – its political, military and religious leader – assisted by ministers, advisers, ambassadors and military chiefs, and so on. The historical truth probably lies somewhere in between. In the view of Nasr Abu Zayd, the exiled Egyptian professor, Islamists' characterisation of Madina as a fully fledged state is "a projection of the present over the past":

> We cannot really think of Madina as a state in the modern sense. It was multi-communities – the community of the believers, the community of the Jews and the community of the pagans – the Arabs – so the Madina document [often referred to as a "constitution"] is some sort of an agreement for these communities to live together. Of course, gradually the community of believers became stronger and took over the city and then took over Arabia. But I wouldn't go so far as to say this was a state ... I don't think it is a state in the proper sense.[62]

The historical arguments over Madina are unlikely ever to be resolved to everyone's satisfaction. For secularists, though, this does not really matter. For them, Madina was a one-off because whatever system existed during the Prophet's lifetime, it was changed irrevocably by his death – one reason being that he never appointed a successor or prescribed formal rules for a system of government. From this they conclude that he left it to the believers themselves to decide what to do.

"No other human being can enjoy the Prophet's combination of religious and political authority," Abdullahi Ahmed an-Na'im writes:

> As the ultimate embodiment of this model, the Prophet was accepted by Muslims to be their sole legislator, judge, and commander. That experience was unique and cannot be replicated, because Muslims do not accept the possibility of prophets after the Prophet Muhammad. All rulers since Abu Bakr, the first caliph, have had to negotiate or mediate the permanent tension between religious and political authority, because none of those rulers has been accepted by all Muslims as capable of holding the supreme position of the Prophet, who defined Islam and determined how it could be implemented.[63]

Looking at developments since the death of the Prophet, an-Na'im points out that political regimes in Islamic history have never achieved a total conflation or convergence of religion and state (regardless of any claims they made to the contrary) – and adds that this suited their purposes: it was a convenient impossibility that regimes used to their advantage. Rulers needed a measure of Islamic legitimacy in order to sustain their authority over their Muslim subjects, but Islamic legitimacy, if it was to be at all credible, could only be bestowed upon them by religious leaders who had some degree of autonomy from the state. The result was a kind of fig-leaf "Islamic" state, much like the modern permanently "emerging" democracies where the regime's survival depends on never reaching its declared goal. Once Muslims recognise the practical impossibility of total conflation/convergence between religion and state, an-Na'im says, they will be better placed to move on and "organise and regulate the more pragmatic model of separation".[64]

Nasr Abu Zayd shares an-Na'im's view that Islamists are chasing an impossible dream but says the problem is how to demonstrate the weakness of their case to "the people who are misled or deceived by these kinds of slogans". In Egypt, for example, the Muslim Brotherhood's semi-illegal status allows it to agitate and sloganise but without having to face the realities of everyday politics. At the same time, more secular voices are harassed and suppressed, either by the government or by Islamists themselves. What is needed, Abu Zayd says, is free space for debate and trading opinions:

> Then the Muslim Brothers and the Islamic groups would have to respond to the challenge, have to speak politics, have to have a detailed plan for what they are going to do. Let them be presented in public life. Let them form a [legal] party, and when they form a party they have to present a programme and they have to acknowledge that this is a political programme – it's not the word of God, it's not shari'a.
>
> This is the real challenge. Give them the ground and say "Hey, you are free – come to the light, speak politics." They will fail.[65]

Full exposure to public scrutiny, Abu Zayd argues, would demolish their case because of its inherent contradictions: while insisting that the Qur'an is their constitution, they ignore those parts of it that might be too unpalatable for popular opinion. One example he cites is *jizya*, the poll tax on non-Muslims, which is clearly prescribed in the Qur'an:

> Fight those who believe not in Allah nor the Last Day, nor hold that forbidden which hath been forbidden by Allah and

> His Messenger, nor acknowledge the religion of Truth, (even
> if they are) of the People of the Book, until they pay the *jizya*
> with willing submission, and feel themselves subdued.[66]

The original idea behind *jizya* was that non-Muslims, since they did not serve in the military and were living under Muslim protection, should pay for their protection through a special tax. It has long been abandoned and is generally regarded as obsolete. However, this presents a serious difficulty for Islamists, since they regard the Qur'an's injunctions as binding. Strict adherence to Qur'anic principles, therefore, would require them to reinstate *jizya*. In 1997 the Muslim Brotherhood's Supreme Guide at the time, Mustafa Mashhur, did indeed suggest reintroducing it but, in a country with around 6 million Christians, this caused uproar and the movement later back-tracked.[67] The militant Gama'a Islamiyya, meanwhile, has said it accepts Egypt's abolition of *jizya* on the grounds that the nineteenth-century decree abolishing it had been issued by the country's ruler – thus sidestepping questions about the principle of *jizya* itself.[68]

The more Islamist groups are forced to address practical issues such as this, the more contortions they have to perform in order to get round the difficulties caused by their own religious doctrine.[69] For non-Islamist Muslims, *jizya* presents no great problem: they can justify its abolition on the basis of historicity – that the circumstances in which the tax was imposed no longer exist today. For Islamists, though, this is much more difficult because the words of the Qur'an and the practices of the earliest Muslims form the core of their argument. "If they concede historicity," Abu Zayd said, "all the ideology will just fall down ... the entire ideology of the word of God."

If the case for Islamism is fragile but not yet seriously damaged, the case for secularism has always been disadvantaged by suspicions of harbouring an anti-religious agenda. Much as Muslim secularists may deny it, the charge has generally left them on the defensive. An-Na'im, however, addresses the problem head-on in his book, *Islam and the Secular State*, which begins with the challenging statement: "In order to be a Muslim by conviction and free choice, which is the only way one can be a Muslim, I need a secular state."

An-Na'im makes clear that he is not advocating a secular *society* but a state which is neutral with regard to religion – a state whose institutions "neither favour nor disfavour any religious doctrine or principle";[70] a state that has no enforcing role in religious matters, though it can have an enabling role.

> When observed voluntarily, shari'a plays a fundamental role in shaping and developing ethical norms and values that can be reflected in general legislation and public policy through the democratic political process. But ... shari'a principles cannot be enacted and enforced by the state as public law and public policy solely on the grounds that they are believed to be part of shari'a.[71]

Sudanese-born an-Na'im is a graduate of Khartoum University who eventually became a professor of law at Emory University in the United States. As a student in Sudan, his ideas were strongly influenced by the teachings of Mahmoud Muhammed Taha, a political activist and unorthodox religious thinker who was executed by the Nimeiri regime in 1985.[72] In *Islam and the Secular State*, published in 2008, an-Na'im advances the debate about Islam and secularism in several very significant ways – in particular by acknowledging a legitimate role for religion in the public life of Muslim countries. In particular, he distinguishes between the state and politics. He accepts that such a distinction is not always easy to make but regards it as an objective that must be pursued.

Separating Islam from politics, in his view, is "neither necessary nor desirable".[73]

This may seem an odd argument to readers in the more heavily secularised European countries (though less so in the United States, where one has only to look at the debates about abortion and gay marriage to see that religious belief is still an important factor in politics). In Muslim countries, however, where religion is very much a part of everyday life, an-Na'im's argument makes a lot of sense. In essence, by admitting Islam into politics, he shifts the debate away from secularism and turns it into a debate about the role of shari'a in a modern state: the religiously neutral state is not a goal in itself but provides the permissive background against which that debate can take place or, as he puts it, the future of shari'a can be negotiated. (He is talking here about shari'a in its broad sense, as "the door or passageway into being Muslim",[74] rather than a system of justice). Accepting a place for religion in politics does, however, require important safeguards:

> Muslims and other believers should be able to propose policy and legislative initiatives emanating from their religious beliefs, provided that they can support them in free and open public debate by reasons that are accessible and convincing to the generality of citizens regardless of their religious or other beliefs. But since such decisions will in practice be made by majority vote in accordance with democratic principles, all state action must also conform to basic constitutional and human rights safeguards against the tyranny of the majority. This is because democratic government depends not only on the rule of the majority view but also on the fact that the will of the majority is subject to the rights of the minority, however small.[75]

Acknowledging the public role of religion in this way, he says, can encourage debate and dissent within religious traditions, making it easier to challenge – and ultimately overcome – religion-based abuses of human rights since these "cannot be eliminated without addressing the commonly perceived religious rationale."[76] Couched in those terms, the debate is not only about secularism and the relationship between religion and the state but also about the kind of religion practised by Muslims – now, and in the future.

5   Vitamin W

AHMED DRIVES AN old truck, transporting goods around the Moroccan countryside. On market days he leaves his village in the hills behind Essaouira especially early so as to reach the main road before 6am – the time the police set up their checkpoint. If the police arrive at the junction before he does, Ahmed has to pay.

In Morocco taking *baksheesh* from drivers on country roads is almost a routine part of police work. Everyone knows it goes on and the police make only the most cursory efforts to hide it. On a long-distance bus journey between towns it is likely to happen several times. As the bus comes to a halt at the checkpoint, the ticket collector folds up a banknote, steps out and strolls to greet the policeman who is standing behind the bus, out of sight of the passengers. As the ticket collector and policeman shake hands, the money passes from palm to palm. Then, with a cheery wave from the policeman, the bus sets off again.

Not all drivers pay up so readily but the reluctant ones are liable to be informed there is something wrong with their vehicle – a worn tyre, perhaps – or that they have committed some kind of traffic offence, and they soon realise that if they want to avoid a lot of hassle a small sweetener to the policeman will do the trick.

This unofficial tax collection system had been supplementing the incomes of Morocco's badly paid police for years, much to the annoyance of almost everyone else and with little effort by the authorities to stop it. But suddenly it was thrown into disarray by one young man armed with a video camera. The Targuist Sniper (as he called himself) secretly filmed the police pocketing bribe after bribe from motorists at a checkpoint near his home in the Rif mountains – and then posted clips on YouTube.[1] In the videos most drivers seem to know what is expected of them. Some are so well prepared that they are already holding money out of the car window as the policeman approaches. But one man, in a blue van, is less willing. He gets out of his van and appears to start arguing with the two policemen.[2] One officer pulls out a notebook and opens it as if to make a report. At this, the driver dips into his pocket and hands something to the other policeman. Problem solved. The notebook is put away and the van drives off.

The Targuist Sniper's action may not have put a stop to police corruption but it did trigger unprecedented debate in Morocco's non-state media. It also forced the authorities – for once – to treat the issue seriously: nine officers were arrested, others were transferred, and the police themselves reportedly dispatched plainclothes video teams to root out corruption. Meanwhile, the Sniper gave an interview to *TelQuel* magazine, saying he was "just a Moroccan citizen who dreams of a better Morocco, and of security services worthy of the name, whose priority would be to protect the people and not to pick them clean as is the case today."[3] As one YouTube viewer pointed out, though, the Targuist Sniper was only attacking the small fry: "You are hounding small-time policemen who take twenty dirhams [around $2.60] because life is hard. We need snipers for the big thieves who are making a huge bonanza ..."[4]

Of all the problems within their society, corruption is probably the one that Arabs complain about most – in private if not always in public. Resentment at official corruption has become a galvanising factor for opposition movements, especially the Islamist opposition, providing them with opportunities to claim the moral high ground.

Rampant corruption in the Palestinian Authority, for example, is generally regarded as a key factor behind the unexpected electoral victory of Hamas in 2006.

"Corruption starts top-down," said Aida Saif al-Dawla, an Egyptian political activist and professor of psychiatry. "If I'm corrupt the only way to ensure that I am safe is to corrupt my juniors. When you go higher up, it is called commission – it has a nicer name."[5] Whatever name it goes by, corruption flourishes at all levels where the social climate is conducive. It ranges from petty "survival" corruption where government employees supplement their meagre salaries by extracting money from the public in small amounts, to "structural" corruption involving government contracts and "commissions" on them, often with the knowledge and blessing of the highest echelons of power.

In general, the bigger the contract the more scope there is for making money on the side – and in the Middle East oil money has made matters worse. With booming revenues from the 1960s onwards, the Gulf states had plenty to spend on vast infrastructure projects and military aggrandisement, and western governments and companies were happy to supply their needs. But securing a contract was not simply a matter of offering the best service at the most competitive price. Shortly after David Owen took over as Britain's foreign secretary in 1977 he received a confidential letter from the British embassy in Jeddah explaining the complexities of doing business with the Saudis:

> The exact nature of the Saudi decision-making machinery is obscure but certainly much is settled by agreement between the senior princes. To secure a contract, a company must secure the support not merely of a senior prince, often through an established agent through whom very substantial commissions

have to be paid, but also of many ministers and officials down the line.[6]

Western governments and companies connived in this, apparently without serious qualms, because they knew their export sales depended on it. It was also difficult to avoid when rivals were resorting to bribes and the use of fixers too. In the words of Sir Ian Gilmour, a former British defence secretary, "You either got the business and bribed, or you didn't bribe and didn't get the business."[7] Naturally, the murkier parts of these deals were kept out of sight but a document from 1970, later made available in the British national archive, sheds light on the workings of the system. At stake was a £100 million ($190 million) contract to supply British-made Vickers tanks to Kuwait. Britain had supplied them before but now the French were trying to muscle in with their new AMX 30 tank, and were depending on high export sales to recoup the development costs.[8]

In the document – a letter to the British ambassador in Kuwait, headed "Confidential" – an official at the Foreign Office in London discusses how to fend off the French. "The Vickers tank is unquestionably superior to the AMX 30 and it would be ludicrous for the Kuwaitis to introduce a third type of tank into their army," he writes. In this, Britain had been counting on the support of General Mubarak (the Kuwaiti chief of staff), Abdullah Ali Reza (a "thoroughly respected" Saudi-Kuwaiti businessman with an "entrée to government ministers"[9]) and Mohammed Khalaf, who ran the Kuwaiti military affairs office in London.

The letter explains that Khalaf is the main problem: he appears to have been nobbled by the French. "I understand that while Vickers pay a percentage on any deal, which is shared between General Mubarak, Ali Reza and Khalaf, the French are prepared to pay Khalaf far more." It continues:

MOD [the Ministry of Defence] were satisfied after three days' study of Vickers' revised offer that it was fair; in fact Khalaf was upset by the offer purely because it interfered with the plans to buy French. The AMX 30 has always cost more than the Vickers; the French have now given a lower price for the first time, planning presumably to recoup with exorbitant charges for spares and ammunition afterwards. To prestall similar moves by Vickers, Khalaf, whom MOD describe as "most efficient in his wickedness", has got quotations from individual component manufacturers here to compare against Vickers' quotation for overall spares supply. MOD (Sales) are, however, satisfied that Vickers' profit levels are reasonable.[10]

The letter considers ways of cutting out Khalaf by making a direct approach to Shaikh Sa'ad (the Kuwaiti defence minister) and discusses whether this should be done by a Vickers company director or a high-level defence ministry official. "There is of course some danger in by-passing Khalaf," the letter says. "We assume that a Vickers director would in fact be seen by Shaikh Sa'ad and for more than just a courtesy call, and would get a reasonable reception, even if he had outflanked Khalaf in this way." On the other hand, "the prestige of the British MOD would perhaps have more chance of overcoming Khalaf's influence over Shaikh Sa'ad than a Vickers delegation."

In the meantime, the British ambassador is urged "to impress upon General Mubarak and Shaikh Sa'ad the folly of introducing a totally different type of tank into their armoured force: the consequential problems of three types of ammunition and spares would be likely to render their army non-operational at an early stage in any emergency." The letter also suggests sounding out Ali Reza about the possibility of sending a defence ministry official and adds drily that presumably

Ali Reza "is using all his considerable influence in Kuwait in *his own* and Vickers' interests" [italics added].

One way or another, this strategy proved successful. But selling tanks to Kuwait was a modest business compared with the al-Yamamah arms deal struck in 1985 between Margaret Thatcher's government and Saudi Arabia. As in Kuwait, the British were initially competing against the French and the contract was secured after intensive lobbying which included a meeting between Mrs Thatcher and the Saudi king. According to a defence ministry briefing paper written at the time ...

> Since early 1984, intensive efforts have been made to sell Tornado and Hawk [warplanes] to the Saudis. When, in the autumn of 1984, they seemed to be leaning towards French Mirage fighters, Mr Heseltine [the secretary of state for defence] paid an urgent visit to Saudi Arabia, carrying a letter from the prime minister to King Fahd. In December 1984 the prime minister started a series of important negotiations by meeting Prince Bandar, the son of Prince Sultan [the Saudi defence minister]. The prime minister met the king in Riyadh in April this year [1985] and in August the king wrote to her stating his decision to buy 48 Tornado IDS and 30 Hawk.[11]

More purchases followed and al-Yamamah turned out to be Britain's largest-ever export agreement, earning more than £40 billion for the main contractor, BAE Systems, over a twenty-year period. Very soon after the initial contract was signed, allegations began to circulate of large-scale corruption – bribes paid to members of the Saudi royal family, government officials and possibly individuals on the British side too. Successive British governments have fiercely resisted demands for a thorough investigation, on one occasion citing a "real and serious threat to national security" as the reason,[12] but a lot of embarrassing information has seeped out over the years.

In 2004 details emerged of a £60 million slush fund used by BAE Systems from which Prince Turki bin Nasser and his family appeared to be the main beneficiaries. Prince Turki, who besides being a major-general in the Saudi air force was a son-in-law of the defence minister, handled the al-Yamamah file on the Saudi side until 2000. A travel agent called Peter Gardiner told BBC2's *The Money Programme* that for more than a decade he had provided lavish benefits worth up to £7 million a year for the prince and his entourage – all paid for by BAE. These included a three-month family holiday costing £2 million; a £170,000 Rolls-Royce as a birthday present for Prince Turki's wife; chartering a Boeing 747 cargo plane to carry home shopping for his wife and her entourage; a £99,000 skiing trip in Colorado for the prince's son and friends; and a £200,000 wedding video for the prince's daughter. In addition to that, Mr Gardiner said he was also instructed to provide money – sometimes in cash, sometimes as bank transfers to pay off credit card bills. The bank transfers, he said, averaged $100,000 a time.

Using the travel agent as an intermediary meant that none of these payments showed up directly in BAE's accounts. Mr Gardiner simply sent a one-page invoice each month to BAE's "customer relations executive" headed: "Accommodation services and support for overseas visitors". BAE systems, meanwhile, insisted that it had complied "with the laws of the United Kingdom and all other countries in which it operates".[13] However, these payments faded almost into insignificance a couple of years later amid allegations that BAE had secretly paid more than £1 billion to Prince Bandar, a son of the Saudi defence minister, while he served as ambassador to the United States. The *Guardian* reported:

It is claimed that payments of £30m were paid to Prince Bandar every quarter for at least 10 years.

It is alleged by insider legal sources that the money was paid to Prince Bandar with the knowledge and authorisation of Ministry of Defence officials under the Blair government and its predecessors. For more than 20 years, ministers have claimed they knew nothing of secret commissions, which were outlawed by Britain in 2002.

An inquiry by the Serious Fraud Office (SFO) into the transactions behind the £43bn al-Yamamah arms deal, which was signed in 1985, is understood to have uncovered details of the payments to Prince Bandar.

But the investigation was halted last December by the SFO after a review by the attorney general, Lord Goldsmith.

He said it was in Britain's national interest to halt the investigation, and that there was little prospect of achieving convictions.[14]

According to a BBC *Panorama* programme, money from BAE Systems was paid into two Saudi embassy accounts in Washington after being authorised by the British defence ministry. "These accounts were actually a conduit to Prince Bandar for his role in the 1985 deal," the BBC report said. "The purpose of one of the accounts was to pay the expenses of the prince's private Airbus." David Caruso, an investigator who worked for the American bank where the accounts were held, told the BBC Prince Bandar had been taking money for his own personal use out of accounts that seemed to belong to his government: "There wasn't a distinction between the accounts of the embassy, or official government accounts as we would call them, and the accounts of the royal family."[15]

THERE IS NO doubt in the minds of most Arabs that corruption is rife. More than 90 per cent of participants in a survey for the Arab

Human Development Report believed it to be pervasive. Though the survey covered only five countries – Algeria, Jordan, Lebanon, Morocco and Palestine – "it is not expected to be less widespread in those countries that were not part of the survey," the report said. It noted that in the countries surveyed "politicians, businessmen and high-ranking officials head the list in the spread of corruption", while corruption is also considered prevalent among the judiciary and in social relations.[16] In another survey, conducted in Lebanon, 74 per cent of Lebanese felt that "bribery is necessary to secure a contract from any public institution" and a quarter of those questioned believed that "all Lebanese politicians are corrupt".[17]

Such problems are certainly not confined to the Arab world, but in international comparisons the Arab countries fare badly. In the Corruption Perceptions Index for 2008 compiled by Transparency International, only one Arab country ranked among the top thirty (out of 180). Qatar, twenty-eighth in the list, was regarded as the least corrupt, while Iraq and Somalia were the most corrupt.[18] This annual survey also assigns a score between one and ten, with ten regarded as highly clean and zero as highly corrupt. Several countries, such as Denmark, Finland, New Zealand and Sweden regularly score nine points or more but in 2008 only five Arab countries managed to reach above the half-way mark:

Corruption Perceptions Index for 2008

Country	Score	Ranking
Qatar	6.50	28
UAE	5.90	35
Bahrain	5.40	43
Oman	5.50	41

Country	Score	Ranking
Jordan	5.10	47
Kuwait	4.30	65
Tunisia	4.40	62
Morocco	3.50	80=
Saudi Arabia	3.50	80=
Algeria	3.20	92
Lebanon	3.00	102=
Djibouti	3.00	102=
Egypt	2.80	115=
Mauritania	2.80	115=
Comoros	2.50	134
Libya	2.60	126
Yemen	2.30	141
Syria	2.10	147
Sudan	1.60	173
Iraq	1.30	178
Somalia	1.00	180

For obvious reasons, actual levels of corruption are notoriously difficult to measure on the basis of hard evidence. Transparency International's index relies on the assessments of experts and business people – "those who are most directly confronted with the realities of corruption in a country". It focuses specifically on perceptions of corruption among public officials and politicians.[19] A different approach to corruption measurement comes from the World Bank, which publishes its Worldwide Governance Indicators every year. Six indicators are considered, all of which have some bearing on corruption levels: accountability, political stability, government effectiveness, regulatory quality, rule of law and control of corruption.[20] Extrapolating from the World Bank's figures, the Arab Human Development Report of 2004 compared the Arab countries with six other regions of the world: Africa, Asia, Europe, North America, Latin America and Oceania. In terms of accountability the Arab countries were the worst by a wide margin, while in terms of political stability, government effectiveness, rule of law and control of corruption, only Africa was worse than the Arab countries.[21]

In practical terms corruption has many harmful effects. It is intrinsically unfair; it undermines democratic processes, distorts free markets, denies people equality of opportunity and in general creates obstacles to progress. Though petty corruption (small payments to low-level officials) is often regarded as unimportant, evidence compiled by Transparency International shows that the poorest in all societies are the ones hit the hardest by bribery: "They face the most demands for bribes and they are more likely to pay. This in turn means that corruption acts as a regressive tax that increases income inequality. Denied their basic rights and free access to public services, the poor suffer most in corrupt environments."[22] Petty corruption also has the effect of making inefficient bureaucracies even more inefficient: delays and obstructions proliferate in order to maximise the revenue from bribes that circumvent them. Where bribery is used to circumvent legitimate requirements (to override safety regulations, for example) it has the effect of lowering standards and undermining government policies. Knowledge that the state's official representatives are also engaged in corruption not only encourages others to do the same but lowers respect for the legitimacy of government.

In a culture where bribery is treated as a routine way of solving problems, it can also be difficult to distinguish between "honest" bribe-takers and others who solicit bribes but have no intention of delivering what they promise. This opens the way to numerous scams. In 2006, for example, the US embassy in Damascus reported that "groups of Syrians were impersonating [government] price control squads in the local markets and collecting large sums of money in the form of bribes from shopkeepers".[23] It happens in schools, too. Egyptian blogger-activist Hossam Hamalawy recalled: "In my school, I got a phone call from a friend three days before the Arabic exam. He said: 'I was promised the exam paper if we manage to raise LE1,600 ($300). Do you think we can get this money?' I thought the guy was lying. There are so many scams about this. Sometimes it's true and on other occasions it's a scam."[24]

In 2008 fourteen Egyptians – including the head of the examinations board in Minya province, a headmaster and a policeman – were jailed following a scandal over the sale of exam papers.[25] Children of senior officials were said to have bought copies of the mathematics and English papers in the *Thaanawiyya Aama* (the final secondary school exam) for LE800 each. In public, government officials insisted this was an isolated case but an education ministry official who spoke to *al-Ahram Weekly* anonymously described the problem as "prevalent all over the country and in all governorates without exception". He continued: "The difference is that authorities in Minya were quick to act and did not bury their heads in the sand and turn a blind eye to the problem as some other officials in other governorates do."[26]

Higher-level corruption involves much larger amounts of money, often in the form of kick-backs on government contracts. The problem here is not just the percentages creamed off into private hands but the way contracts can be shaped at the country's expense to maximise private gain. As Dieter Frisch, the former director-general for development at the European Commission has noted:

> The corrupt decision-maker may well be tempted to accept a substandard quality of service which will make his personal profit all the greater. Thus, with a road-building project for example, complicity between government departments and contractors may result in corner-cutting with regard to agreed standards of quality so that the savings made may be shared out between the two parties.
>
> At their very worst, the disastrous effects of corruption mean that the conception of a project, and ultimately its very choice, are determined by corruption. As far as conception is concerned, a good example would be the purchase of a technology which is wholly unsuited to the particular needs of a country or the choice of a capital-intensive project – more lucrative in terms of corruption – rather than a labour-intensive one which would nevertheless be far more beneficial to that nation's development.[27]

The peak of perversion, Frisch continued, is when government priorities are shaped in a way that generates the greatest personal gain for the decision-makers – as in the case of the Lebanese law that helped a minister sell fire extinguishers.

Such practices are seriously at odds with standard Islamic teaching which stresses the need for integrity in financial affairs. The IslamOnline website says: "Allah forbids all unclean and corrupt means of making money, such as dishonest trading, gambling, and bribery. Bribery and usury ... are totally prohibited and forbidden and those who are guilty of them have been condemned by Allah and His Prophet."[28] It quotes a verse from the Qur'an which says: "Oh ye who believe! Eat not up each other's property by unfair and dishonest means."[29] A saying attributed to the Prophet – that God has "condemned alike the giver of bribes, and the taker of bribes in deciding cases" – is also often cited in this context.[30] In a similar vein, the Islamic Conference of Foreign Ministers in 1990 stated: "Authority is a trust; and abuse or malicious exploitation thereof is absolutely prohibited, so that fundamental human rights may be guaranteed."[31]

Despite religious disapproval, there are specific factors in Arab countries that exacerbate the problem of corruption and make it so prevalent:

> The politico-legal structure of some Arab states makes it difficult to differentiate between corruption in its conventional form (abuse of public office for personal gain), and an inherent failing (rigged rules) in the system itself. For example, in some states both law and custom decree that the land and its natural resources belong to the ruler, and fail to distinguish at this level between the private and public life of the ruler, while the private property of the ordinary citizen becomes a grant from the ruler. In such a situation, it is difficult to talk of corruption in governance, for whatever the ruler does, he is disposing of his own property.
>
> Some regimes set up economic institutions attached to their military or security apparatus, to finance their activities. Here again matters become confused; it becomes difficult to draw the line between the exercise of an official function (since individual corruption may be but a reflection of the corruption of the whole situation) and what can be described as personal corruption.
>
> In addition, there are ways to manipulate laws that, in many Arab countries, do not allow senior officials to carry out private business while they occupy an official post. Many officials circumvent the law by allowing members of their families to set up companies and enterprises that often benefit from the official's position and relations.[32]

Abundant tales of unscrupulous behaviour at the highest levels obviously give a green light to those below, but Jordanian-based business consultant Jehad al-Omari believes the real problem lies with the system. "This is a cut-and-paste culture," he said. "You have all the apparatus of modernity but you don't have the content of it."[33] In other words, the institutions may exist – often transplanted from elsewhere – but without having been absorbed into the culture they do not function properly. When the machinery of government grinds slowly and inefficiently, people look for ways to short-circuit it – and one way is with money. Realising that slowness and inefficiency can be lucrative, officials – often on low salaries – thus have every incentive to be as obstructive as possible until payment is in prospect. Such practices can be found in many countries but, according to Khaled Diab, an Egyptian whose years spent outside the country have perhaps given him a broader perspective than many of his compatriots, they are especially pervasive in the Arab world:

> Whenever you have to deal with Egyptian bureaucracy, it's shocking how much low-level corruption there is. You are *expected* to bribe. It's almost like tipping in a restaurant when dealing with petty civil servants. I've tried to resist it my whole life, but I sometimes resort to leaving a little sweetener because someone is so blocking my paperwork that the only way to get it done is to pay something. But I've only ever done that in cases where something is absolutely my right or someone is standing in the way of that in order to get a tip. It's so easy in the monolithic bureaucracy that is Egypt for someone to really be a hindrance, because for each document you may need five signatures and maybe the fifth signature might not work – so you pay a sweetener.[34]

Ghada Kabesh has been driving in Egypt for years without taking a test: she simply purchased a licence. "I paid LE60 [less than $18 at the time], but that was in 1997," she said. Since then, prices have gone up a lot. Recently, she had to renew her licence and the papers for her car:

> I got it sorted out while I was waiting outside in my car, for LE400 ($75). I did that instead of going and waiting in lines and begging employees to sign this paper, then stamp that paper – you need, like, a hundred signatures. The employees probably take LE300 [a month] as a salary, so seeing me as a young woman dressed nicely, they would just not finish my stuff [unless I paid them].
>
> Someone told me I also had 1,000 tickets [for driving offences] – which I never did because I am very careful. So I asked how much it would cost me not to pay these tickets, and he told me LE200. It happens all the time in any governmental institution.[35]

The preoccupation with social status in Arab countries also infects and undermines their administrative systems. Constitutions may preach that everyone is equal before the law but the reality is different. Whether it is a matter of asking officials to do something – such as granting a permit – or seeking to avoid a penalty, status counts and is recognised by the system, allowing those with the right level of clout to pull rank. "People with a certain status in society think the rules don't apply to them, or they think that even if they do apply in theory, they can just pull a few strings and someone will sort it out," Khaled Diab explained. He continued:

> Say a traffic policeman stops a guy in a Mercedes for speeding, First of all, the policeman will be afraid to do it. He might not stop him. And if he does, the guy might turn around to him and say: "Do you know who I am?"

That's a common response to intimidate the agents of the law. It's not just the state, but those delegated with enforcing the law don't enjoy the status to enforce it because they are lower down the pecking order than a lot of the people they have to deal with.

Defined simply, corruption is "the misuse of entrusted power for private benefit".[36] Corruption occurs when decisions or actions are influenced by extraneous considerations rather than the merits of the case. One particular problem in the Arab countries is that corrupt acts are not necessarily recognised as such – and this applies particularly to nepotism. The obligation towards family members and wider kinship circles (discussed in Chapter 1) means that giving jobs to relatives is often regarded as a duty and a virtue rather than a vice.

"To my mind at least, nepotism is a form of corruption but it's kind of brushed under the carpet – nobody wants to talk about it," Jehad al-Omari said.

> When I came to Jordan as a company manager for an Emirati company I wanted to restructure the company and I wanted to get the company going – it was in a very bad financial state. In a country like Jordan the easy route is to fall back on the safety of your tribe. The easy route is to call your cousin and your uncle and your nephew, and say I need a driver, I need an assistant, I need an accountant. The family, so to speak, will give you that support, be it at a cost, be it sometimes not as you would wish it to be in terms of competencies but at least it's there, it's instant, it initially comes free of charge with no commitments. I certainly did that.

To fill some of the vacancies, he advertised. "You can get qualified people and you can get very unqualified people. But, on so many different issues you still fall back on that family ... Sometimes advertising in the press is only just a show to satisfy a legal requirement of the cut-and-paste culture. It gives the appearance of civility, of order, of procedure, of system, but the reality is not there. So connections, *wasta, mahsubiyya* (patronage, favouritism) – whatever it's called, it's still part of that package." For businessmen like Omari, the problems of nepotism do not end with the recruitment process. Employing members of the same family can make it difficult to maintain discipline. "On a personal level I paid a heavy price in terms of creating animosity amongst my employees," he said. "Suddenly I was mean, rather than firm. When you're running a company of, say, 120 people, the idea that you punish someone for a well-deserved mistake is abhorrent to his relative who might be in a higher position and will fight you for it."

Similar to nepotism, at least in its effects on employment, is the phenomenon of *wasta* which roughly translates as connections, clout, influence or favouritism. Often jokingly referred to by Arabs as Vitamin W, *wasta* is the magical lubricant that smoothes the way to jobs, promotions, university places and much else besides. In fact, with the right connections, it can solve almost any kind of problem. *Wasta*, the blogger known as Secret Dubai wrote, is "arguably the most valuable form of currency in much of the Middle East, far more effective than bribes and certainly more effective than following due process".[37]

"Everything goes through *wasta*," said Salam Pax, the Iraqi blogger. "Whether you are trying to get a good bed in hospital for your aunt, whether it was me trying to dodge military service, you can make your life much easier. It's almost expected." *Wasta*, he explained, is an extension of "this feeling that a family or a tribe will look after each other ... If you are from tribe X, and you meet someone else from tribe X you are expected to help them. If you don't – then, hey!"[38]

Wasta comes from an Arabic root (*w-s-T*) conveying the idea of "middle", and a *wasta* is someone who acts as a go-between. The same word, as an abstract noun, refers to the use of intermediaries. As with nepotism, the intermediary in cases of *wasta* must be someone with influence (in order to secure the favour) but not necessarily a relative or even a close friend; quite possibly just a passing acquaintance or sometimes a complete stranger.[39] By using his influence to perform a service, the *wasta* acquires prestige and honour but, perhaps more importantly, the person receiving the favour incurs a debt of gratitude which may have to be repaid in unspecified ways at some point in the future.

The origins of *wasta* are by no means disreputable. It has a long and generally respectable history as a way of managing relations between families, clans or tribes through intermediaries. In the event of a blood feud, for example, *wastas* – either an individual or a group of elders respected by both sides – could be called upon to resolve the matter through negotiation and compromise while salvaging the honour of the parties involved. In this traditional form of *wasta*, the methods adopted – typically beginning with a suspension of hostilities while discussions take place – bear a strong resemblance to modern approaches to conflict resolution, and this form is still found today in the more tribal parts of the Middle East. Evidence of its continuing usefulness can be seen from time to time in newspaper advertisements, such as one placed in the Jordanian daily, *al-Ra'i*, after relatives of two men who were hit (and presumably killed) in a traffic accident agreed not to seek revenge:

> In the name of God, the merciful and compassionate, special thanks from the Muayteh family to the Mushaqabeh / Bani Hasan family.
>
> The Muayteh family offers bountiful thanks and gratitude

to the Mushaqabeh family generally, and the Baqairat family especially, for their noble stand and their traditional Arab magnanimity which was expressed by giving up all their family and legal rights, especially with regard to the traffic accident in which Khalid Arif and his cousin Nasir Aqil were hit by Noful Muhammad Muayteh. Sincere thanks and appreciation go to Shaykh Khalil Mahmoud Mushaqabeh (Abu Aqil) and Mr Aqil Mahmoud Mushaqabeh and Mr Arif Mahmoud Mushaqabeh, and our thanks and appreciation to all the brethren comprising the reconciliation group, headed by Haj Hamad Ahmad Mahadeen, Shaykh Abdul Karim Muayteh (Abu Salem), Shaykh Khalaf Muayieh, Mr Abdullah Muayteh, and Mudallah Muayteh. May God recompense them with every blessing, and cause the goodness and honour of their family to last for ever.[40]

Unofficial conciliation has its place in every society, but in this case, praiseworthy as the mediators' efforts may sound, they are predicated on the likelihood that an aggrieved family will take the law into their own hands to exact revenge and that if they do so the state will be unable to provide adequate protection for the family under attack. This reflects a serious failure by the state and its institutions. In a well-functioning state there are procedures for dealing with the aftermath of accidents, even tragic ones, without the need for *wasta*; in the meantime, continued reliance on *wasta* makes it more difficult to establish alternative procedures which enjoy the confidence of citizens. Besides mediation, *wasta* is also traditionally used to intercede – for example to approach one family on behalf of another with a view to arranging a marriage – and it is this form which has evolved in insidious ways to become rampant throughout the Middle East. Intercessionary *wasta*, as practised today, is basically a way of circumventing problems rather than confronting them.

The development of Arab states in the twentieth century, far from banishing *wasta*, created new opportunities for it to adapt and flourish. The expansion of the Jordanian civil service during and after the 1960s, for instance, led to a situation where senior officials filled new posts with employees from their extended family or region.[41] Governments were happy to let this happen at the time, since they were less preoccupied with building a smooth-running state than establishing their own legitimacy among the populace – and this was one way of doing so. "That's how *wasta* and nepotism spread and gave birth to thousands of unqualified and unproductive employees who do nothing but wait for their salaries at the end of the month," according to Dr Adnan Badran, president of Philadelphia University in Jordan.[42]

Although *wasta,* as an almost inescapable aspect of daily life, is often depicted in Arabic novels, films and TV dramas, there has been surprisingly little research into the phenomenon apart from two studies published in 1993 and 2002 in relation to Jordan – the latter by the Amman-based Arab Archives Institute (AAI) which had earlier conducted a survey of public opinion.[43] Jordan clearly has a serious *wasta* problem, though the country is by no means unique in that respect.

As in many Arab countries, the public sector in Jordan is the largest employer. An estimated 500,000 people receive salaries from the state – which probably means that as many as one family in two depends financially to some extent on the state. Salaries account for around two-thirds of the national budget.[44] Among the many burgeoning arms of government, the state-run television corporation has long been regarded as the most overblown. According to the AAI report, an internal investigation found that over a five-year period it had hired around 1,000 superfluous employees – and it is easy to see how this happened. On one occasion the director-general was approached by the prime minister to hire "some acquaintances of his". A couple of hours later security staff at the main gate reported that a bus had arrived carrying twenty people who said they had been sent by the prime minister. The director-general then contacted the prime minister: "There are tens of people out there," he remonstrated. But the prime minister was insistent: "Just appoint them, quickly," he replied.[45]

Although Jordanian television has had periodic mass clear-outs of staff, "there were employees of high qualifications among the dismissed ones and many others, appointed by *wasta*, remained at the top of their jobs".[46] Often, there is little or no attempt to conceal the use of *wasta*. Faisal Shboul, a newly appointed director of the state-run Petra News Agency, admitted to the press that he had been appointed through *wasta* – adding that this was no different from the way the eleven previous directors had been appointed.[47]

For politicians, being known as someone who can deliver on the *wasta* front brings obvious electoral advantages while the popularity of any who refuse to play the game is liable to suffer. At an electoral gathering in the northern city of Salt, Abdullah Nsour, a former deputy prime minister of Jordan, revealed that he appointed thousands of people from his district while in office.[48] In a newspaper interview, a former mayor of Amman, Mamdouh Abbadi, condemned *wasta* but admitted to appointing many people from his own tribe.[49] Resisting the expectations of their supporters can be extremely difficult – especially if rival tribes or other districts are seen to be benefiting. On the other hand, politicians who use *wasta* extensively are liable to become overburdened with more and more demands from their constituents. This has a distorting effect on the activities of parliament, diverting members' attention from legislating and monitoring the government's performance, according to the AAI: "Voluntarily or out of social pressure, parliamentarians' role in mediating, or, in other words, using *wasta* between the citizen and the state, is increasing dramatically and becoming their main task."[50] Politicians cannot be blamed for that entirely: it is driven by popular demand, institutional weakness, arbitrary enforcement of laws, lack of transparency and bureaucratic complexity. One member of parliament, Khaled Tarawneh, grumbled that citizens are more interested in obtaining *wasta* than discussing the issues of the day.[51]

Beyond the employment sphere, the story of Selwa, a Jordanian living in Los Angeles, illustrates the multiple uses of *wasta*. She had bought air tickets for herself and her two children to visit her family in Jordan:

> Because her father was very sick, Selwa was forced to stay in Jordan beyond the two months stipulated by the tickets. When she reported to the check-in desk at Amman's Queen Alia Airport, the check-in officer politely asked her to go and change the status of her tickets, which meant that she would have to pay a substantial amount of money for not observing the conditions of her ticket. Furthermore, she was told that she could carry on only two suitcases, not three, and that she had to pay for the excess baggage. Selwa vainly tried to convince the officer that she could not afford to pay the extra amount. Because she did not have the money, she did not take the flight that day.
>
> Selwa telephoned Majid, a steward at Royal Jordanian, who is a good friend of her husband. Majid told her that he was about to take off for the Far East but he would contact his friend Khalid at the check-in station to help her.
>
> Selwa went next morning to the check-in counter, found Khalid, mentioned that she had talked to Majid, and told

him about her problem. Khalid processed her check-in papers quickly, ignoring the excess weight and the schedule violation. He then went with her to the exit tax official who exempted her from it. His help did not end there because when she boarded the plane, she heard somebody asking her to proceed to the cockpit. Selwa went to the cockpit where she was told that Majid had contacted them and asked them to take good care of her. She and her children were moved from the economy section of the plane to first class and given royal treatment.

Describing this episode in their book, *Wasta: The Hidden Force in Middle Eastern Society*, Robert Cunningham and Yasin Sarayrah, point out that as a result of *wasta*, Selwa saved herself an excess baggage charge, the charge for changing the status of her ticket, the airport departure tax, and even got a free upgrade into first class. Apart from the potential safety hazard of slipping overweight baggage on to the plane, the authors note that such practices represent a long-term economic cost to the airline, as well as inefficient use of resources. "If one steward can do this for a friend," they comment, "consider how many stewards, pilots, and clerical staff are employed by the airline, how many other officials work at the airport, and how many friends and relatives each has, which indicates the scope of *wasta* activity at the airport."[52]

Although *wasta* often provides the means for people to obtain a benefit they are not entitled to, there are other situations where, as a result of maladministration or defective governance, *wasta* can help them obtain their rights. This has led to an argument that *wasta* can also be benevolent – a "poor people's weapon" where those lacking the means to deal with the authorities effectively can secure just treatment through intervention by others who have influence. The problem with this approach is that it does not address the underlying reasons for the maladministration and, in the long run, probably makes matters worse by alleviating any pressure to reform the system. Among various people interviewed about this by the AAI, Hakim Harb, a film producer, refused to give examples of "benevolent" *wasta*, saying that whether mischievous or benevolent it should not exist in a society that respects individuals' rights: "When we live in a real society, progressive, and civilised, and when we live in an atmosphere filled with freedoms, democracy and human rights, everyone will obtain his/her rights and the right people will be in the right places without the need for any form of help."[53]

The widespread dislike of *wasta* was highlighted in 2000 by a survey among Jordanians.[54] Eighty-six per cent agreed that it is a form of corruption and 87 per cent thought it should be eliminated. At the same time, though, 90 per cent said they expected to use *wasta* at least "sometimes" in the future and 42 per cent thought their need for it was likely to increase, while only 13 per cent thought their need would decrease.

Respondents were also asked what they would do "if you need to get business done at a government office, company or organisation". Forty-six per cent said they would look for *wasta* before beginning and 19 per cent said they would look for it after beginning. Only 35 per cent said they would deal with the matter directly (ie without resorting to *wasta*). Those who said they would use *wasta* were asked a further question about their reasons for doing so: 50 per cent said it was because of "complicated" procedures, 41 per cent believed they would be unable to complete the business without *wasta* and 5 per cent gave "social standing" as their reason.[55]

Sometimes the reciprocal nature of wasta makes it difficult to avoid. Basem Sakijha of the Jordanian Transparency Forum recalled that when his newly graduated daughters were looking for work, employers would say "Let your father call us". A request from the father to hire them would thus turn their employment into a favour, creating an obligation to repay it later. Sakijha refused and says his daughters were turned down for several jobs because of it. One was eventually taken on by *al-Ra'i* newspaper. "I didn't use *wasta* but they hired her because she's my daughter, definitely. They are friends and colleagues, and my father was at that newspaper as editor-in-chief once. This is the way it is."

Jordan's king, Abdullah II, has spoken out against *wasta* on occasions – though it has made little difference. Appointing a new prime minister in 2000, he wrote: "We should work together to draft a Code of Honour that would put an end to all forms of *wasta*, nepotism and cronyism ... to make every citizen secure and convinced that all these negative phenomena are a shame to all those who believe in them or practise them."[56] Sakijha was among those lobbying to make *wasta* illegal. "The prime minister at that time, and the king himself, agreed that this should be in the law," he said. "They put this article to criminalise users of *wasta* and it went to parliament." But parliament amended the wording to say that *wasta* was a crime, *except when used for justified reasons* – which in effect made the law pointless.[57]

ON PAPER at least, almost all Arab states are committed to fighting corruption. By 2008 all except Lebanon, Oman and Somalia had signed up to the United Nations Convention against Corruption which came into effect at the end of 2005.[58] However, they are still a long way from implementing some of its most basic requirements which include transparent procurement systems, a merit-based civil service, active involvement of civil society in the fight against corruption, an independent judiciary and public auditing procedures.[59]

Arab countries do initiate anti-corruption drives from time to time but they tend to be patchy rather than systematic and are often part of a political game. Such campaigns rarely include measures that will make corruption less likely in the future and usually target those who have fallen out of favour for unrelated reasons. When so many of them benefit from ill-gotten gains, corruption charges provide a simple means to get rid of them if the need arises. Corrupt ministers and officials can also be turned into scapegoats for wider government failures.

Towards the end of the 1990s, while being groomed to succeed his father as president of Syria, Bashar al-Asad played the leading role in an anti-corruption campaign. It was not the first of its kind in Syria, but certainly the most sustained. It was also very necessary, judging by a report in the official *Tishreen* newspaper in June 2000, which said that government corruption was costing the treasury at least $50,000 a day and that thirty-nine cases of fraud had been uncovered by state financial controllers in the first quarter of the year.[60] Although Bashar was said to have a genuine dislike of corruption, the campaign served other purposes too: it raised his profile and won him popularity among the public while also providing a means to clear out untrusted members of the old guard and start establishing his own power base.

The most senior casualty was long-serving prime minister Mahmoud Zu'bi – dismissed in March 2000 and expelled from the Ba'ath party for "actions, behaviour and untrustworthiness which are contrary to the values, ethics, and principles of the party, violate the law, and caused immense damage to the reputation of the party, state, and national economy."[61] Amid hints of embezzlement involving millions of dollars, his assets were then frozen but he never stood trial. When police arrived at his home to arrest him, he shot himself in the head with his own pistol (at least, according to the official account).[62]

Along with Zu'bi, former deputy prime minister Salim Yasin, former transport minister Mufeed Abdul Karim, and a Spanish-Syrian businessman, Mounir Abu Khadour, were accused of receiving illegal commissions on the purchase of six Airbus A320s for the national airline fourteen years earlier.[63] The two ex-ministers were each jailed for ten years but Abu Khadour fled abroad.[64] The basic allegation was that Airbus had been allowed to overcharge for the aircraft, thought to be worth $240 million in total – with the accused pocketing at least some of the proceeds. Airbus, for its part, denied paying bribes.[65]

Though the Airbus case was the most notable, there were other anti-corruption moves in Syria around the same time. A travel ban was reportedly imposed on dozens of former officials to prevent them fleeing the country[66] and the economic security court sought to lift immunity from three members of parliament suspected of embezzling public funds – among them the chairman of the Central Federation of Peasants.[67] While these efforts no doubt helped to consolidate Bashar's accession to the presidency, Syria continues to be perceived as one of the most corrupt Arab countries, surpassed only by Iraq, Somalia and Sudan in the Transparency International index.[68]

Meanwhile, Saudi Arabia appears to have become concerned about its ranking in the index. At seventy-ninth position in the 2007 list, it was perceived as by far the most corrupt among the Gulf Cooperation Council members.[69] In 2008 the interior ministry reported that prosecutions for bribery had increased by 15 per cent during the previous year, with more than 500 cases in Riyadh alone (no figure was disclosed for the rest of the country).[70] Predictably, however, the campaign seemed to be targeting low-to-middle ranking officials rather than corrupt princes.

In July 2008, for example, eight health officials were accused of taking bribes in connection with the licensing of pharmacies. The Jeddah-based Arab News reported that pharmacy owners had been forced to pay bribes ranging from 20,000 to 45,000 riyals ($5,350–$12,000) because officials delayed their paperwork.[71] A couple of weeks later the health minister, Dr Hamad al-Mane, revealed at a press conference that a Saudi company supplying medical equipment had tried to bribe his private secretary in the hope of avoiding an $800,000 penalty payment. The secretary had been offered just over $41,000 – roughly four times his monthly salary. The minister did not name the company involved but said its representative had been arrested, the firm would be blacklisted and its penalty doubled. He added that the king and Crown Prince Sultan (who in 1985 signed the notorious al-Yamamah agreement) had ordered that the secretary be given a financial reward for his honesty.[72]

Whistleblowers are not always treated so well, though. In Egypt, medical staff who raised the alarm about substandard blood bags (supplied to government hospitals by a company belonging to a member of parliament) found themselves transferred to less desirable jobs.[73] Exposing corruption, especially at the higher levels, is also risky for the Arab media – which basically means that governments are left to police themselves.

In the future it is possible that increased computerisation of official paperwork will gradually reduce the scope for petty corruption. Amina Khairy, an Egyptian journalist, is hopeful about that. "I think with the introduction of e-government and so on, it is going to get better," she said, "but not in the near future, because of the [low] percentage of Egyptians who have access to the internet, plus the percentage of Egyptians who are illiterate ... but I think we are moving on the right track." She used the internet herself to apply for a copy of her daughter's birth certificate – which was then delivered to her door by an official seeking *baksheesh*. "He thought it was for a new-born baby and he said '*Mabrouk!*' (Congratulations!) so I had to pay him. But at least I didn't have to go to the police station or one of those government offices, I didn't have to go through the hassle."

She also foresees a decline in Egyptians' use of *wasta*:

> I think there is positive change in the *wasta* phenomenon – at least in some sectors in Egypt. When you used to go to the television building twenty or fifteen years ago it was mainly families who controlled the system – the father who holds a very high-ranking position, then he has his sons and daughters, whether as anchors, presenters, directors, editors and so on. The big government ministries – you have somebody working at the ministry of housing and then he gets his wife to work as a secretary for somebody or his son graduates as an engineer and he goes to work [there] ... I think this is changing because the government is not any longer the main employing body in Egypt. There are more and more job opportunities from the private sector and I don't think the private sector could afford the *wasta*. If I owned a company I wouldn't be able to take your son to work for me unless he or she was qualified to do the job.[74]

In Jordan, though, anti-corruption activist Basem Sakijha thinks it more likely that new private sector businesses will become tainted with the old ways. "*Wasta* is there, even in the private sector," he said. "They can't go on doing their business unless they use *wasta* [in their dealings] with the authorities and with the society as well ... They hire qualified people to do the job but they also have to hire people who don't work – just to keep things going. They have a free choice but they have to deal with the facts on the ground ... So they find themselves eventually getting into this vicious circle."[75]

Much as people may wish to escape from this vicious circle, their capacity to do so will be severely limited so long as a maze of bureaucracy and government restrictions excludes them from more straightforward ways of getting things done.

6   The urge to control

HISHAM KASSEM WAS planning to launch a weekly news magazine. In Egypt that requires the government's permission, so he paid a visit to the Higher Press Council, the official body that grants licences to publishers – if and when it feels inclined to do so.

> A polite bureaucrat met me and explained the licensing procedures. I needed nine other partners holding equal shares to be listed on the licence application. We would need to deposit LE100,000 (approximately US$25,000) for a monthly publication, LE250,000 for a weekly, and LE1 million for a daily.
>
> The money would be set aside in a designated account and no interest would be paid on it while the application was being processed. Applicants could withdraw the money at any time, but in that case the application would immediately be nullified ...
>
> The problem was, as I explained to the polite bureaucrat, that I did not know nine other people who might be interested in investing in a startup press business with me. He told me I was lucky, because a recent amendment had reduced the total of founding members from two hundred to ten.
>
> I asked him about the time frame for processing the application and he replied that he had not the slightest clue...
>
> I asked, "When was the last time a publication was granted a licence?" He said he could not remember.
>
> I asked when the Higher Press Council had last convened. "Two years ago," he said.[1]

The question here is why, in any sensibly run country, such rules should be thought necessary. Obviously a new magazine needs funds to cover its production costs – otherwise it cannot be published – but why should publishers be obliged to demonstrate the fact by providing the government with an interest-free loan until the Higher Press Council can summon up the energy, at some indeterminate point in the future, to hold a meeting? Why should a publishing company need ten investors, all holding equal shares, let alone two hundred? Why, indeed, should anyone wishing to publish a weekly magazine need the government's permission at all?

Recognising that in the previous ten years only four political weeklies and one monthly had been granted licences, and that the founders of all four weeklies had strong connections with the government, Kassem decided not to bother applying for a licence. Instead, he did what most independent publishers in Egypt do, and established his magazine, the *Cairo Times*, across the sea in Cyprus. Flying the printed copies back to Cairo was expensive and turned it into a "foreign" publication (meaning that each issue had to be approved by the censors before being allowed into the country), but at least it made publication possible.[2]

The Egyptian press law, like those in most Arab countries, is designed to make independent publication difficult, to keep public debate in the hands of "responsible" elements and to provide an excuse for punishing those who stray over the red lines of permissible expression. The press, though, is only one element caught up in a web of absurd restrictions that also stifle creativity in films and theatre and regulate the activities of political parties, trade unions, professional bodies and all kinds of non-governmental organisations.

At one level the purpose of this is very clear: to keep a lid on political discourse and activity – especially any that might be perceived as a threat to the established order. At another level, though, it reflects a very old-fashioned notion of the function of governments and what they can legitimately seek to control. It may also fill a psychological need of the regimes themselves, generating a sense of power that helps to allay doubts about the level of support they actually enjoy. Meanwhile, their heavy-handed regulation means that people continue to be treated as sheep. Instead of encouraging them to become mature citizens, engaged in the affairs of their country and capable of making their own judgments, Arab states still play the role of a remote father-provider who forbids and permits, protects his children from their own foolishness and the bad influences of others, and occasionally grants privileges which can be taken away again if the children misbehave or appear not sufficiently grateful.

"[Forming] civil society organisations in Saudi Arabia that work in politically-sensitive areas, such as human rights and corruption, requires the permission of the king himself," said Kareem Elbayar, Middle East legal adviser at the International Center for Not-for-Profit Law. "You would basically have to go and petition the king and the king would make a determination on whether or not he approved the group. There are very few groups for that reason."[3] In 2003, under pressure for reform,[4] the king finally gave permission for a non-governmental human rights committee to be set up, which his foreign minister insisted would be "totally independent", with its independence guaranteed by the king.[5] Others have been less fortunate. In 2006 Musa al-Qarni and three other men petitioned King Abdullah for permission to form an Islamic organisation to discuss "freedom, justice, equality, citizenship, pluralism, [proper] advice, and the role of women." They never had a reply. A few months later, Qarni was arrested and carted off to jail after secret police commandos stormed a villa in Jeddah where several men "widely known for their advocacy on issues of social and political reform" were meeting.[6]

Although freedom of association is enshrined in international law, many ordinary Arabs share their rulers' view that it is not a natural entitlement. Hoshyar Malo, a lawyer and director of the Iraq-based Kurdish Human Rights Watch, noted:

> In many countries, especially in the Middle East, neither the governments nor the people believe that the rights of association and assembly are among the fundamental rights ... Even where the government allows individuals to establish associations, this is seen more like a gift or a bonus from the government to the people than a recognition of the human rights protected by international conventions ... This false understanding of human rights in the Middle East is due to many factors – mainly cultural, religious, and historical – that prop up the idea that the government grants rights and freedoms to the people.[7]

The right of people to act collectively for the sake of shared interests, purposes and values is one of the building blocks of freedom, and exercising that right is the essence of civil society activity.

> Civil society commonly embraces a diversity of spaces, actors and institutional forms, varying in their degree of formality, autonomy and power. Civil societies are often populated by organisations such as registered charities, development non-governmental organisations, community groups, women's organisations, faith-based organisations, professional associations, trades unions, self-help groups, social movements, business associations, coalitions and advocacy groups.[8]

Definitions of civil society usually treat it as a separate space, distinct from the state, the family and the market – and therein lies its value. Civil society, Ziad Abdel Samad notes, is "situated between state and market, monitoring the powers and roles of each to assure a balance between them". In a Middle East context, clans and tribes are considered to be "family". Abdel Samad, who is executive director of the Arab NGO Network for Development,[9] continues: "Accordingly, just as civil society monitors the powers of the state and the market, it also has the potential to monitor tribal and clan relations in order to assure a balance among market, state, and family."[10] That can only happen, of course, if the state recognises the value of civil society and provides a suitable framework for it to function properly. A booklet of legal guidelines published by the Open Society Institute begins:

> The governmental and political structure of an open society may take many forms, but fundamental to them all is the principle that the state exists to serve the people, not the people to serve the state or the party that controls it. Achieving such a society requires laws that protect the rights of individuals to express their views freely and to come together freely to organise their efforts in pursuit of a common objective. The freedoms of expression, association, and peaceful assembly are the hallmarks of an open society. Law alone cannot create an open society, but no open society can exist unless the law gives meaningful protection to these and other fundamental freedoms. The law must recognise the right of individuals to join together to pursue shared interests or to pursue shared notions of the public good, free of state interference.[11]

This, it need scarcely be said, is anathema to most Arab regimes – which helps to explain why civil society in the Middle East is so weak.[12] A flourishing civil society promotes active citizenship, undermining the idea that the ruling elites know best – with the result, as Abdel Samad notes, that they become "defensive and jealous" at the prospect.[13] Active citizenship also advertises that government is not all-powerful. Even charitable work, unthreatening and apolitical as it might seem, can be a sensitive matter if it highlights the state's own failure to provide basic services. One way to neutralise that is for the ruling elite to claim the credit for themselves, often by establishing the ruler's wife as prime mover behind the nation's charitable efforts. Suzanne Mubarak,[14] Asma al-Asad,[15] Queen Rania of Jordan[16] and Shaikha Mozah of Qatar[17] are all notable examples. Independent initiatives are easily commandeered or stifled, either by taking them over or setting up a government-controlled organisation with a similar name and purpose – a practice known in Yemen as cloning. "This is very, very common throughout the region," Elbayar said:

> There will be an environmental group in Jordan and then the king will set up a *royal* environmental group with much more money. It's very common for gathering international attention and support, especially in a country like Jordan which is taken to be a liberal regime.

These are not civil society bodies in the normal sense and, though they often resemble non-governmental organisations, they cannot properly be described as NGOs (since that would be a contradiction in terms). With hefty government backing, though, they can easily co-opt and squeeze out genuine domestic NGOs. In Qatar and the Gulf states, most NGO-type organisations are government-run, Elbayar continued: "In Bahrain there are at least five national human rights organisations and three of them are government-run, so they say things are great – the government's human rights record continues to improve."

Most Arab constitutions pay lip-service to freedom of association but in practice the regimes use a variety of devices to restrict it. Worldwide, civil society organisations usually start out as informal groups of people who have banded together for a common purpose. Many remain like that, without any practical need to be formally constituted. However, those that become larger and employ staff or seek grants and donations benefit from having a formal legal status – which can open the door to government interference. Almost all the Arab countries require non-governmental organisations to be registered whether they wish to or not, and legally speaking this can apply even to children's clubs and hobby groups.[18] Abdel Samad writes:

> Despite the numerous initiatives for modernisation and democratisation in the region, most Arab governments still heavily restrict, through law and procedure, the establishment and activities of civil society associations. Laws in most of these countries prevent any group of people from conducting public activities unless they are registered as an association. In some cases, associations are subject to excessively cumbersome registration procedures. An association's activities are restricted to those set forth in its founding documents, which cannot easily be altered. Moreover, the types of organisations are often defined by their activities as perceived by the state, regardless of the perceptions and objectives of a given association's members and constituency.
>
> In many countries, the government demands that the association obtain advance permission each time it organises any public activities. Permission is also required if the association wishes to join any regional or global network or to receive funding from foreign donors. The government also

has the right to monitor the financial status, public activities, and private activities of the association's members, and it may dissolve the association for any reason.[19]

The difficulty of registering a civil society organisation varies from country to country. In some it means seeking official approval (and the possibility of rejection), while in others, at least in theory, the law treats it as little more than a formality.[20] However, one common tactic for blocking applications, reported in Syria and Saudi Arabia, among other places,[21] is simply to ignore them – which also spares the authorities the bother of having to think up reasons for a refusal.

In Lebanon, Egypt and Tunisia the law anticipates that applications may well become "lost" in the bureaucracy and states that if the authorities fail to make a decision within a specified period the application is deemed to have been approved. This is what happened with Helem,[22] the Lebanese gay and lesbian organisation. Presumably because of its controversial nature, the authorities did not respond – which meant that Helem could operate lawfully though without an official registration number. Among other things, the lack of a registration number meant it was unable to open a Lebanese bank account.[23] In Tunisia, however, officials circumvent the legal time limit by refusing to give receipts for applications. A report by the US State Department described this as routine practice: "Without such a receipt, NGOs were unable to counter the government's assertions that they had not applied to register and therefore were not allowed to operate. In such cases NGOs could be shut down, their property seized, and their members prosecuted for 'membership in an illegal organisation.'"[24]

Often, there are complex and vaguely worded rules which allow the authorities to refuse permission if they disapprove of an organisation's aims or the people involved, or to close it down subsequently if they dislike the way it is developing. In Bahrain and Oman, for example, they can refuse to register an organisation on the grounds that "society does not need its services" or, in the case of Oman, "for any other reasons" decided upon by the Ministry of Social Affairs.[25] In Qatar, which like most Gulf states depends on its large foreign workforce, non-Qataris are effectively excluded from freedom of association: the law allows them to participate in "private societies" only where this is deemed necessary. Participation by non-Qataris requires approval from the prime minister himself and non-Qataris must not exceed 20 per cent of the total membership.[26]

In Egypt the revised law on non-governmental organisations,[27] introduced in 2002, "created a legal regime that gives the state excessive latitude to dissolve, reject, or slowly choke any organisation financially, should it wish to do so," according to Human Rights Watch. "Worse still is the significant but unwritten role of the security services, which routinely reject applications to register new groups or candidates for board member elections, despite having no legal basis for doing so. Even groups that have successfully registered continue to endure close monitoring and sometimes harassment from security service agents."[28]

The problems often start with obstructive quibbles about the application:

> [They] kept sending back our papers with changes. For example, we could not have activities in "Egypt," we had to say "Cairo". The most significant thing in the application is that you must list all your activities. For the six activities we specified, they asked us to add "after approval of the relevant authorities". Six times! We wouldn't. We eventually settled on the fact that we would only apply for approval if we did a trade fair.
>
> They wanted to have it as an open field for them [to

intervene]. They would keep on sending us back the papers with written amendments. They were on paper, in pencil, no personal communication about it. They finally agreed to accept the papers on October 28. It had taken us five months to complete the forms.[29]

Article 11 of the Egyptian law forbids non-governmental organisations from "threatening national unity" and "violating public order or morals" – which provides an excuse for meddling by the security services. Threats to national unity, public order and morals are interpreted very broadly: the New Woman Foundation, for example, was informed that its list of objectives (research, publication of periodicals and research papers, providing expert advice on women and human rights, opening of a cultural centre; training programmes and conferences on women's issues, different kinds of public events; charity markets and exhibitions of women's handiwork, and other projects and services that serve the organisation's goals) included "items that breach Article 11". As often happens in such cases, there was no further explanation. An NGO's choice of board members is also subject to approval by the authorities:

> If an individual has a history of peaceful social activism, has spoken out on political issues, or was a member of a political organisation, for example, a student political group, then he or she appears likely to trigger security force objections.[30]

Organisations that successfully negotiate these hurdles face continuing supervision by the Egyptian authorities in what Human Rights Watch likens to a parent–child relationship. The numbers of board members and their terms of office are set by the authorities, as are procedures and quorums for annual general meetings, procedures for executive committee, fundraising requirements and methods of record-keeping. "At best these requirements are heavy-handed. At worst they provide ample means for selective enforcement and blatant political interference," Human Rights Watch says.

The level of detail in this regulatory framework provides ample scope for government intervention and even harassment – either by junior officials seeking bribes in return for leaving them alone, or at a higher level. A surprise inspection of the Nadim Centre in Cairo, which provides medical and other support for victims of torture, was apparently triggered by a senior health ministry official coming across its website and disliking what he saw. It was then threatened with prosecution on a host of charges, including possession of a questionnaire about torture and books about human rights, without a permit. Following a public outcry the list was reduced to just two alleged violations: not having a first aid kit or a fire extinguisher (both of which were on the premises at the time). Not all NGOs are treated in this way, however. As in other parts of the Arab world, if they stay clear of human rights and other issues that impinge on politics, if their organisers do not have a history of political activism and the authorities have no other reason for wishing to discourage them, they are likely to meet fewer obstacles.

Some countries have begun to recognise that the bureaucratic complexities surrounding NGOs can hamper social development and, at the time of writing, Oman, Yemen, Iraq and Egypt were said to be preparing new and, it is to be hoped, less restrictive laws. "The emerging trend is to remove many of the major obstacles for civil society but to keep one major one in place – and that is foreign funding restrictions," Elbayar said.[31] Restrictions on foreign donations are one of the key features of the Law on Societies which took effect in December 2008. Article 17 states that if a society "wants to obtain any contribution, donation or funding from non-

Jordanians, whatever its form, it must submit an application to obtain the approval of the relevant minister". Since no criteria for approving or rejecting foreign donations are specified in the law, whether or not to allow foreign funding appears to be entirely at the minister's discretion.[32]

Some governments seek to justify this on the grounds that they are trying to prevent money laundering and terrorist financing but that argument, Elbayar says, does not hold water. The amount of money entering Arab countries via NGOs is very small compared with the amount coming in through business transactions, and if the aim is to stop money laundering it should be done through a general law applied across the board, not by singling out NGOs for special scrutiny. A more plausible motive for restricting foreign donations emerged in 2006 when the Jordanian government announced a series of new restrictions for non-profit companies which included a prohibition on receiving foreign donations without the cabinet's approval. This was intended to close a loophole used in Jordan and some other Arab countries whereby organisations working in controversial areas such as human rights and press freedom register themselves as non-profit companies rather than submitting to the hazards of registering as an NGO. Those that had registered in this way in Jordan included Mizan (a lawyers' group for human rights), the Amman Centre for Human Rights Studies, the Centre for Defending Freedom of Journalists, and the Adaleh Centre for Human Rights Studies.[33] Explaining the new restrictions in a newspaper article, Jordan's controller-general of companies wrote:

> These [non-profit] companies [have] become a Trojan horse for spotlighting criticism and for insulting national and official institutions ... on the pretext of promoting human rights [through] written reports sent to [foreign] donors pretending

> to show ... that they are a watchful eye on what is going on
> with the issue of freedoms [and] rights.[34]

In the poorer Arab countries there is not enough funding from local sources for most NGOs to survive, so they often depend on western donors or the UN. By vetting all foreign donations governments thus acquire the power to strangle NGOs more or less at will.

THE CONTAIN-AND-CONTROL techniques for dealing with NGOs that have been described here illustrate the approach of Arab governments towards independent initiatives by their citizens more generally – including the development of political parties and non-government media. Outright suppression is one way to limit freedom of association and expression but it tends to attract bad publicity. Bureaucracy is a more subtle weapon, and often no less effective. Its pettiness and inefficiency may have developed more by accident than design but can be harnessed for a purpose. The obvious, if unstated, aim is regime survival while the stated aim is a paternalistic one: protecting a supposedly naïve and gullible public from "undesirable" influences. Among many other things, this leads to a requirement that newspapers and magazines, sometimes along with printing presses and even journalists themselves, must be licensed. As with the compulsory registration of NGOs, licensing is the cornerstone of a regulatory system which facilitates various kinds of government interference – the ultimate sanction being withdrawal of a licence. This provides the authorities with a variety of tools for exercising control in ways that appear less crude than formal bans and direct censorship – though the effect is much the same. It means newspapers can be disciplined on technical grounds for breaking the law or infringing the terms of their licence, even if the real reason is that they have offended the government.

The closure of *Addomari* (the Lamplighter), a satirical weekly in Syria, was one example. Launched in 2001 shortly after Bashar al-Asad became president, it was the country's first independent newspaper in thirty-eight years and for a while each issue sold more copies than all the official dailies put together.[35] By 2003 the regime had taken a dislike to it and the information minister demanded to see the content of each issue before publication. Its owner, Ali Farzat, refused and temporarily suspended publication. Later, when he tried to publish another issue without submitting it for approval, the authorities prevented its distribution. A government decree then rescinded its licence on the grounds that *Addomari* had "violated laws and regulations in force by failing to appear for more than three months" as required by the conditions of its licence.[36]

In terms of ownership, newspapers in the Arab countries fall into three categories: those that are government-owned (together with semi-official papers such as *al-Ahram* in Egypt), party newspapers (including those of opposition parties in some countries), and the independent press. In some of the Gulf states all newspapers are classed as independent, though the term can be misleading. Qatar, for instance, has six newspapers – all of them technically independent but actually owned by members of the ruling family or businessmen with close ties to the ruling family.[37]

Basically, licensing creates an appearance of freedom by allowing independent newspapers to exist without direct government censorship, while using the threat of punishment to encourage self-censorship. As with the registration of NGOs, obtaining a licence ranges from straightforward to almost impossible, depending on the country and/or the background of the applicant. In a free society, though, there is no reason why anyone should need a licence to publish anything: many countries get by perfectly well without.

Though Arab journalists often call for the press laws to be reformed, the real need is not for reform but their abolition. Since the right of free speech applies equally to everyone, it is invidious to make a distinction between what the press can legally say and what ordinary citizens can legally say, or vice versa. If ordinary citizens do not need a licence to speak their mind there is no reason why newspapers and magazines should need one either.[38] Few would argue that freedom of speech can ever be absolute because there are occasions when it conflicts with other human rights – as in the case of incitement to violence – but the idea that people require a licence to publish approaches the problem from the wrong direction: it should start with an assumption of total freedom and then consider what restrictions might be legitimate.

Arab attempts to control the press have parallels elsewhere, both modern and historical – even in the west. Soon after the arrival of printing in Britain, its subversive possibilities were recognised and between 1500 and 1700 there were numerous efforts to restrict the number of printers, with little success. Between 1700 and 1820 the preferred course was to imprison journalists and pamphleteers or, where appropriate, to bribe them. Robert Walpole, generally considered to have been Britain's first prime minister, spent £50,000 bribing newspapers – an extraordinary sum in the early part of the eighteenth century. Another technique was to make it expensive to buy or publish newspapers. Publishers were required to deposit a bond of £200–£300 with the government as surety against any future conviction for seditious or blasphemous libel. Newspapers were also subjected to a stamp duty (described by its opponents as "the tax on knowledge") which priced them beyond the reach of ordinary people. This had the opposite effect to what was intended: illegally published unstamped newspapers thrived while those that complied with the law saw their circulations fall, and in 1855 the tax was finally abolished.[39]

As far as what can actually be said in the Arab press is concerned, the restrictions not only tend to be very broad but are often vaguely drafted, allowing ample scope for arbitrary interpretations. The Yemeni Press and Publications Law approved in 1990, for example, included the following prohibitions:

> Anything which prejudices the Islamic faith and its lofty principles or belittles religions or humanitarian creeds;
>
> Anything which might cause tribal, sectarian, racial, regional or ancestral discrimination, or which might spread a spirit of dissent and division among the people or call on them to apostasise;
>
> Anything which leads to the spread of ideas contrary to the principles of the Yemeni revolution, prejudicial to national unity or distorting the image of the Yemeni, Arab or Islamic heritage;
>
> Anything which undermines public moral [*sic*] or prejudices the dignity of individuals or the freedom of the individual by smears and defamation;
>
> To criticise the person of the head of state, or to attribute to him declarations or pictures unless the declarations were made or the picture taken during a public speech. This does not necessarily apply to objective, constructive criticism.[40]

These reflect the typical areas of sensitivity in most Arab countries. Similarly, the "reformed" Kuwaiti press law, issued in 2006, criminalises the publication of material criticising the constitution, the emir, or Islam or inciting acts that will offend public morality or religious sensibilities. This might be considered an improvement on the previous law in that offenders now face heavy fines instead of jail sentences.[41]

When functioning properly, the media plays the role of a sceptical, inquisitive, persistent, loud-voiced and often troublesome citizen, asking awkward questions and teasing out the answers. Despite some significant steps forward during the last decade or so, this is a goal that the Arab media, considered overall, is still a long way from reaching. It is also a role that it would still be ill equipped to perform even if all the government restrictions were suddenly lifted tomorrow.

One reason is that Arab newspapers are in a parlous state: hardly any of them pay their way financially. The official press is heavily subsidised, both directly and indirectly. In Syria, for example, only a tiny fraction of the official newspapers printed are sold to the public on the streets; vast numbers are purchased by the civil service and the military in the hope that soldiers and pen-pushers will feel dutiful enough to read them. "Independent" newspapers are subsidised too, either by their owners for reasons of prestige and influence, or by other means. Lebanon, with its multi-faceted politics, has a tradition of media diversity and relatively little control by the state, but that does not necessarily bring independence. Magda Abu-Fadil, director of the Journalism Training Programme at the American University of Beirut, explained:

> When there was only print, assorted Lebanese newspapers were the mouthpieces of regional governments – pretty much all of them. Lebanon being such a free country, they all started bashing each other through Lebanese media. They couldn't do it on their own turf, and Lebanon was the perfect playground for that back in the 1950s and 1960s, what with Arabism and all the different "-isms".

Paying newspapers to provide the required slant – by ignoring some stories and covering others, or covering them in a certain way – is a long-standing practice and "par for the course", according to Abu-Fadil.

> When the Lebanese civil war broke out some of those media moved to Europe and carried on the tradition. In fact, they wouldn't have survived otherwise because it's just so expensive to operate in Britain and France and Italy where they established their respective headquarters.

Payments would be channelled through proxies so as not to be directly attributable to their source, though the real source was usually obvious from the content of the papers. Along with the newspapers themselves, writers and editors sometimes received subsidies too: the Saudis in particular were noted for their "envelope parties" for Arab journalists working in London. To what extent these practices continue today is difficult to judge, though gossip within the profession suggests they are not particularly uncommon.

How many Arab newspapers actually make a profit? Very few, according to Abu-Fadil. Asked if she could name any that definitely do, she replied:

> Not really. I'll tell you why, because in most of the Arab world the main media are state-owned – the subsidy comes from the government. What exists as so-called independent media can barely eke out a living (a) because they don't have enough of a following, (b) because of government restrictions, bans, constraints, harassment and assorted other obstacles, (c) because advertising isn't enough and they certainly don't have enough circulation [revenue] if we're talking about print.
> It's even more difficult for broadcast and unless they have adequate subsidies – usually from different sources – there's

only so much in the advertising pie. If there is a falling out between one country's government and another, advertising from that country dwindles to a trickle.

Advertisers' influence can have a damaging effect on the media's independence anywhere in the world but the problem is exacerbated in the Arab countries because their advertising markets are more politicised than most. Advertisers in the west do not generally treat their spending as a form of subsidy or support: they are interested in reaching their target audience at an economic price, so deciding where to place their ads is essentially a commercial decision. The same applies to some extent in the Arab media too but a significant portion of their advertising depends on political rather than business considerations. (On one occasion I took part in a discussion programme on a small satellite channel run by a Tunisian dissident. Before the discussion started, the station showed a film of Kuwaiti folk-dancing in traditional costumes. During the discussion, every advertising slot was taken up by the Kuwaiti airline. Considering the relative obscurity of the channel, I found it hard to believe that this was purely a commercial decision on the part of the airline: the Kuwaitis were clearly subsidising the station.)

Not only are publishers and broadcasters susceptible to pressure from advertisers but advertisers themselves are susceptible to pressure from governments and politicians. In addition to that, governments and people associated with them are often major advertisers in their own right. This is one reason why al-Jazeera, despite its vast region-wide audience, has trouble attracting advertising. Al-Jazeera, of course, is lucky in that it can survive without – thanks to a generous benefactor in the shape of the emir of Qatar. A small weekly magazine in Lebanon, however, was less fortunate. "At one point it was very left-wing and very anti-Hariri [the late Lebanese prime minister],"

Abu-Fadil recalled. "Being the multi-billionaire that he was, who bristled at criticism like any other politician, Hariri saw to it that advertising halted – what little advertising there was for the magazine. So they almost went under." At that point, Hariri came to the rescue and bought up the magazine. "After that it was all accolades and praises and cheerleading for Mr Hariri."

Without financial viability or a hands-off benefactor it becomes extremely difficult for the media to assert any kind of independence. That, in turn, lessens credibility in the eyes of the public – which keeps sales low and perpetuates the need for subsidies. Unfortunately, though, it is not the only problem. To do their job properly, journalists need facts, and for Abu-Fadil this raises a series of questions: "Do they know how to dig for facts?", "Have they been trained adequately?", "What facts are there that can be obtained?" In most cases, she said, facts are few and far between – "and especially from official sources, basically because people like to cover up misdeeds and all sorts of problems". As with the economics of the media, this creates a vicious circle: when facts are hard to come by there is not much point in making the effort to find them. The result, much of the time, is a bland style of reporting based on statements, meetings, conferences and other set-piece events, with little attempt to probe beneath the surface by explaining the significance and the issues at stake or scrutinising the validity of what has been said.

If the Arab media lack the ability to battle for government transparency and accountability, at least there is hope that inquisitive citizens may carry that struggle forward. Trawling through planespotting websites, a Tunisian blogger called Astrubal was intrigued to discover photographs of the presidential Boeing 737 at a variety of European airports: Brussels, Geneva, Lisbon, Madrid, Malaga, Malta, Milan and Paris. "After observing more than two dozen photos," Astrubal wrote, "the first finding that emerges is the many destinations that the local press never talks about ... Tunisians know that their president does not make many official trips ... Were these trips for private purposes? In that case, isn't the use of the presidential plane an abuse of power?"[42] Astrubal posed three questions:

> Who is using the presidential plane, since it is not the head of state?
>
> What purpose does this aircraft serve, paid for and maintained by the Tunisian taxpayer?
>
> Who controls the "reasonable" use of this facility, described by some as the "symbol of the state's prestige"?

These were all questions that in a free country the media would be raring to investigate but, as Astrubal noted, "those are taboo questions in Tunisia, and we do not ask them." He continued:

> Apart from the troubling aspect of these destinations of the plane in question, as long as media silence lasts with regard to mentioning the presidential lifestyle, a presumption of guilt will be the norm ... To mention only the case of the two photos of Friday February 9 and Sunday February 11, 2007, I simply point out that there is nothing, not a single word in the Tunisian media (except short-sightedness on my part) that could explain the presence of the Tunisian presidential plane in Geneva's airport.

Another Tunisian, Sami Ben Gharbia, took up the detective work and confirmed that only two of the photographs (taken at Malta in June 2005) could be matched with press reports of an official presidential visit. "The rest of the pictures were taken at European airports at times when Ben Ali was not there officially," Ben Gharbia wrote.[43] Both bloggers strongly hinted that many of the plane's recorded journeys were in fact shopping excursions by the president's wife, who is reputedly a shopaholic.[44]

Blogs, increasingly, are becoming a source of news in their own right. Bloggers who flout the customary taboos also highlight the deficiencies of the mainstream media and, here and there, they are beginning to embolden the independent press. Egyptian blogger-activist Hossam el-Hamalawy commented:

> Blogs have become one of the main news sources about what's going on in Egypt – for reporters and experts, pundits – whether locally or abroad – and, increasingly, the local population.
>
> What we write is picked up by the local and international mainstream media, and that's how we spread the message to an even bigger off-line audience. *Al-Badil, al-Masri al-Youm, al-Dustour* – these newspapers are following the blogs and hardly a day will pass without them having a news report about something that a blog said or a story where they picked up the lead from a blog.

Mainstream journalists, he said, sometimes break politically sensitive stories by giving them to bloggers first and then reporting what the blog said – in effect, getting the blogger to carry the initial risk:

> A friend of mine who was working in an independent Egyptian publication would come to me or to others, and say: "I have this information but my boss is scared shitless, so can you post it and then we'll be quoting it." In our case we're more than happy to do it – we're activists at the end of the day.[45]

The spread of camera phones throughout the Arab world has provided another weapon in the bloggers' armoury, allowing ordinary people to record incidents that the authorities would prefer to deny and then post the results on the internet. One Egyptian blogger, Wael Abbas,[46] became famous in 2006 for reporting on a mob who sexually molested women in downtown Cairo. (The interior ministry said the attacks could not have happened because no one had complained to the police, and a pro-government newspaper said the story was a product of Abbas's "sick fantasies".)[47] Abbas and Hamalawy were among the first Egyptian bloggers to post a video, made on a mobile phone, which showed police sodomising a minibus driver with a stick. As a result of the video, two officers were later charged with torture and jailed for three years each.[48] A succession of police brutality videos followed, generating unprecedented public debate. Ironically, this trend was started – accidentally – by the authorities themselves, according to Gamal Eid of the Arabic Network for Human Rights Information. The minibus driver had been arrested when he tried to intervene in a dispute between the police and other drivers. The officers involved made a video of his torture which they circulated as a warning to his friends, not expecting it to be picked up by bloggers. "After that bloggers started to say 'We can use it also to video the kind of cases where they don't known we are [filming]'," Eid said. [49]

Amid the welter of restrictions on thought and expression in the Middle East, the internet looks enticingly liberating and its technology is so simple that anyone can publish anything, without the need for intermediaries. This do-it-yourself aspect is giving citizens a voice all over the world. The eventual consequences of that remain to be seen, though in the Arab countries, unaccustomed to such freedom, they could prove especially far-reaching. For Hamalawy, one of the most memorable videos on YouTube was made by two kids in the Egyptian city of Tanta, with a mobile phone. "They were filming the police assaulting a street vendor, and you hear one of the kids telling the other: 'Send it to Wael Abbas, send it to Wael Abbas!' and the other says: 'No, no, no, I'll upload it to YouTube tonight' – and it's there online."

THE TECHNIQUES USED for controlling the press and NGOs can also be seen at work in controlling political parties (at least, those that are not parties of government). In Bahrain, Kuwait, Libya, Oman, Qatar, Saudi Arabia and the UAE, parties are simply not allowed. Elsewhere, opposition parties function not so much by right as through the grace and favour of the regime. Once again, the familiar licensing/registration systems usually apply and licences can be, and sometimes are, taken away. In 2004 the Arab Human Development Report observed:

> States which allow party activity ... try to trip up the opposition parties, by depriving them of resources and media exposure, controlling nomination and election procedures, using the judiciary, the army and security services to curtail their activities, hounding their leaders and activists while tampering with election polls.
>
> Some states have witnessed a massive rise in the number of political parties (27 in Algeria, 26 in Morocco, 31 in Jordan and 22 in Yemen). Some see this as a reflection of the divisions among political and cultural elites, or of the ruling regime's manoeuvres to divide the opposition, rather than a sign of democratic vitality. Fragmented as they are, these parties are incapable of rallying popular support to achieve the objectives for which they were created. Indeed, this proliferation has engendered an aversion to political activity among citizens, a fact evident in their obvious reluctance to take part in the electoral process. On the other side, governments deliberately freeze and ban parties that rally popular support: in Egypt 7

out of 17 licensed parties have been frozen, in Mauritania 6 out of 17 and in Tunisia 3 out of 11.[50]

Most established democracies have systems for registering political parties but registration is often voluntary and confers certain benefits, such as protecting the party's name and logo from imitations. Registration in these countries is normally a straightforward and apolitical process: in Britain, all it requires is some basic information such as the party's name and address, and the name and address of its leader and nominating officer.[51] Many established democracies also have rules about party funding – for example, requiring large donations to be publicly disclosed. Apart from that, though, how the parties conduct their business and what policies they adopt is a matter for themselves, and for the electorate. However, Arab laws governing political parties often stray beyond ensuring they are properly constituted and funded into questions of their general suitability and acceptability. The Yemeni law, for example, says that a party's "principles, objectives, programmes, and means" must not contradict:

a) Islamic precepts and values;

b) The sovereignty, integrity, and unity of the country and the people;

c) The republican system, and the objectives and principles of the September and October Revolutions, and the Republic's Constitution;

d) The national cohesion of the Yemeni society;

e) The basic freedoms and duties, and the international declarations on human rights;

f) The Yemeni society's affiliation to the Arab and Muslim nations.[52]

At first sight this is unnecessary, since any party in Yemen that did reject Islamic values, the republican system, and so on, would have virtually no prospect of being elected. The point of including such stipulations in the law, though, is that it transfers the responsibility for judging a party's merits and demerits in these areas from voters to the registering authorities.

The Yemeni law goes on to say that a new party's policies and programmes must "not replicate those of other (existing) parties and political organisations".[53] Egypt has a similar rule that parties' platforms must "constitute an addition to political life according to specific methods and goals" and must not contradict "the requirements of maintaining national unity [and] social peace".[54] Again, this creates an opportunity for the regime, rather than the voters, to pass judgement on their policies. In Egypt the task of interpreting these vague requirements is entrusted to the Political Parties Committee (PPC), a body where eight of the nine members are presidential appointees. The PPC has frequently rejected applications to license parties on the grounds that their policies are "not sufficiently distinct from those of existing parties", while others have been rejected for espousing "a radical ideology". One party – al-Karama (Dignity) – was rejected on separate occasions both for being too similar to other parties and also too radical. Over a twenty-seven-year period from its creation in 1977, the Egyptian PPC rejected sixty-three parties' applications and approved only two.[55]

Following an amendment to the law in 2005 new parties no longer have to seek the PPC's approval; they can announce their formation and the PPC then has ninety days to object. However, the PPC still has the power to temporarily suspend any party and to reverse any of its "delinquent decision[s] or act[s]" in consultation with the Interior Ministry. If a party is deemed to be no longer "an addition to political life" or not helping to maintain national unity and "social peace", the PPC can dissolve it and liquidate its funds. As one opposition politician put it, "Under the terms of the political parties law, the ruling party has the right to select its opposition, on its own terms."[56]

ARAB REGIMES, IT need scarcely be said, have an almost insatiable urge to control. But there is a paradox here that foreigners often fail to grasp. Arab regimes may legislate and regulate endlessly but their desire for control is often not matched by an ability to exercise it. Though they may succeed in keeping a lid on open dissent, though they may establish large armies and security forces and employ vast bureaucracies, their ability to effect change and influence the behaviour of their citizens is far more limited than it looks. As Nazih Ayubi noted in his ground-breaking book, *Over-stating the Arab State*:

> Their capabilities for law enforcing are much weaker than their ability to enact laws, their implementation capabilities are much weaker than their ability to issue development plans.[57]

Possession of arbitrary powers and the absence of constitutional restraints is of little use, Ayubi argued, if the regime's will cannot be translated into a sound political or social reality: "The Arab state is therefore often violent *because* it is weak."[58]

Where survival of the regime becomes the chief priority of government it is hardly surprising that the power of the state should be directed towards controlling dissent, and that this is the area where it is deployed most forcefully and effectively. Exercising power in this way is often mistaken for a sign of strength when in reality it is an acknowledgment of vulnerability. In areas where regime survival is not perceived to be at stake the picture is somewhat different: the same "control mentality" exists in the form of laws, decrees and regulations but in a far more tokenistic way since the regime often lacks the capacity, and sometimes also the inclination, to enforce them.

One illustration is the contrasting attitudes towards enforcing laws that serve the public good – environmental protection, health and safety, etc – and those that serve the good of the regime. Ayman Nour's real offence was that he had dared to contest the first "free" presidential election in Egypt without the regime's approval, and he was sentenced to five years in jail for what the prime minister described as serious crimes. He had been accused of forging some of the signatures required by the law in order to register his political party. The charges against him were generally regarded as trumped up but, even if true, they were only a violation of an unfair law designed to make the formation of opposition parties as difficult as possible. Mamdouh Ismael, on the other hand, was the owner of a Red Sea ferry, *al-Salam Boccaccio,* which caught fire and sank in 2006 with the loss of more than 1,000 lives. A parliamentary inquiry blamed the ferry company for the disaster and, according to a recovered data recorder, the company had over-ruled the captain's request to return to port after fire broke out on board. Ismael, a well-connected member of the upper house of parliament, was allowed to flee Egypt – allegedly with help from senior officials. He was tried in his absence two years later along with four others and acquitted of all charges.[59] Ismael's acquittal caused public uproar and an appeals court eventually convicted him of involuntary manslaughter and sentenced him to seven years' jail, but he remained abroad. The issue here is not the guilt or otherwise of Nour and Ismael but the regime's priorities: more concerned about a challenge to its authority than a shipping company's duty of care towards its passengers.

In *Over-stating the Arab State,* Ayubi drew an important distinction between "strong" and "hard" states. Unlike a strong state, a state that is hard may also be weak. A hard state tends to be highly centralised and interventionist, seeking (though not necessarily successfully) "to enforce a detailed, standardised regulation of the economy and the society". A strong state, meanwhile, is complementary to society and operates in partnership with its citizens. Its strength lies not in subjugation but in "its ability to work with and through other centres of power in society".[60] By these criteria, most Arab states can be described as predominantly "hard but weak".[61] In comparison, European states lean more towards the "strong but soft" – strong because they are generally capable of effecting change and implementing laws, and soft because they can do so without much need for coercion.

The key here lies in the different relationships between states and their people – in particular, concepts of citizenship and the responsibilities that go with it. EU citizens, for example, enjoy more freedom than those in Arab countries and yet in many ways the regulation of their lives is far more extensive. Everyday activities such as work and business practices are subject to a multiplicity of rules that simply do not exist in most Arab countries. This type of regulation, though, is not so much an attempt to curtail their freedom as to balance competing freedoms: the freedom of businesses to make money, for example, versus the freedom of their employees not to be exploited. In general the aim is to protect the weak from the strong and to shield the individual from malpractices, health and safety hazards, and so on.

The types of regulation found in EU countries are not only different in character but compliance is higher. High levels of compliance depend not just on the existence of laws but on public acceptance of the rationale behind them. Prospects for compliance are also improved if the processes for introducing new laws and regulations are perceived to be legitimate. That requires a culture of public scrutiny and debate where interested parties and the media can express their views freely (it helps too, of course, if the ultimate decision rests with a properly-elected body). Where there is general acceptance of a law, enforcement becomes a last resort rather than the first line of defence. The mere *threat* of enforcement can often be enough to ensure compliance but that only works where non-compliance is known to be futile – where the police, the courts and enforcement officials cannot be influenced by bribery or pulling rank.

This is not to trumpet European countries as models of perfect governance – no system is perfect – but to show why, by comparison, Arab countries have such problems with compliance. In line with the "father knows best" approach to government, Arab laws tend to be handed down from on high by diktat and the lack of critical scrutiny before they are approved often results in vague or ambiguous language that makes them more difficult to implement. With less debate, there is less opportunity for the public to be persuaded of the rationale behind new laws – a difficulty which is compounded by the general perception of government as a creator of obstacles rather than a facilitator and a partner with society in solving problems. In addition to all that, there is the perception, at least among those with money and influence, that compliance may be optional.

In 2000 the Egyptian parliament updated its road safety laws. Drivers and front-seat passengers were required to wear seat-belts, motorcyclists were required to wear helmets and use of mobile phones was prohibited while driving. Several years later, and despite police crackdowns, all these rules continue to be flouted on a monumental scale. In Egypt even the basic premise – that seat-belts save lives – is disputed. "What do we need seat-belts for?" Ashraf Ismail, a Cairo taxi driver told the *New York Times*. "We never really get moving in these endless traffic jams; I'm lucky if I get out of second gear all day." The paper noted that his opinion appeared to be shared by the majority. Many of the older cars in Egypt had never been fitted with belts, or had had them removed to avoid a tax on "luxury" vehicles. Once belts became compulsory, the price shot up from around $22 a pair to over $100. This in turn spawned a cottage industry producing cheap but ineffective belts that would not withstand an accident.[62] To save money, some drivers fitted half-straps which look like real seat belts from outside the car. ("Please, hold this," a Cairo taxi driver once said to me. I was expected to sit with the piece of webbing stretched across my chest "in case a policeman sees us".) Attitudes towards seat-belts are also shaped by a widespread sense of fatalism – that God alone determines whether we live or die. Many cars have colourful stickers on their dashboard saying, in Arabic calligraphy, "*Ma sha' Allah*" ("Whatever God wills"). In most Middle Eastern countries if you get into a taxi and attempt to disentangle the seat-belt, the driver – if he is in a good mood – is likely to say "Don't worry, there's no need." The more macho ones treat it as an affront to their driving skills.

It is a similar story with female genital mutilation (FGM) – a practice that Egyptian governments have been trying to stamp out for more than half a century. *Al-Hayat* journalist Amina Khairy recalled a ceremony at a small village in Aswan which was about to be declared an FGM-free zone. Since this entailed a rare visit from senior officials, the villagers treated it as an opportunity to lobby them about other matters – in fact, anything except FGM:

Everybody was inside the main hall – the governor, the head of the Council for Motherhood and Childhood – and everybody was clapping. Outside the hall, all the women of the village were standing with applications because they knew very important people were going to be there – somebody asking for electricity, someone whose daughter was ill and dying of a heart problem, and so on.

When I asked them about FGM, they said of course we have to circumcise our daughters but we do it through a doctor. Whether this was because of religious belief or social belief, I had the feeling that they just closed their ears when somebody was coming talking to them about FGM.[63]

THE GAP BETWEEN what Arab regimes would like to control and what they can actually control has widened significantly since the mid-1990s and is likely to continue widening, regardless of any efforts to stop it. As often happened in the past with social and political change, this gap is driven by new technology. The technology required for economic development can also be used to develop political freedoms and while regimes may seek to restrict its use, ultimately – as was seen with earlier attempts to control printing presses, typewriters and photocopiers in various parts of the world – that is not sustainable.

The first serious cracks started appearing in the 1990s with the spread of satellite television. For the first time large numbers of Arabs could watch programmes that had not been produced under the control of their own governments. Arab governments did not take this lying down. In particular, the Qatar-based al-Jazeera station and its staff faced various kinds of harassment, and the near-impossibility of blocking satellite transmissions sometimes prompted desperate measures. On one occasion, according to Faisal al-Qassem, presenter of the weekly debate programme, *al-Ittijah al-Mu'akis* (*The Opposite Direction*), the authorities in Algiers cut off electricity supplies "so that people could not watch the programme because we were talking about the military generals and how they are wasting the money of Algerians". Elsewhere, including Jordan, Kuwait and post-Saddam Iraq,[64] the station's local bureaus were forcibly closed. It happened so many times in different countries that Jihad Ballout, head of al-Jazeera's media relations, reckoned he could predict when a closure was coming. First the government would plant nasty stories about al-Jazeera in the local newspapers, he said, then the secret police would start tailing reporters, making it obvious that they were doing so.[65]

The formula for *al-Ittijah al-Mu'akis* was so basic that most TV stations in the west would never dream of making it their flagship programme. For Arab viewers, though, it was a radical innovation, attracting audiences in the tens of millions. For seventy-five minutes, Qassem – wearing spectacles, with his hair combed sideways to minimise the bald spots, and looking more like a university lecturer than a TV star – would sit at a table strewn with papers, while his two guests argued. The protagonists would shout, gesticulate and try to drown each other out, with Qassem sometimes appealing for calm, at other times provoking them further. On occasions, they even stormed out. In the control room above the studio, it took a team of five people, working frantically, to keep the flailing arms in shot.[66]

Viewers could also join the fray via emails and phone calls (according to al-Jazeera staff, many would claim to be calling from non-Arab countries such as Sweden – presumably for fear of retribution by the authorities). The calls were not filtered and there was no time-delay to protect against abusive language. It was all live: anything could happen and frequently it did. Qassem himself once casually remarked on air that all Arab leaders are bastards and the furore lasted for weeks.

In Qassem's view, the secret of the show's popularity was that it broke so many of the Arab world's taboos. "We tackle the most sensitive issues, be they political, religious, social, cultural or economic. We were the first to do a hot debate on secularism and Islam," he said. "In the past, in the Arab world, you couldn't even talk about the price of fish, because that might endanger national security as far as the security services were concerned."[67]

Technically, al-Jazeera was just another state-owned channel. It had been founded in 1996 by a decree from the emir of Qatar and was lavishly funded by him but, in Arab terms, it enjoyed an unprecedented measure of journalistic independence (though it has often been accused of shying away from controversial stories relating to Qatar). Many of its original staff had previously worked for the BBC's Arabic language broadcasts and brought with them the BBC's tradition of balanced reporting. This ethos was reflected in the station's slogan: "*al-Ra'i ... wal Ra'i al-Akhr*" ("Opinion ... and the Other Opinion"). Unlike many Arabic channels, for example, it was never averse to broadcasting interviews with Israeli politicians.

This more open approach quickly established al-Jazeera as the most popular and trusted source of news and political debate in the Arab world – a development that the hidebound state-run channels have still not come to terms with. In 2003, at the moment when American forces swept into Baghdad and Iraqis began attacking the symbols of Saddam Hussein's rule, Syrian television interrupted its live coverage of the war to bring viewers a programme about Islamic art and architecture. The scenes in Iraq, apparently, were deemed unsuitable to be shown on a state-run channel, so the war vanished from sight for five whole hours at its most crucial point. "There are plenty of statues to be found in Syria that are not unlike the one that was toppled in Baghdad," a western diplomat observed wryly.[68] In

April 2005 a bomb attack in the Khan el-Khalili district of Cairo was promptly reported by al-Jazeera but it took a further two-and-a-half hours for Egyptian state television to pluck up the courage to mention it. According to reports in the independent press at the time, this was because the state television's news director had switched his mobile phone off and could not be contacted to give permission.[69]

The big question, of course, is what contribution Arab satellite television is making towards political and social change. There can be little doubt that it has significantly undermined governments' ability to control the supply of information and dictate the shape of public discourse. One obvious prerequisite for a properly functioning democracy is informed citizens who can freely exchange ideas. Certainly debate has become far more open over the last ten to fifteen years and satellite television has played a large part in that, but as yet it is debate that has nowhere to go: the opportunities for channelling it towards political ends are still severely restricted. Nevertheless, Marc Lynch, an American expert on the Arab media, views it as a positive development:

> The Arab media cannot create democracy by itself, but I think it's actually doing something which is really more important than creating democracy. It's creating pluralism, it's creating the possibility of meaningful public dissent in which it's OK to disagree; you're not a traitor to the Arab identity, you're not a traitor to the Arab cause if you disagree ...[70]

However, Imad Karam, a Palestinian journalist-turned-academic adds an important note of caution, pointing out that "most of this new Arab space for criticism and debate is one-dimensional":

> A closer look shows it to be dominated by one set of issues, while many others pertaining to the daily lives of Arab

citizens are largely ignored. The public sphere that the Arab
satellite channels create is largely taken up with discussion
of international politics and issues relating to Arab relations
with Israel, the US and other western states. This leaves
little room for domestic issues, such as national political
reforms and development indicators, policies on poverty and
unemployment, or a plethora of social and health problems
including AIDS, drugs and the increasing divorce rate.[71]

Karam's own analysis of the most popular discussion programmes
on al-Jazeera over a ten-week period in 2005 – *Al-Ittijah al-Mu'akis
(The Opposite Direction)*, *Akthar min Ra'i (More than One Opinion)*
and *Bila Hudud (Without Limits)* – showed that debate was heavily
weighted towards international affairs rather than internal Arab
issues. Only three out of the thirty broadcasts were directly related
to the principles and practice of democracy, reform or development.
"The remaining twenty-seven dealt with issues such as the post-
Arafat era in Palestine, Syrian withdrawal from Lebanon, Sudan,
international politics, and US and foreign interventions in Arab
affairs. Thus, although it is quite true to say that al-Jazeera talk
shows provide a platform for the criticism of Arab governments ...
the shows make little contribution to a concrete democratic agenda
within which people develop a vision of how to act."[72]

THE INTERNET, LIKE satellite TV, is no respecter of national
boundaries and is even more difficult to control. Although television
– both satellite and terrestrial – can allow some public participation
through phone-ins, interviews and discussion programmes, it is
basically a one-directional medium, delivering news, opinions and
entertainment in a highly structured way to a passive audience . The
internet, on the other hand, is unstructured, unfiltered, anarchic

and – most importantly – multi-directional. It requires active users who not only seek out the information they want but who can also become providers and exchangers of information themselves. In societies where independent action is frowned upon and no one is supposed to speak out of turn, this is potentially very subversive.

One of the benefits of the internet for political activists is ease of communication. Whereas a decade or more ago they might have had to gather in clandestine meetings or surreptitiously hand out small numbers of photocopies to a few acquaintances, nowadays they post information on the internet where anyone can see it. "Most of them know how to create a blog, organise a chat group, make phone calls through a computer and use a proxy to get round censorship," Reporters Without Borders noted in its annual report for 2007. "The web makes networking much easier, for political activists as well as teenagers."[73]

The Arab countries, however, have lagged behind most of the world in adopting the internet. One factor, until the late 1990s, was the technical difficulty of using Arabic on the internet (and on computers more generally) which tended to restrict access to those who could use English or, in some cases, French. Another factor was cost (including high connection charges, often through a government-controlled monopoly). Saudi Arabia and Iraq were the last Arab countries to provide public internet access, in 1999 and 2000 respectively.

By the middle of 2008 more than 38 million Arabs were believed to be using the internet at least once a month and overall internet penetration (users as a percentage of population) had reached 11.1 per cent. This was still only about half the world average (21.9 per cent) but all the signs pointed towards continuing rapid growth. The largest numbers of users were in Egypt (8.6 million), Morocco (7.3 million) and Saudi Arabia (6.2

million). As might be expected, the highest penetration levels were found in some of the wealthy Gulf states: the UAE (49.8 per cent), Qatar (37.8 per cent), Bahrain (34.8 per cent) and Kuwait (34.7 per cent) – all well above the world average. Further down the list, Lebanon, Saudi Arabia and Morocco were near or slightly above the world average.[74]

Internet use in the Arab countries

Country	Population	Users 2000	Users 2008	% of total	% Increase	Penetration
Algeria	33,769,669	50,000	3,500,000	9.13	6900	10.4%
Bahrain	718,306	40,000	250,000	0.65	525	34.8%
Comoros	731,775	1,500	21,000	0.05	1300	2.9%
Djibouti	506,221	1,400	11,000	0.03	686	2.2%
Egypt	81,713,517	450,000	8,620,000	22.48	1816	10.5%
Iraq	28,221,181	12,500	54,000	0.14	332	0.2%
Jordan	6,198,677	127,300	1,126,700	2.94	785	18.2%
Kuwait	2,596,799	150,000	900,000	2.35	500	34.7%
Lebanon	3,971,941	300,000	950,000	2.48	217	23.9%
Libya	6,173,579	10,000	260,000	0.68	2500	4.2%
Mauritania	3,364,940	5,000	30,000	0.08	500	0.9%
Morocco	34,343,219	100,000	7,300,000	19.04	7200	21.3%
Oman	3,311,640	90,000	300,000	0.78	233	9.1%
Palestine (WB)	2,611,904	35,000	355,000	0.93	914	13.6%
Qatar	928,635	30,000	351,000	0.92	1070	37.8%

Country	Population	Users 2000	Users 2008	% of total	% Increase	Penet- rations
Saudi Arabia	28,161,417	200,000	6,200,000	16.17	3000	22.0%
Somalia	9,558,666	200	98,000	0.26	48900	1.0%
Sudan	40,218,455	30,000	1,500,000	3.91	4900	3.7%
Syria	19,747,586	30,000	2,132,000	5.56	7007	10.8%
Tunisia	10,383,577	100,000	1,765,430	4.60	1665	17.0%
UAE	4,621,399	735,000	2,300,000	6.00	213	49.8%
Yemen	23,013,376	15,000	320,000	0.83	2033	1.4%
TOTAL	344,866,479	2,512,900	38,344,130	100.00	1426	11.1%

Source: Internet World Stats, 2008.

Having accepted the inevitability of the internet, the first instinct of Arab regimes was to look for ways to control it. This was based partly on their fears of political subversion but also on the fears of conservative and religious elements that it would undermine "traditional" values – fears that in both cases were well-founded. The favoured approach often reflected the broader mindset of the regimes concerned: the Saudis opted for an extravagant high-cost, high-tech solution, while Iraq under Saddam Hussein surrounded internet use with barely penetrable bureaucracy.

In Iraq UN sanctions made personal computers scarce and expensive, and modems – essential for connecting to the internet – were banned by the regime until 1999. Public access was eventually granted through the General Company of Internet and Information Services, a government monopoly. Outgoing and incoming emails were routed through the censorship department, which meant they could take several days to be delivered. Those who could afford an internet subscription (which at $750 a year was prohibitively expensive for most Iraqis) had to sign an application which said:

> The subscription applicant must report any hostile website seen on the internet, even if it was seen by chance. The applicants must not copy or print any literature or photos that go against state policy or relate to the regime. Special inspectors teams must be allowed to search the applicant's place of residence to examine any files saved on the applicant's personal computer.[75]

There were also sixty-five permitted web cafes (known in Iraq as "internet centres") with unlimited powers to supervise usage:

> Before a visitor could use the internet centre, they had to be interrogated by those running the centre about the web pages they intended to surf. When using a computer, visitors had to turn the monitor towards the centre's door and were prohibited from deleting the history that records the web pages they accessed ...
>
> If visitors were actually allowed to use the internet after agreeing to these conditions, they typically found themselves presented with either Saddam Hussein's picture (which was on the majority of the permitted web pages) or a large "X," informing them that the web page was banned in Iraq. This was, of course, only if they were allowed to use the internet: those in charge of the centres could arbitrarily bar visitors from using a connection if they did not know the visitor or if they didn't like the way the visitor looked. Authorities could decide that someone had no reason to use the internet and order them to return home.[76]

This may have given the Iraqi regime some comfort, but it was scarcely watertight. Following the 1991 Gulf war, Saddam had lost control of the Kurdish provinces in northern Iraq, where internet access was unrestricted. Young Iraqis who wanted to use the internet without government monitoring simply travelled north, sometimes in groups. Around 10 per cent of the customers in Kurdish web cafes were said to be visitors from the south.[77]

In Saudi Arabia, meanwhile, the council of ministers issued a set of internet rules which, among other things, prohibited users from publishing or accessing:

> Anything contravening a fundamental principle or legislation, or infringing the sanctity of Islam and its benevolent shari'a, or breaching public decency;
>
> Anything contrary to the state or its system;
>
> Reports or news damaging to the Saudi Arabian armed forces, without the approval of the competent authorities;
>
> Anything damaging to the dignity of heads of states or heads of credited diplomatic missions in the kingdom, or that harms relations with those countries;
>
> Any false information ascribed to state officials or those of private or public domestic institutions and bodies, liable to cause them or their offices harm, or damage their integrity;
>
> The propagation of subversive ideas or the disruption of public order or disputes among citizens;
>
> Any slanderous or libellous material against individuals.[78]

It was unclear from this how users could ascertain that information was not false or damaging to Islam or the dignity of heads of state, etc, before viewing it. The rules also included various other prohibitions against advertising and commercial activity on the internet except with "the necessary licences". Internet service providers (ISPs) were required to keep detailed records of users, including "purpose of use", "the time spent, addresses accessed or to which or through which access was attempted, and the size and type of files copied", and "provide the authorities with a copy thereof, if necessary". Most importantly, though, ISPs were required to route all traffic through the Internet Services Unit (ISU) at King Abdulaziz City for Sciences and Technology in Riyadh.[79]

The ISU houses the largest and most sophisticated internet-censoring system in the Middle East – based on technology that western companies eagerly competed to provide.[80] In principle this is very similar to the filtering systems that parents and schools can purchase to prevent children accessing unsuitable websites, except that in accordance with Saudi Arabia's paternalistic approach to government it is done on a national scale. The ISU justifies this on religious grounds with a quotation from the story of Yusuf in the Qur'an.[81] Yusuf (Joseph in the corresponding Bible story) is resisting sexual advances from the wife of al-Aziz (Potifar in the Bible) and she threatens to have him thrown in jail unless he agrees. Yusuf then appeals to God for help:

> He said: O my Lord! Prison is more dear than that unto which they urge me, and if Thou fend not off their wiles from me I shall incline unto them and become of the foolish.
>
> So his Lord heard his prayer and fended off their wiles from him. Lo! He is Hearer, Knower.[82]

This is a very strange passage to cite in support of government censorship. If it has any relevance at all to resisting the temptations of the internet, its message is surely that God will protect those who seek His help – which ought to make intervention by the ISU unnecessary. The ISU's second line of argument in favour of censorship is "confirmation from modern scientific studies" (all of them American) which are said to demonstrate that suppression of pornography leads to a reduction in rape cases – a claim that is by no means universally accepted. The ISU makes no attempt to justify censorship of non-pornographic websites, which is done "upon direct requests from the security bodies within the government". It says it has "no authority in the selection of such sites and its role is limited to carrying out the directions of these security bodies".

The ISU's system relies on frequently-updated lists of "undesirable" sites provided by Secure Computing's SmartFilter, plus additions by the Saudis themselves. There is also some input from the public: users who try to access a blocked page can ask to have it unblocked (with the attendant risk of drawing the authorities' attention to their activities). Users can also ask to have unblocked pages blocked. In 2001 the ISU was receiving more than 500 blocking requests from the public every day (about half of which were eventually acted upon) and more than 100 requests to have pages unblocked.[83] By 2004 the number of blocking requests was reported to be running at 200 a day, with only a "trickle" of unblocking requests.[84] This suggests that some sections of the Saudi public are considerably more enthusiastic about censorship than the ISU itself.

After testing 60,000 web addresses for blocking by the Saudi authorities over a three-year period, the OpenNet Initiative (ONI) reported:

> We found that the Kingdom's filtering focuses on a few types of content: pornography (98% of these sites tested blocked in our research), drugs (86%), gambling (93%), religious conversion, and sites with tools to circumvent filters (41%). In contrast, Saudi Arabia shows less interest in sites on gay and lesbian issues (11%), politics (3%), Israel (2%), religion (less than 1%), and alcohol (only 1 site).[85]

Although only a few religious sites were blocked, ONI found that most of those blocked "involved either views opposed to Islam (especially Christian views) or non-Sunni Islamic sects (including Shi'ism and Sufism)". A "significant minority" of Baha'i sites were also blocked but the ONI found no blocking of sites related to Judaism, "and very few sites with Jewish or Hebrew content". Some sites relating to the Holocaust were blocked, "though this occurs primarily because SmartFilter categorises many of these sites as having violent content".[86] Several sites supporting al-Qa'ida were found to be blocked as well as the sites of al-Manar (the Hizbullah TV station) and the Palestinian al-Quds brigades. In the religious area, the blocking of Shi'i websites is perhaps most significant because it further marginalises the kingdom's own Shi'i minority (thought to be around five per cent of the population).

In the political area, ONI found blocking of "several sites opposing the current [Saudi] government along with a minority of sites discussing the state of Israel, or advocating violence against Israel and the west, and a small amount of material from Amnesty International and Amnesty USA". In the media area, no major news outlets were blocked, though some e-zines were.

Although the Saudi filtering may not appear particularly aggressive except in terms of protecting internet users' "morality", it does result in unknown numbers of "innocent" pages being accidentally blocked. One early example was the blocking of information about breast cancer because of the objectionable word "breast".[87] A women's human rights site was also classified as "nudity" because of one image of a naked woman showing torture marks.[88] "Internet filtering is inherently error-prone," the ONI report said. "We found incorrectly categorised pages in every area we tested extensively." This obviously causes inconvenience to users, even if they are not seeking to break the rules laid down by the authorities. A survey by the ISU itself in 1999 found that 45 per cent of users thought the blocking was excessive (41 per cent thought it reasonable and 14 per cent thought it was too little).[89] In another ISU survey 16 per cent cited blocking as a "common problem" when using the internet.[90] More recently the acting general manager of the King Abdulaziz City for Science and Technology told Arab News: "Of those who log on to the internet, 92.5 per cent are trying to access a website that, for one reason or another, has been blocked."[91]

In due course Saudi internet blocking will probably be remembered, along with the prohibitions on satellite dishes and camera phones, as just one in a long line of futile attempts to stop the clock for the sake of "traditional" values. However, it has possibly served one useful purpose by allowing the internet to take off in the kingdom without arousing undue ire from the most reactionary elements. It is worth recalling the furore over the introduction of television, which was eventually accomplished in 1965 after King Faisal promised that the principles of "Islamic modesty" would be strictly observed, and that the broadcasts would include a large proportion of religious programmes. With the internet, these problems were averted by ensuring that a filtering system was in place before the public were granted access. Reassuring the traditionalists may be one reason why the ISU is uncharacteristically open about its activities, frequently trumpeting its "success" in blocking pornography.

It is also worth pointing out that, even with the filtering, the internet has given Saudis access to far more information and ideas than they ever had before. The "old media", such as print, are still subject to more stringent – if sometimes erratic – control. Journalist Molouk Ba-Isa described one everyday occurrence:

Last week, in the post, I received two catalogues from a US company, Lands' End. The cover and all the pages through [to] page 42 of one catalogue had been torn off. The missing pages in the first copy of the Lands' End catalogue contained some discreet photos of women in swimsuits. I know this because the second Lands' End catalogue came through the post intact. Both catalogues were exactly the same. Even sillier, by simply clicking to the company's website, I could see all the swimsuits.

At a time when we have a desperate need as a nation to allocate resources to education, infrastructure and health care, somewhere a group of Saudis is spending their days tearing pages out of magazines and catalogues to protect my morality – and getting paid for it. My psyche wasn't permanently damaged by seeing the swimsuit photos in the second catalogue. I've seen worse just by visiting the swimming pool at almost any housing compound in al-Khobar.

Despite the efforts of the ISU, and despite the nuisance caused, internet filtering does not prevent Saudi users from accessing blocked pages if they seriously want to do so. According to IT journalist Robin Miller, writing in 2004, the head of the ISU conceded that filtering is "a way to protect children and other innocents from internet evils, and not much more than that".[92] One obvious, if expensive, way of circumventing the system is to use dial-up connections in neighbouring countries. Another method is to get some technical help. In 2001 Arab News reported that government blocking had created new business opportunities for those who know how to get round it. A reporter who presented himself as wanting access to blocked sites "had no trouble at all in finding willing hackers in every computer centre in Riyadh", the paper said. "They also offered access to personal email accounts and sold pornographic DVDs."

Charges for providing access to blocked sites ranged from SR100 to SR250 ($27–$67).[93]

The most popular method, for those with the expertise, is to connect to an open proxy server outside the kingdom.[94] Although the government firewall sees the user connect to the server it does not see subsequent requests for blocked pages. Naturally the authorities are aware of this practice and they try to add proxy and anonymiser sites to their blocking lists, but ONI notes: "Finding and blocking open proxy servers is a labour-intensive task since these servers change domain names and IP addresses frequently to evade such filtering." In 2004 ONI found that only 27 percent of the proxies and 41 percent of the anonymisers it tested were blocked.[95] After trying this out for himself during a visit to the kingdom, Robin Miller concluded:

> The Saudi Internet filters are easy to defeat. I found at least a dozen anonymous surfing sites that let me view all the porn anyone could want in less than thirty minutes, and I have viewed more online porn while testing the Saudi content filters than I had looked at in my entire life before this experiment.

Although Saudi Arabia's internet censorship has attracted a lot of attention (and criticism), ONI found evidence of broad filtering in six other Arab countries: Oman, Sudan, Syria, Tunisia, the UAE and Yemen. Four more – Bahrain, Jordan, Libya and Morocco – were found to carry out "selective filtering of a smaller number of websites". No evidence of blocking was found in Algeria, Egypt or Iraq.[96]

However, technical advances, more diverse ways of accessing the internet, wikis, blogs, RSS feeds, dynamic web pages, plus growing use of multimedia – podcasts and videos as well as plain text – all make the censor's task more difficult and probably, in the end, futile. Centralised filtering (often through a state monopoly on internet access) also creates technical vulnerability: "Sending all internet traffic in the whole country through a single chokepoint obviously creates a single point of failure," Miller notes. Besides Riyadh, the Saudis have a second gateway in Jeddah, "but this is nowhere near the level of fail-safe connectivity major US online companies expect from their bandwidth providers".[97] Time is probably not on the side of the censors. Jonathan Zittrain and John Palfrey, two Harvard experts on internet law, explain:

> Regardless of whether states are right or wrong to mandate filtering and surveillance, the slope of the freedom curve favours not the censor but the citizens who wish to evade the state's control mechanisms. Most filtering regimes have been built on a presumption that the Internet is like the broadcast medium that predates it: each website is a "channel", each web user a "viewer". Channels with sensitive content are "turned off", or otherwise blocked, by authorities who wish to control the information environment.
>
> But the Internet is not a broadcast medium. As the Internet continues to grow in ways that are not like broadcast, filtering is becoming increasingly difficult to carry out effectively. The extent to which each person using the internet can at once be a consumer and a creator is particularly vexing to the broadcast-oriented censor ... the changes in the online environment give an edge to the online publisher against the state's censor in the medium-to-long run.[98]

In the end, though, these technical difficulties may be outweighed by other considerations. The internet differs from the press and broadcasting in that government attempts to control it have far more impact on business activity; especially the modern, international,

IT-based types of business. The problem of reconciling censorship with the need for unfettered business access is illustrated by the UAE, where one internet provider serving most of the country uses filtering extensively while the other, mainly serving the Dubai free zone, does not.[99] How long these two conflicting approaches can survive side by side in the same country remains to be seen.

The Egyptian government, despite its predisposition to control freakery, recognised the internet as a special case when it embarked on its Economic Reform and Structural Adjustment Programme (ERSAP) under the sponsorship of the IMF and World Bank in the early 1990s. One of the cornerstones of this was to make Egypt an IT hub to compete with India in out-sourcing IT jobs. Hossam el-Hamalawy, an Egyptian blogger-activist said:

> Mubarak brought in all these western-style technocrats and staffed the Ministry of Telecommunications. They laid down a fantastic infrastructure for the internet. These technocrats played a role in blocking the security services' efforts to establish the internet infrastructure Tunisian style, because they said this is not business-friendly. It's not business-friendly to start blocking websites. You are not going to attract Microsoft and the other big companies – especially because you are not a big market like China, where Google and all the others can make compromises. So here is the contradiction. If they start blocking our blogs and our websites, and they start tightening the censorship here and there, they are going to scare off the big IT players that they want to attract.[100]

"The government is facing a crisis in adapting its old means of control to the new situation," Hamalawy continued. Egyptian bloggers do often get arrested, but rarely for their blogging activities alone. "We're talking hundreds, because in any demonstration downtown [in Cairo] or now, increasingly, in the provinces, there will always be a good number of bloggers detained among them. The Egyptian bloggers have one foot in cyberspace and the other foot is in the street. We're not like your average IT geeks who are sitting all day in front of a computer – we mix the two. Our blogging is related to our organising on the ground. This is the uniqueness of our experience here in Egypt and the source of our strength."

Bloggers are also harassed by telephone, Hamalawy said:

> Our friend Noha runs the Torture in Egypt blog – this famous one.[101] There is a state security officer who calls her up. He says his name – Osama – and he says that he calls from the State Security headquarters. He would call up and ask 'How are you?', 'How's your family?' – trying to be nice. Other times he would be all aggressive. [Other] people would also receive phone calls but officers would not say their names. Sometimes they would call up as if they were like thugs and start issuing threats towards you and your family ... we're going to do this to your mother, blah, blah, blah.

By 2007 the only Egyptian blogger to have been convicted solely in connection with his blogging was Kareem Amer, sentenced to three years' imprisonment for "spreading information disruptive of public order and damaging to the country's reputation", "incitement to hate Islam" and "defaming the president of the republic". The trial appears to have been prompted by his critical views of Islam and his account of sectarian riots in Alexandria rather than politics.[102] In the same year Fouad al-Farhan, who blogged in Saudi Arabia under his real name, was arrested and detained without trial for more than four months, allegedly for "violating non-security regulations".[103] In 2006 a Syrian, Mohammed Ghanem, was sentenced to six months in jail on charges of "insulting the president, undermining the state's dignity, and inciting sectarian divisions". Ghanem ran a news website in Arabic called Surion which proclaimed itself as "national, democratic, independent, free". He appeared to have upset the authorities by criticising the Ba'ath Party and advocating political and cultural rights for Syria's Kurdish minority.[104]

Cases of this kind are still quite rare, however, suggesting that the authorities have not found an effective way to crack down on blogging. Bloggers can take measures to preserve their anonymity and some are out of reach in foreign countries. Worse still for the authorities, their numbers are growing all the time. The bloggers who get into trouble are usually those already known to be activists, and harassing them for their political activities rather than their blogging puts the authorities on more familiar territory. Arrest and imprisonment also halts their internet activities, at least temporarily. Often, they face charges that are difficult to challenge on grounds of human rights or free speech. The case of Mohammed Abou, a Tunisian human rights activist and anti-corruption lawyer, was fairly typical. In 2005 he was jailed for eighteen months for "insulting the judiciary" and two years for allegedly assaulting a woman lawyer.[105] Both charges were widely regarded as spurious. His arrest came one day after he published an article on tunisnews.net criticising President Zine el-Abidine Ben Ali for having invited Ariel Sharon, the Israeli prime minister at the time, to a conference in Tunis. In the article he mentioned corruption allegations surrounding relatives of both Sharon and Ben Ali (a subject that is taboo in Tunisia). In an earlier online article he had also compared Tunisian prisons to Abu Ghraib, the notorious US-run jail in Iraq.

Potentially, an even bigger problem for the authorities is the way popular social networking sites such as Facebook can become a vehicle for activism and communication on a large scale. In 2008 a

Facebook group calling for a general strike in Egypt attracted more than 70,000 members.[106] The strike itself turned out to be a damp squib, partly because it lacked backing from the main opposition parties,[107] and one commentator questioned whether the internet can really connect with the Egyptian masses.[108] Nevertheless, the Facebook protesters had opened up another new area for activism beyond the state's control – one that others will surely develop further in the future.

However, oppressive government is only one side of the coin. The other side (as the next chapter shows) is where people oppress each other and governments fail to intervene or show a lead.

7 A sea of victims

THE ARABIC WORD for "slave" is *'abd*. It is a word that Nesrine Malik heard often during her childhood in Sudan. "In fact," she said, "it was so common that I had no awareness of its negative connotations until well into my teenage years." Her father's family, from a proud northern Sudanese clan, used it to refer to anyone who had darker skin than themselves, from southern Sudanese house servants to migrants from Darfur.

"Sometimes there was a clear intent to demean, but at other times it was used almost affectionately – for example, when addressing a particularly dark-skinned or thick-lipped child. This was a kind of racism that no one ever challenged or addressed, and through a child's eyes it was very straightforward. On a scale of colour, lighter was good, darker was bad."

Though lighter-skinned girls in northern Sudan are considered more marriageable than those with a darker skin, Nesrine thinks the real issue for her father's family was not so much colour as preserving their tribal identity and a "pure" blood line. She continued:

My father's family is very obsessed that we're the Maliks. We have land, our ancestor was the founder of this tribe ... You're indoctrinated with the superiority of the tribe. My father's tribe, they say things like: "We're taller and our skin is softer." What does that mean? It means nothing.

My dad's family would say: "This guy doesn't look like he's free" – meaning: "Were his family slaves?" If there is even a hint, then it's a problem. It can be appearance – if you have a slightly bigger nose, slightly kinkier hair, if you are less Ethiopian, less Eritrean-looking, more southern Sudanese, you've got a problem, even if you have no slave background at all ... My father's family, until my father's generation, had slaves. They had entire families that worked for them as slaves. They weren't paid, they were basically given housing and shelter. This was in the 1930s and 1940s.

These issues would come particularly to the fore whenever a marriage was contemplated. In Nesrine's view, it was all about maintaining a consistent family tree:

Birth and lineage, at least from what I've seen in Sudan – it's a massive thing. Because you know that you are from a pure stock, it gives you a sense of superiority and snobbery. It's so accepted, so normal.

People would limit their choice of partner and their choice of who you mixed your blood with. They were trying to control it to almost within the block where you lived, I was thinking you can't – we're the same nationality, the same language, the same religion, the same colour, and you're looking for something – that some grandmother in the person's past was Egyptian or was somebody's slave at some point. Basically it's a fear, a terror of this blood line being polluted, and I think it's entirely in people's heads. It's a tribal legacy.

The Malik family's confidence in their social status was shaken, however, when they later moved to Saudi Arabia where ideas of "pure" breeding are taken to even greater extremes. "In Saudi, it was 'Do you know who your great-great-great-great-grandfather was?' – because if you don't God knows what's happened in between," she recalled.

My little sister, she's got a really fat nose. The first week we were there, we were sitting in a car and a little Saudi girl walked by with her mother. The Saudi girl pointed to her and said to her mother: "*Abda! Shufi abda!*" ("Look! A slave-girl!"). My little sister was just ... she was in tears, coming from this really proud Sudanese family. She was teased in school and they used to call her "*khubza mahruqa*"– which means burnt bread – because she was dark.

Girls from Shi'i families faced much the same treatment, if not worse:

In Saudi, Shi'ites are treated like they are dirty; like they would physically sully you if you touched them. There was a Shi'i girl in class and they would say: "Just so you know, she's Shi'i" – the first thing, so that you would not go to her house, not ask her over. They were very clearly discriminated against. They were not just considered weird Muslims but hundred per cent non-Muslims.

You get this "Islam is the perfect religion" and "Islam is fair" and "Everybody is the same as the teeth of a comb" and all that bullshit. It's pure propaganda, because it's not effectively practised. I'm not saying Islam espouses racism but it certainly hasn't made a dent in the racist attitudes of Muslims, and when you try to tackle it, people think you are attacking Islam.

It was a similar story a few years later when Nesrine continued her studies at university in Egypt and shared a female dormitory with a mixture of Sunni Muslims and Coptic Christians:

The Sunni girls wouldn't eat with the Coptic girls and they wouldn't take their clothes off – they wouldn't change – in front of the Coptic girls, because they had this kind of fear that they were impure, the devil was in them, or something like that, and there was very, very clear friction between the two – which I felt was odd because in Sudan when I was at school we had lots of Coptic people and it was fine. There wasn't the discrimination against Copts in Sudan that I felt was in Cairo.

The Copts themselves were very parochial – it was reciprocated. It wasn't just discrimination by Muslims. It was also Copts thinking Muslims are retarded and barbaric – massive stresses that I don't think people talk about a lot. I saw lots of hatred and almost tribal tension between the two – girls spitting in each other's faces, tearing their hair, calling each other dirty – and this wasn't a school, it was the American University in Cairo. We were in our late teens and early twenties.[1]

"SOCIAL DISCRIMINATION is the greatest of all ailments facing Arab societies today," Hussein Shobokshi, a board member of the Mecca Chamber of Commerce, observed during one of the Doha Debates.[2] Discrimination based on race, religion, ethnicity, gender, sexuality, tribe, family or place of birth is certainly widespread and deeply entrenched. Arabs rightly point out that discrimination is by no means unique to their own countries but the real issue is the lack of effort to confront it. Discriminatory practices are so common and take so many forms that they tend to be accepted as the norm and have become, to some extent, institutionalised. Apart from discrimination against women, such practices are rarely challenged and according to Nadim Houry, Human Rights Watch's researcher for Syria and Lebanon, many simply pass by, unrecognised for what they are:

People that would be up in arms, let's say, about a law that discriminated against Muslims in western Europe would not be up in arms about a law that discriminated against a [particular] group of Muslims or other religions in their own home countries. Somehow, the hypocrisy and the double standards haven't really been incorporated. The people that get offended because a migrant worker in Europe would be treated a certain way don't see it applying to their own societies where they have migrant workers.

Houry describes this as a case of "recognising the debate but keeping it afar":

People here in Lebanon, the more educated people, will have a perfectly normal discourse against discrimination – it's bad, we shouldn't discriminate – but they often use examples from the west ... discrimination is bad against Muslims in Europe, look at what happened in the States with the African-Americans, and all these things. Somehow they never manage to use examples from the region where they live, even though examples would be rife. There is this sort of division ... they have accepted that these are important concepts – they would never agree to racial profiling while flying in the United States. They are very aware of these issues ... yet somehow they don't manage to transpose that debate into their [own] country.

Part of the explanation, perhaps, lies in the way human rights issues have become entwined with international politics. "The debate around the veil in France got a lot of play in the Arab world," Houry said, "whereas in the debate around the veil in Turkey – and one could say Turkey is a lot more harsh about it – there were almost no voices in the Arab world criticising Turkey. You could find legions and legions of people that criticised France." He continued:

That doesn't apply just to discrimination, it applies to any sort of human rights violation. You go to talk to an [Arab] official about torture of someone and they'll talk about Abu Ghraib and Guantanamo. Then when you say "OK, granted this has been documented, what about the torture in prisons in the Arab world?" – that is where the disconnect happens. I believe this is the real battle. You've got to transpose these concepts that I think people are aware of. They've heard about them, and they would argue for them when it applies to other countries.[3]

Ghassan Makarem, a founder of Helem, the Lebanese gay and lesbian rights organisation,[4] believes the real issue is not the legitimising of discrimination but "de-legitimising human rights as something universal that we all agree on". He said: "It has been de-legitimised on two levels. The first level is because it's being used by the United States, by the west, in some cases for political reasons – but that's never an excuse. The second level, and this is something that you face every day in any activist work in Lebanon, is: who is actually [up] holding these principles in society in the Arab world? Who is talking about human rights, about democracy? If you look at Lebanon it's a very thin layer of intellectual elite."[5]

Hossam Bahgat, director of the Egyptian Initiative for Personal Rights,[6] believes a large part of the problem is the lack of an anti-discrimination culture in Arab countries. "People can immediately spot injustice and stand up for the oppressed," he said, "but it's not the same thing as discrimination or inequality. They don't spot inequality as easily. They can see why torture is wrong, why the imprisonment of a journalist or a political activist is wrong. They see the abuse. But just because someone is not getting exactly the same treatment as another person is not as shocking to their moral system as simple abuse." He continued:

People would not necessarily argue that it's OK to torture or mistreat a Sudanese refugee but they would not necessarily see that this Sudanese refugee is entitled to the same rights and freedoms as others. Part of it, I think, is that this has just not been a big component of the public discourse. It is probably also an accumulation of discrimination against women, racial discrimination, religious discrimination, etc – the failure to address these sub-systems of discrimination contributes to the inability to see discrimination in general as a moral transgression.

In abstract, people would say everyone should be treated equally. Most constitutions in the region have an equality clause but in practice it is not very intuitive for people to see a case of discrimination. For example, how come we have never had a single president of a public university [in Egypt] who was Christian? People would argue endlessly that this is not discrimination. Or the fact that women are not entitled to sit as judges (or were not until recently) in Egypt.[7] They would not see this as discrimination – it's just the custom. What's implied here is that women are too emotional, especially when they have their periods. You have presidents of courts, judges, saying this publicly, the newspapers reporting this, and it doesn't really shock people. You have columns in the press saying there are too many black Africans allowed to enter Egypt now, and that these people are all infected with AIDS and are a threat to public health. They get away with this because the threshold for moral outrage against bigotry and prejudice is still very low.[8]

Discrimination works both ways, of course. While some people are discriminated against, others get preferential treatment for equally discriminatory reasons. This introduces a complicating dimension in Arab societies. *Wasta* and other forms of favouritism, together with the feeling that everyone has a duty to help those with whom they have some affinity – whether the ties are based on kinship, a shared faith or simply having been born in the same district – encourages positive discrimination, as if it were a virtue. The fact that others more entitled or better qualified to receive a benefit may be excluded in the process tends to be overlooked.

The full range of discrimination, from positive to negative, can be seen in attitudes towards non-Arabs. In Lebanon (as elsewhere in the Arab world) foreigners are judged basically according to the lightness of their skin and the fatness of their wallets. Houry said:

> If you happen to be white, then you're OK – you shouldn't wait as long in the queue, etc. The whiter you are as a foreigner the better you are treated, and there are these hierarchies. It's not a caste system – there is no sort of formal structure to it – but public perceptions.
>
> Some say it's just ignorance, people not knowing the "other". That explains part of it but I don't think it explains the entire picture. In Lebanon, it's hard to think that people don't know better – many Lebanese have lived abroad, and they wouldn't act that way abroad. Why do they find it acceptable to act that way here [in Lebanon]?

The foreigners at the bottom of the scale are African and Asian migrant workers. Domestic maids – common among the better-off Lebanese families – are normally referred to as "Sri Lankans" even if they come from the Philippines or Nepal. As recently as the 1990s some of the swimming pools in Lebanon had signs saying housemaids were not allowed to use them. "There's a famous incident – I've heard it from different people though I don't know if it's an urban legend – about the wife of the Sri Lankan or Philippines ambassador," Houry said. "She was having a swim in one of the fancy beach resorts and was asked to get out of the pool. That sort of discrimination is definitely very prevalent. Examples come out every day. These are what I call the clear-cut cases of discrimination: you're not allowed

to do this, we don't want migrant domestic workers swimming ..."
He continued:

> Another example which I find striking is discrimination
> within prisons among prisoners. If you go to the Roumieh
> prison in Lebanon, the largest prison, you'll have Sri Lankan
> or south Asian prisoners acting as cleaners for Lebanese
> prisoners. That's often driven by economics but it's also driven
> by the perception that this is their role. They might get paid or
> they might get a couple of cigarettes but they are supposed to
> clean the cells of better-off Lebanese. So even within micro-
> societies like prisons you see some of the same patterns of
> discrimination.

As employees of a household, live-in maids exist in a sort of limbo as "marginal insiders and intimate outsiders"[9] forming a socially invisible presence, yet privy to many of the family's secrets. This can lead to strained relationships where a maid is viewed as slightly less than human and/or as a cunning manipulator who could jeopardise the family's cohesion. With little or no privacy and even less opportunity to develop sexual relationships, many are consigned to sleeping on balconies or kitchen floors. Often they are regarded as asexual beings, though in some households they are viewed as a source of temptation for husbands and teenage sons.[10]

A lot of employers are reluctant to give them adequate leisure time for fear of how they may spend it. According to Houry, "When you talk to them about guaranteeing a day off where migrant workers can go and do whatever they would like to do – a real day off, not a day off where they basically accompany their employer to the restaurant to take care of the kids," the reaction is: "You want them to go out and have sex and come back pregnant?"

I was at a meeting with an official from the ministry of labour and he kept pushing this point and I said: "You expect someone to stay in Lebanon and live for eight or nine years – you don't think at some point they will have a desire to have sex?"

It brings back some of the images of racism in the States that we saw in the 1950s and 1960s – the idea that you deny someone's sexuality because you don't really recognise that they might have desires, while at the same time [imagining] that if you somehow let them loose, if you release your control, they are these uber-sexual beings that are going to go and whore the entire Sunday afternoon.[11]

CENTRAL TO THE issue of human rights – indeed, the essential principle on which all human rights are based – is the concept of equality. The Universal Declaration of Human Rights, approved by the UN general assembly in 1948, spells out in clear and uncompromising language "the equal and inalienable rights of all members of the human family". In the words of Article 1: "All human beings are born free and equal in dignity and rights." Article 2 continues:

Everyone is entitled to all the rights and freedoms set forth in this declaration, without distinction of any kind, such as race, colour, sex, language, religion, political or other opinion, national or social origin, property, birth or other status.[12]

There are no half-measures here: either the equality principle is accepted in whole or it is not. Human rights should apply equally to everyone, everywhere, at all times and there is no room to discriminate by selectively excluding some human beings on the pretext of local circumstances or cultural norms. Equality, Houry says, is "one of these concepts that haven't really seeped through".

> I don't want to over-simplify it ... but when you talk about equality you assume things like equality before the law, equality of opportunities. That simply doesn't exist, and people don't even necessarily claim it exists.
>
> People accept that if you're born into a more privileged family then of course you will find it easier to get into university ... It's not really a system that's under challenge. In Lebanon there's an expression, "*Shatir bi Shtartu*" – which basically means: "If you know how to get around the system, good for you. We're not going to criticise it."
>
> There isn't a sense that somehow society needs to ensure equality ... People will shrug their shoulders if you ask them a question like "Do you think if you have more money or if you come from a bigger [more important] family it should be easier for you to do x, y and z?" People say "Oh no, we should all be equal," but when you ask them about specific examples ... they accept the way it is – that each person tries according to their means, whoever their contacts are. Why take a stand on protecting equality for all?

Equality and discrimination are also linked to questions of identity. The more people feel a need to assert their identity – perhaps in the face of challenges from competing identities – the more they are liable to discriminate for and against others on that basis. The most obvious way to assert an identity is by conforming to the norms (dress, behaviour, etc) associated with it. But as far as equality is concerned, expressing an identity in this way is a double-edged sword. It brings a measure of equality among those who share the same identity but can also reinforce inequalities between them and people outside the group. For example, the *hajj* – the annual pilgrimage to Mecca – is often cited as a great leveller where the high and mighty, along with the poor and powerless all become (temporarily) indistinguishable, clad identically in a simple white cloth. Here, conformity produces both a highly visible identity and a sense of equality – but only within the group. It also, very deliberately, sets them apart from others. That, in itself, is not necessarily a problem but it becomes a problem if others outside a particular identity-group (and, indeed, any within the group who are thought to be not conforming "properly") start to be treated as inferior or are denied an equal right to assert an identity of their own choosing.

Most Arab states pay some lip-service to notions of equality. The constitution of Jordan, for instance, says:

> Jordanians shall be equal before the law. There shall be no discrimination between them as regards to their rights and duties on grounds of race, language or religion.[13]

And the constitution of Yemen:

> The state shall guarantee equal opportunities for all citizens in the fields of political, economic, social and cultural activities and shall enact the necessary laws for the realisation thereof.[14]

Such statements are not untypical. In practice, however, Arab governments do little or nothing to prevent discrimination or promote equality, though there are some significant exceptions in the field of women's rights (Morocco, for example, introduced a quota system for female members of parliament).[15]

"In most of the region there are no laws that criminalise discrimination or even make it something that you can sue against," Hossam Bahgat said. "In Egypt, I cannot take an employer to court for printing an ad in the newspaper asking for males only." As in most Arab countries, the principles of equality spelled out in the constitution are not backed up by relevant legislation. There is no law in Egypt to prevent recruitment on the basis of gender or religion, and in practice it happens a lot. "Christian businesses do not employ Muslims, except maybe for the driver, the doorman and even then sometimes they don't recruit Muslims at all," Bahgat said. Even so, overt religious discrimination in recruitment ads is frowned upon, though gender discrimination is accepted.

Legislation aside, Arab governments are notably bad at managing communal relations, especially where discrimination and the rights of minorities or other marginalised groups are concerned. Governments' interest in them basically begins and ends with the question of whether they are likely to pose a threat to public order or national security. When problems flare up the response is often heavy-handed and in more normal times, when work might be done to address the underlying issues and avert future crises, they are not given priority. This is partly a result of the state's weakness: actively combating discrimination, and the entrenched attitudes that lie behind it, risks bringing the regime into conflict with powerful social forces – for no obvious gain, at least in the short term.

A far bigger impediment, though, is that open debate about communal relations is still mostly taboo. One reason is the cultural abhorrence of *fitna* – a term with religious connotations meaning "discord" or "civil strife"[16] – which results in a tendency to conceal problems for fear of making them worse rather than examining them frankly and trying to resolve them. The official picture, therefore, is of a cohesive, harmonious and united society, and any disruption of that (short of open warfare as seen in Iraq) must be the work of a handful of misguided troublemakers. Syria, for example, has long denied the existence of ethnic tensions involving its Kurdish minority. After several days of rioting in Kurdish areas which left dozens dead in 2004, officials variously blamed politically motivated "troublemakers", "foreign influences" and an old vendetta between tribes. A statement from the Syrian embassy in Paris formally denied any suggestion of inter-ethnic tension while referring to it obliquely: "It is certain that the perpetrators of these troubles will quickly discover that total harmony between ... different ethnic groups in Syria is much stronger ... than they believe."[17]

The reluctance to acknowledge ethnic diversity is also closely linked to ideas of national identity and pan-Arabism. The "Arab" world, as it is normally referred to, contains a variety of non-Arab ethnicities – Armenians, Assyrians, Berbers, Kurds, Sahrawis, Tuaregs and Turkmen among them. Most Arab states, in the form we know them today, were created during the last century and their boundaries were determined, sometimes quite arbitrarily, by imperial powers, and since independence Arab governments have had to grapple with the consequences, trying to weld a hotchpotch of tribal, ethnic and religious groupings into nations. One example among many is Syria:

> Syrian national identity has been a serious problem from the very beginning of the country's independence. The modernity and artificiality of Syria's borders and its multi-ethnic and religious make-up have made identity a complex affair. The struggle for Syrian independence from France was primarily fought in terms not of a "Syrian" nationalist discourse, but of "Arab" nationalism. Since 1961 the official name of the country has been the "Syrian Arab Republic", hence denying recognition of non-Arabs and instead placing Syria at the heart of a broader Arab nation. Pan-Arab nationalism continues to be the official ideology of Syria today and has had severe

implications for the non-Arab minorities of Syria, most of all the Kurds.[18]

Kurds form the largest ethnic minority in Syria and are thought to number around 1.75 million – roughly ten per cent of the total population. They live mainly in the north around Aleppo and in the Jazeera region of the north-east and have suffered official discrimination over many years, starting in the 1930s but increasing noticeably with the rise of Arab nationalism in the 1950s and 1960s.[19] This has mainly taken two forms: marginalisation and "Arabisation". One method was to suppress the Kurdish language, Kurmanji, and other expressions of their identity – for example by restricting celebrations of the Kurdish new year. A ban on printing and publishing materials in Kurmanji has been in place for more than half a century and in 1987 was reportedly extended to Kurdish music cassettes and videos.[20] In the largely Kurdish province of al-Hasakah businesses are banned from having Kurdish names and since 1992 this has also been applied to registering new-born children with "non-Arab" names.[21]

In 1962 the Syrian government embarked on a policy of Arabisation of Kurdish areas which peaked in the 1970s with the "Arab Belt" initiative. A report by Human Rights Watch described the process:

"The government wanted to eliminate 150,000 Kurds and bring in Arab settlers," a Kurdish political activist in Hasakah told us. "It wanted to force the Kurds to leave the governorate, which was seventy to eighty per cent Kurdish. Beginning in 1973, they moved Arab settlers to the border area with Turkey ...

The Arab Belt initiative included the expropriation of prime Kurdish land as part of a national agrarian reform plan, and the settlement of Syrian Arabs in model villages that each contained 150 to 200 homes. Kurdish residents resented the state's favourable treatment of the settlers. A Kurdish engineer from the area said this:

> "The government built them homes for free, gave them weapons, seeds and fertiliser, and created agricultural banks that provided loans. From 1973 to 1975, forty-one villages were created in this strip, beginning ten kilometres west of Ras al-'Ayn. The idea was to separate Turkish and Syrian Kurds, and to force Kurds in the area to move away to the cities. Any Arab could settle in Hasakeh, but no Kurd was permitted to move and settle there."

The settlement campaign was halted by President Hafez al-Asad in 1976, according to Fouad Ali Kuh of the Democratic Unity Party in Syria, but the status quo was not reversed. Not all of the Arab settlers remained permanently in the area, according to Kurdish sources. "There are two types of settlers: those who stayed, really integrated and now speak Kurdish, and the temporary residents who do not invest here, are not comfortable here, and live here only during the planting and the harvest," the engineer noted. Kurds claim, however, that until now the government inflates population statistics for the Arab villages along the border while underestimating the number of Kurdish residents.[22]

The official line from the Syrian government is that the Kurds are full Syrian citizens with the same rights and opportunities as other ethnic or religious groups. The fact that numerous Kurds hold positions of power or influence is often cited by Syrian Arabs as evidence of Kurdish equality. However, as a Chatham House briefing paper pointed out, "these Kurds tend to be urban and affluent, to speak Arabic rather than Kurmanji and to be reconciled to the 'Arabness' of their identity. As such they command little respect among the

Kurdish population, especially in the north." Essentially, Kurds are excluded from social, political and economic advancement "unless they are prepared to become effectively Arabs in all but ethnic origin. This requires abandoning Kurmanji in favour of Arabic and accepting Arab cultural and political values and goals."[23]

Some of Syria's Kurds, though, do not even have the option of becoming Arabised. An estimated 200,000 of them are officially stateless because of a special census carried out in al-Hasakah province in 1962 as part of the Arabisation policy. The declared purpose of the census was to identify "alien infiltrators" who had illegally crossed the border from Kurdish areas of Turkey, but in reality it did something else:

> By many accounts, the special census was carried out in an arbitrary manner. Brothers from the same family, born in the same Syrian village, were classified differently. Fathers became foreigners while their sons remained citizens. Kurds who had served in the Syrian army lost citizenship while families who bribed officials kept theirs.[24]

Altogether, about 120,000 Syrian Kurds were stripped of their citizenship, but the problem has grown since then:

> One Kurdish resident of Hasakah governorate told us that when his father, who was born in Syria, lost his nationality in the 1962 census, he and his three brothers – all born in Syria – became "foreigners" as well. The four brothers have since married, and their thirty-three children, all born in Hasakah governorate, are not Syrian citizens. In Darbasiyyah, located west of Qamishli, there are approximately 59,000 Kurdish residents in the town and its 200 surrounding villages, according to a well-informed local source. He told us that 20 per cent of the Kurdish residents – some 12,000 people

– are not Syrian citizens although they were born in the country.[25]

Today, these Syrian-born "foreigners" face many obstacles in their daily lives. They have no political rights; they are not allowed to own property or businesses or to work in the public sector or practise as doctors or engineers. They are not entitled to the same education or health care as Syrian citizens, and cannot legally marry a Syrian citizen. Without the standard Syrian identity card they cannot receive state benefits or stay in a hotel, and with no passports or travel documents they are unable to leave the country: they are trapped in a permanent limbo.

Though the Syrian government's handling of the Kurdish issue has been ham-fisted to say the least, the underlying problem dates back to the imperial powers' carve-up of the Middle East after the First World War. This broke up the Kurdish-inhabited territory and assigned it to four different countries: Turkey, Iraq, Iran and Syria. Since then, Syrian and Iraqi Arabs have tended to view the Kurds as a threat to the "Arab nation" and are fearful of the Kurds' own national aspirations.

The overthrow of Saddam Hussein in 2003 and the political gains made subsequently by the Kurds in Iraq intensified nationalist sentiment among Syria's Kurds, as well as apprehension among Syria's leaders. It is probably no coincidence that the riots of 2004, officially portrayed as the work of a few troublemakers, came just a few days after the Transitional Administrative Law was agreed in Iraq, recognising Kurdish control over the northern region:

> The trouble began at a football match in Qamishli in the Jazira [region] on 12 March when hostilities between Kurdish and Arab supporters ended with the security forces shooting dead

at least seven Kurds. This was followed by further shootings at their funerals.

Thousands demonstrated in Qamishli and in Kurdish areas across Syria – the Jazira, Afrin, Aleppo and Damascus. Some protests turned into riots, government and private property was ransacked and burned and a police station was attacked in Amude. Depictions of Hafez al-Asad were vandalised, the Syrian flag was burned and banners daringly proclaimed 'Free Kurdistan' and 'Intifada until the occupation ends'.

Ajanib [the Kurds with no citizenship] appear to have been especially enthusiastic participants. The Syrian authorities reacted with customary brutality, beating, arresting and imprisoning large numbers of Kurds. The army moved into Kurdish regions in force, tanks and helicopters appeared in Qamishli and a week later calm was restored. It is not known how many Kurds died at the hands of the military and later in custody, but estimates reach around 40 plus over 100 injured. More than 2,000 Kurds were jailed. Five Syrian Arabs also died, including one policeman.[26]

The riots of 2004 were widely regarded as a watershed in relations between the Syrian government and its Kurdish minority. Encouraged by events in Iraq, the Kurds were clearly becoming more assertive and less easily cowed.[27] On the government side, too, there was recognition that the old policies would not work and concessions would have to be made. The Ba'ath Party congress in 2005 made conciliatory noises, promising steps to help the Kurds – but without specifying what they would be. Though the government has formally acknowledged the need for a different approach, it seems unsure how to proceed without appearing weak or opening up questions about the ideological basis of the Ba'athist state. In the absence of a clear alternative Syrian security forces marked the Kurdish new year of 2008 in their traditional way – by shooting three people dead at a bonfire party:

> Two hundred people gathered around 6:30 pm on a road in the western part of Qamishli. They lit candles on the side of the road and a bonfire in the middle, around which some performed a Kurdish traditional dance. "This was a celebration of Nowruz, not a political demonstration," one of the participants told Human Rights Watch.
>
> Firefighters appeared on the scene to extinguish the bonfire while police and intelligence officers fired teargas canisters and live ammunition in the air to disperse the crowds. Two participants told Human Rights Watch that when the celebrants failed to disperse, individuals wearing civilian clothes and driving in a white pick-up truck of the type usually used by intelligence officials fired their assault rifles into the crowd. "Without any warning, they started firing to the ground and suddenly bullets started flying indiscriminately," an eyewitness told Human Rights Watch.[28]

National legal systems, the Arab Human Development Report noted in 2004, "do not protect members of groups outside the mainstream, which are often marginalised". Their rights are often violated but ...

> These individuals may also suffer additional violations at the hands of the law or the administration or as a result of entrenched social practices, simply because of their background. Violations of human rights in Arab countries are more pronounced when cultural, religious or ethnic dimensions are present, particularly since marginalised groups have fewer opportunities to protest their rights. Repression directed specifically at such groups reflects an odious

"minority mentality" in parts of society and in oppressive regimes alike.[29]

Depriving people of their citizenship is an extreme form of discrimination. Depriving them of the means to *prove* their citizenship may be less dramatic but has much the same effect. In Egypt, everyone over the age of sixteen is required to have an identity card. Without the card they cannot work legally, study beyond secondary school, vote, operate a bank account, obtain a driver's licence, buy and sell property, collect a pension or travel. Thus, when officials refuse to provide someone with a card for supposedly administrative reasons, the consequences are severe.

Among the information recorded on Egyptian ID cards is the holder's religion. Besides being an unnecessary infringement of privacy,[30] this potentially opens the way to discrimination in situations where the card has to be shown. Worse, though, a long-standing policy operated by the interior ministry limits a person's choice to the three "heavenly" religions (as they are referred to in Arabic) – Islam, Judaism or Christianity. The policy is not based on any Egyptian law but is derived from the ministry's interpretation of shari'a and has been criticised as discriminatory and illegal by a United Nations special rapporteur:

> The mention of religion on an identity card is a controversial issue and appears to be somewhat at variance with the freedom of religion or belief that is internationally recognised and protected. Moreover, even supposing that it was acceptable to mention religion on an identity card, it could only be claimed that the practice had any legitimacy whatsoever if it was non-discriminatory: to exclude any mention of religions other than Islam, Christianity or Judaism would appear to be a violation of international law.[31]

Apart from those who would prefer not to be associated with any religion, the people most affected by this policy are members of the Baha'i faith, thought to number around 2,000 in Egypt. The Baha'is originated in Iran during the nineteenth century and by the early twentieth century also had a flourishing community in Egypt. Although the Baha'i faith is often regarded as an heretical offshoot of Islam, the Egyptian community was initially tolerated but its position worsened in the 1950s – partly because of its accidental connections with Israel. In 1868, after being banished from his native Persia, the founder of the faith, Baha'u'llah, was exiled with his family and a small band of followers in the Turkish penal colony of Acre. As a result of this, the faith's international headquarters was established in the Acre/Haifa area which later became part of Israel.[32]

In the 1960s President Nasser issued a decree which, in effect, withdrew state recognition from the Baha'i community and confiscated their property. Nasser's decree was reaffirmed by the Supreme Court in 1975 in a ruling which said that only the three "revealed" religions were protected by the constitution: the Baha'is were entitled to their beliefs but practice of the Baha'i faith was a "threat to public order" and therefore fell outside the constitutional protection for freedom of religion.[33]

So long as Egyptian identity cards continued to be produced manually, there was some flexibility in the system and Baha'is could often persuade officials to enter a dash in the "religion" section or leave it blank. This changed in 1995 when the government gradually began replacing the manually-produced cards with computerised ones which did not allow the option of a dash or a blank – with the result that no ID card could be issued to Baha'is unless they were prepared to lie about their religion.

In 2006 two Egyptians, Hossam Ezzat Mahmoud and his wife,

took the issue to court and won the right to register themselves and their two daughters as Baha'is. This ruling – hailed by human rights groups as a step forward – upset conservatives and Islamists, so the government decided to appeal. The Supreme Administrative Court then overturned the lower court's decision, on the grounds that Baha'ism is not a recognised religion and that Muslims who adopt it are apostates[34] – much to the delight of the rabble present in court, according to a blogger who was there:

> Two bearded men in suits started shouting: "Allahu Akbar! Islam is victorious!"
>
> Another veiled woman joined in the chanting. "God's religion is Islam! Baha'is are infidels! They are infidels! Allahu Akbar!" The woman then knelt and kissed the floor. She then stood up, and continued her hysterical outcry outside the court room in the corridor. "Baha'is are the cause of problems in Iraq! They also destroyed Lebanon!!" she kept on screaming.
>
> I had no clue what the heck she was talking about, and did not know if I should laugh or cry. It was pure bigotry. "They are a cancer in our society!"
>
> As I was standing to watch the ongoing circus, a civil servant who worked at the court building approached me.
>
> "What is this business of Baha'is?" he asked. "Is it a new movement?"
>
> "No. It's a religion," I answered.
>
> He paused for a few seconds, looked at the Baha'is in tears outside the court, and then looked back at me. "They'll go to hell, the sons of —."[35]

These views also had support in the Egyptian mainstream. The Grand Mufti, Ali Gomaa – often regarded as a fairly open-minded cleric – asserted that Baha'is do not deserve recognition, while Muhammad

Abdel Hafez, a columnist on *al-Gomhouriya* newspaper, fulminated: "If Baha'ism is officially recognised, worshippers of cows, the sun and fire will want to jump on the bandwagon."[36]

In January 2008 Baha'is brought two further cases before the Court of Administrative Justice which ordered the interior ministry to place a dash in the religious affiliation section on ID cards and birth certificates for Baha'i citizens. On this occasion the government did not appeal, though three months later the people concerned were still waiting for their new documents.[37]

The largest group of non-Muslims in Egypt are the Christians. Mostly members of the ancient Coptic church, they are thought to number 6 million or more (up to 10 per cent of the total population). Obviously, on occasions, people wish to change their religion – sometimes purely out of conviction, though perhaps more often when marrying someone from a different faith. The numbers of converts in Egypt are difficult to estimate but one thing is clear: converting from Christianity to Islam, and registering it with the authorities, is a very straightforward matter – so simple that legal safeguards against over-hasty conversion are sometimes ignored, while converting *from* Islam is fraught with administrative difficulties and can even be hazardous:

> Egyptians who are born Muslim but convert to Christianity face considerable social opprobrium as well as official harassment. For these reasons, very few if any Muslim converts to Christianity have initiated the necessary formal steps to revise their identification documents to reflect their change in religion, as permitted by the Civil Status Law. An undetermined number have emigrated to other countries, or live anonymously and surreptitiously with forged documents ... Some who nonetheless have made their conversion public say that security officials have detained them on charges of

violating public order and, in some cases, have subjected them to torture.[38]

In theory, conversion from one faith to another should be no problem. The Egyptian constitution is very explicit. It says "the state shall guarantee freedom of belief and the freedom to practise religious rites".[39] In addition, the Civil Status Law of 1994 allows citizens to change information on their identity documents, including the religious affiliation, simply by registering the details with the interior ministry's Civil Status Department (CSD). Clear as that might seem, the position is complicated by Article 2 of the constitution which says "Islam is the religion of the state". One of the practical effects of this is that the courts and government officials interpret it as a licence to act in the name of Islam and refuse to do anything that would amount to government approval of "sin". Since conversion away from Islam is generally regarded as apostasy, they argue that a Muslim state cannot officially acknowledge or endorse it.

A further argument is that conversions from Islam or other expressions of unorthodox religious views jeopardise public order. Article 98(f) of the penal code criminalises the use of religion "to promote or advocate extremist ideologies ... with a view toward stirring up sedition, disparaging or showing contempt for any divinely-revealed religion, or prejudicing national unity and social harmony". In the eyes of some officials, conversion to Christianity is in itself a disparagement of Islam and therefore a breach of the law. Despite some very loose interpretations of the penal code, however, fears about a threat to public order are well founded:

> Societal attitudes towards religious conversion, by both Muslim and Christian communities, remain highly negative and hostile. The last few years have witnessed an

increase in sectarian tensions in Egyptian society, and one of the manifestations of this sectarianism is the extreme politicisation of the issue of conversion. Conversions have often led to Muslim-Christian violence, especially when they have been accompanied by rumours of forced abduction of young women by men of the other religious communities or proselytising by enthusiasts of the other faith.[40]

Trying to prevent conversions, though, is no long-term solution to the threat of disorder. A more sensible and sustainable approach would be to actively counter the expressions of intolerance when conversions occur, but that is scarcely possible while the government continues to pursue discriminatory policies of its own.

Egyptian Christians sometimes find themselves officially converted to Islam against their will. Under Islamic law, children are assumed to have the same religion as their parents, though Islam takes precedence: if one parent is Muslim the children are automatically classified as Muslims too.

Fadi Naguib Girgis was born into a Christian family in Alexandria but when he was five years old his father converted to Islam, left home and adopted a Muslim surname (Girgis, the Egyptian equivalent of George, is one of the names that clearly identifies its holder as Christian). Fadi, however, continued to be known by his original surname – the one shown on his birth certificate – and regarded himself as a Christian. At the age of nineteen he moved to Cairo for work and applied for one of the new ID cards:

My [paper] ID was falling apart, and I wanted the national identity card ... They pulled up my name; it was listed not as Girgis but 'Abd al-Hakim [his father's new Muslim surname]. And the religion was wrong [listing Fadi as a Muslim]. They charged me with forging my ID, my birth certificate, my diplomas, and said I was trying to convert from Islam to Christianity. They confiscated my documents and transferred me to the public prosecution office.[41]

He was detained for five days then released after intervention by the Coptic pope. The public prosecutor eventually dropped the forgery charges for lack of evidence and advised him to reapply for an identity card; he did so and the application was again refused.

Yusif Fandi was another victim of involuntary conversion. His father had become a Muslim but Yusif himself remained Christian in faith. A few months after becoming engaged to a fellow-Christian, in preparation for marriage he applied for an ID card at the Civil Registry Office in the Cairo district of Imbaba. Instead of issuing him with a card, the office director confiscated his birth certificate (which described him as a Christian) and sent him to the police. After a night at the police station, the police passed him to the public prosecutor's office where he was held until later the following night. Though he was eventually released without charge, officials continued to refuse him a card showing his religion as Christian and, in the meantime, his marriage prospects were wrecked:

> Our engagement was broken, only because of this ID problem. Now a Christian girl's family won't accept me because I'm [officially] a Muslim, and a Muslim girl's family won't accept me, knowing I'm really Christian.[42]

IT IS NO EXAGGERATION to say that discrimination – in all its many forms – is endemic in the Arab countries. But where, exactly, does the blame lie? "Ultimately," said Nadim Houry, "the state or the society you belong to is supposed to ensure that you have equal opportunities." He continued:

It's not that people haven't heard of these concepts. Most laws – and constitutions as well – are framed in a way [that says] "we are against discrimination, we are for equality and all citizens are born equal" – but all these slogans ring hollow when you look at them more closely.

I would venture to say it's not simply because of lack of practice by the state, I think even within society the sense of equality or non-discrimination is absent. It's not just the state that is the culprit here. Most examples of discrimination are between people, but no one is really going to take a strong stand to push for that equality.

Equality, as a principle, also has to compete with other social principles – often more powerful ones – pushing in the opposite direction: the obligation to help your own kind; the high value placed on conformity and the low value placed on diversity; the desire to assert identity; and the need to keep up appearances of national unity (whatever the underlying reality) in the face of perceived threats from outside. For Hossam Bahgat, it is the sheer pervasiveness of discrimination that makes it difficult to address:

If you want to mobilise moral outrage against discrimination, you [need to] wake this sense of outrage in the minds of the majority, and that's built on the premise that as people enjoying our [own] rights we should all stand with the oppressed. This majority doesn't exist because injustice and inequality is so widespread in Egypt. It affects everyone almost, apart from the lucky few.

You can talk to many Egyptian Muslims and they would argue out of strong conviction that Copts are enjoying more rights than Muslims in Egypt. Really, this is a very widespread notion – that Copts in Egypt are a spoilt minority, they control the economy and they are the luckiest minority in the world, and look at how the west is treating Muslims – Copts here should feel really grateful.

Another part of the problem is that it's all a power game, so a middle-class, middle-aged civil servant in the ministry of transport who is working in inhuman conditions and gets very poor treatment from his superiors would immediately take this out on his wife or his children or his Coptic neighbour. This sense of injustice gets exercised in different ways. In a sea of victims it's really hard to find one victim and to make a big case about their victimhood.

Nevertheless, recognition of equal rights is one of the keys to change in Arab societies – perhaps the main one because it affects so many aspects of daily life. Accepting the equality principle undermines patriarchy, clannism and autocracy. It gives people an equal right to express themselves. It allows them to practise religion, if they so wish, according to their own conscience rather than the demands of others. It requires tolerance and acceptance of diversity. It insists on equality of opportunity and opposes corruption – the use of money and influence to deny people their rightful opportunities. More than calls for democracy and free elections, focusing on equal rights provides a basis for addressing the region's problems across a broad front. At the same time, no one should underestimate the difficulty of winning acceptance for such a basic principle, obfuscated as it often is by arguments about cultural imperialism and cultural relativism.

8   Alien tomatoes

THE HUMBLE TOMATO is a normal – even "traditional" – ingredient used by cooks almost everywhere, but it wasn't always so. The tomato is a native of Central and South America, and its spread around the world started with the Spanish *conquistadors*. Though swiftly adopted in southern Europe from the middle of the sixteenth century, tomatoes were at first regarded with suspicion by the British and North Americans. Some believed they were poisonous, while Puritans thought them a dangerous aphrodisiac. It was a similar story when tomatoes reached the Syrian city of Aleppo at the end of the nineteenth century:

> Aleppo's residents first refused to consume tomatoes, let alone cultivate them, because their red colour contradicted the idea that they are vegetables ("greens" in Arabic). Thus, they called them "Satan's backside" and the city's mufti banned their consumption.[1]

The ban did not last long, however, and soon the best-quality tomatoes in Aleppo were known as *baladiyya* ("local" or "domestic"), though a reminder of their foreign origin survived in the Syrian word for "tomatoes": *banadura* – a corruption of the Italian name, *pomodoro*.

Globalisation – and hostility towards it – is not a new phenomenon: "At a basic level, it has been an aspect of the human story from earliest times, as widely scattered populations gradually became involved in more extensive and complicated economic relations."[2] In recent history the first major wave of globalisation came in the nineteenth century, associated with colonialism, and was followed by another wave in the second half of the twentieth century. Since the 1980s the pace of globalisation has accelerated rapidly – which the World Bank attributes mainly to two factors:

> The first is technical progress especially in information technology, international communication and global transportation. Not only goods but also services and knowledge can flow much more easily because of innovations such as the internet.
>
> The second major development is the shift in policy orientation as governments everywhere have reduced barriers that had curbed the development of domestic markets and their links to the international economy.[3]

Despite the widespread debate about globalisation there is no precise and universally accepted definition of its meaning. The World Bank describes it as "the global circulation of goods, services and capital, but also of information, ideas and people".[4] Syrian-born writer Georges Tarabichi, meanwhile, suggests globalisation simply means "the world becoming one".[5] Whatever the preferred definition, there is general acceptance that it involves a breaking down of barriers (particularly between states), increased activity across national boundaries and the growing influence of international bodies, multinational companies and the like. Although globalisation is often thought of primarily as an economic process, it has many other effects too, and the main purpose of this chapter is to consider its social and political impact in the Arab countries.

Public discussion of globalisation by Arabs almost always starts with the assumption that it is a threat to their way of life – a common post-colonial critique, popular from Asia to South America.

"Globalisation is another term for capitalism and imperialism, and all Arabs and Muslims need to consider it an imminent danger that is endangering our political, social, cultural and economical stability," Jassim Asfour, general secretary of the Egyptian cultural council, informed a symposium in 2002. "Globalisation contains a lot of aspects that are related to the phenomenon of Americanisation. So in order to fight this phenomenon and protect our national identity and revive our Arabic and Islamic culture, we need to protect our culture by understanding what globalisation is and know how to fight it."[6] More colourfully, Arab-American journalist Ramzi Baroud informed readers of *al-Ahram Weekly*:

> I have seen little Arab kids, innocently celebrating the end of Ramadan in a special Burger King tent [to] the rhythm of hip-hop lyrics detailing an oral sex encounter. As appalling as this may sound, the unfiltered global market culture is undoubtedly forging a collective identity crisis among the young generation in the Arab world that now has naïvely, albeit joyfully reduced western civilisation to the character of Britney Spears, a badly-cooked cheeseburger and online pornography.[7]

The Arab debate about globalisation has fallen prey, in the words of Tarabichi, to "ideological inflation" – the result of a "chronic divorce between thought and fact":

> Globalisation did not [initially] manifest itself in the Arab world's stock exchanges, in open markets (let alone the closed ones), in the portfolios of shareholding companies (let alone its companies owned by families or individuals) or in delocalised factories. Rather, globalisation was first witnessed in the brains of its intellectuals ... The concept of globalisation

in circulation in the Arab world is primarily the product of intellectuals and primarily for their consumption.

Keeping the debate abstract and separating it from reality in this way has given rise to the idea that globalisation not only *ought* to be resisted but that it *can* be resisted. Certainly the effects of globalisation may be negative as well as positive but globalisation itself is a fact of life. It is not something that can be sensibly opposed or supported; it exists in much the same way that rain exists. Nobody is foolish enough to oppose rain. The question is how to keep dry when it falls and how to benefit from the water it provides.

Dealing with globalisation in the abstract has also, as Tarabichi puts it, allowed the debate among Arabs to "simmer without any restraint". He notes too that many of the arguments mustered against globalisation are basically a re-hash of earlier complaints about cultural imperialism, modernity and "alien" influences, with a large dose of conspiracy theory thrown in. A few examples illustrate some typical objections:

> *Abdel-Ilah Balqaziz (Morocco):* Globalisation is "an act of cultural rape and symbolic aggression on other cultures, a synonym of forceful and technology-equipped penetration, thus destroying culture's sovereignty in the societies reached by globalisation."[8]

> *Mutaa Safadi (Syria):* "Globalisation is an attenuated description of the comprehensive attack on all countries of the world [to subdue them] to the will of the big capitalist ... Imperialism today is not military; it is financial. It is the imperialism of the absolute in hands that consider themselves absolutely free to act as they wish with the world's fortunes and economy."[9]

> *Yumna Tarif Khawli (Egypt):* "It is a ferocious attack by western civilisation to oppress the Arabic language. We are the only people in the world who speak the same language of our holy book ... The only means for realising the western dream of destroying the Arab nation is what is going on now through the destruction of the Arabic language. After 100 years, the Arabic language will suffer Latin's fate. In fact, language is the haven, the refuge and the final life support if we are to survive."[10]

Such opinions are not, of course, confined to Arabs, and Arabs often have little hesitation in adopting western critiques uncritically. One example towards the end of the 1990s was the *The Global Trap: Globalisation and the Assault on Prosperity and Democracy* by Hans-Peter Martin and Harald Schumann, translated from German into Arabic and greeted with enthusiasm by much of the Arab media – an interesting case of anti-globalisation sentiment becoming globalised.

Inevitably, the more apocalyptic views heard in the Middle East ignore some obvious but inconvenient facts. Arabs constantly portray globalisation as something that is done to them by others, and yet there is no need to look further than oil production, where Arab countries supply almost one-third of the world's needs,[11] to see that it is anything but a one-way process. Huge oil revenues in the Gulf states have led in turn to the reinvestment of Arab petrodollars in western enterprises through a mixture of sovereign wealth funds and private investors. The first sovereign wealth fund was established by Kuwait in the 1950s with the aim of providing an income when the oil runs out. Since then, other countries have followed suit (including Russia and China) and the importance of these state-controlled funds has grown enormously. The largest is thought to be that of the United Arab Emirates, worth around $875 billion.[12]

As one of the less-visible aspects of globalisation, Arab investments in the west do not usually attract much attention though paranoia sometimes surfaces over possible threats to national security and the power that Arabs could wield if investment decisions were shaped by politics rather than commercial interests.[13] One highly publicised example came when Dubai Ports World, a company ultimately controlled by the ruler of Dubai, sought to acquire the British shipping company, P&O. As part of the deal the Dubai company would have taken over the management of six major ports in the United States. Protests followed in the US, based mainly around supposed "security concerns", which *New York Times* columnist Thomas Friedman described as "borderline racist".[14] One "concern" raised was that several of the ports in question were used for shipping nuclear material – with the unspoken implication that if the sale went ahead some of this might fall into the hands of terrorists.[15] Others argued that foreign states could not be trusted with "strategic American assets" – even though most US ports at the time were already run by foreign companies, with the US Coastguard continuing to control all aspects of security and the US Customs Service in charge of inspecting cargoes. The issue was eventually resolved when the Dubai company transferred the port management contracts to a New York-based asset management company.[16]

Arabs' other notable role in globalisation has been religion. The call to Islam (*dawa*') transcends national boundaries in much the same way that multinational corporations do and from small beginnings in the Arabian heartland, Islam now has an estimated 1.2 billion adherents and is growing faster than the world's population.[17] Modern air travel and the growth of Muslim communities beyond the Middle East have turned the annual *hajj* – the pilgrimage to Mecca – into a global event attended by some 2 million believers.

It is only by ignoring these multi-directional processes and characterising it as an imposition by the outside world that "globalisation" can be turned into a rhetorical weapon and then deployed, often very selectively, against influences or changes that are disliked for other reasons. The classic example of this selectivity is in the globalisation of food and drink: complaints about "McDonaldisation" and "Coca-Colonisation" are rife in the Arab countries, as they are elsewhere. But the real argument is not globalisation or even foreign influences in general: it is about American influence in particular, and these products (even if in reality they are produced by locally owned franchises) provide a convenient and easily politicised symbol of it. Meanwhile, the United States itself is assumed to be so dominant that it is immune to foreign influences – though even in the US immigration and travel have had their effect on popular tastes:

> Ethnic cuisine has become an integral part of the American way of life, and more and more people are experimenting with spices that were once considered exotic. In fact, according to the American Spice Trade Association, 1995 American spice consumption amounted to 3.1 pounds per person, an increase of a pound from the 1976 per capita consumption.[18]

In the Arab countries at least, arguments about "McDonaldisation" and the like are driven more by politics than the desirability or otherwise of hamburgers or even the preservation of local traditions. By far the most controversial are American products – or rather, those that have iconic status – and products associated with Israel. Other countries make a guest appearance from time to time – Denmark, for example, in the wake of the "Prophet cartoons" affair.[19] The politicisation can also be seen in the way products associated with less controversial countries, such as Italy and Japan, are treated. While "McDonaldisation" raises hackles, the "pizzafication" and "sushification" of Arab takeaways proceeds with scarcely a murmur of protest.

Sweden also figures in the "nice and harmless" category. Indeed, it was singled out in a video message from Bin Laden as one of the countries that al-Qa'ida had chosen not to attack[20] – which is fortunate for the Swedish company Ikea, whose self-assembly furniture is very popular in Saudi Arabia. There were extraordinary scenes in 2004 when Ikea opened a new store in Jeddah and offered vouchers ranging from $27 to $134 for the first 250 customers. Although Saudi Arabia is usually regarded as the most resistant of all the Arab countries to foreign influence, around 20,000 people gathered at the store on its opening day. Three people died in the ensuing stampede and sixteen more were injured.[21]

Although campaigns against "foreign" businesses and products are often driven by international politics, the causes can sometimes be much more local. The arrival of Kentucky Fried Chicken in Damascus in 1999 – to much fanfare and with two US congressmen in attendance – was one example. The KFC franchise was owned by the son of Syrian vice-president 'Abd al-Halim Khaddam, who at the time was in the midst of a quarrel with Bashar al-Asad, the president's son. Shortly after the opening, an article in *al-Hayat*, by the paper's Damascus bureau chief, criticised the vice-president for his involvement with a symbol of American "imperialism", and the story was taken up by other Arab newspapers. Open criticism of such a senior figure was highly unusual and Khaddam later claimed that the story had been planted by Bashar in the hope of undermining his political position. The issue was eventually resolved when the Damascus KFC changed its official name from Kentucky Fried Chicken to Kuwaiti Food Company – thus retaining the initials but removing the American reference.[22]

Around the same time the British supermarket chain, Sainsbury's, ran into difficulties when it expanded into Egypt and rumours spread that the company had Jewish connections and supported Israel (which it emphatically denied). However, as with the KFC episode in Syria, the real motivation for the anti-Sainsbury's campaign lay elsewhere: the rumours were said to have been started, or at least encouraged, by small shopkeepers who feared – perhaps justifiably – that its price-cutting policies would drive them out of business. Mosque preachers and pro-Islamist newspapers also joined in by denouncing the company and there were several incidents where school students, protesting at Israel's treatment of the Palestinians, threw stones at Sainsbury's branches.[23] After just two years the company pulled out, blaming heavy trading losses, though not the boycott, as the reason for its decision.[24]

Episodes such as these are a sideshow to the real globalisation debate and need to be separated from it. Much of the talk about westernisation, hegemony and cultural imperialism is similarly confused. In an article headed "*Damsels in distress? The west should stop using the liberalisation of Muslim women to justify its strategy of dominance*," Soumaya Ghannoushi writes:

> ... just as there is a military machine of hegemony, there is a discursive machine of hegemony. When armies move on the ground to conquer and subjugate, they need moral and ideological cover. It is this that gives the dominant narrative of the "Muslim woman" its raison d'etre.
>
> No wonder then that the "Muslim woman" liberation

warriors, the likes of Nick Cohen, Christopher Hitchens, and Pascal Bruckner [three writers], were the same people who cheered American/British troops as they blasted their way through Kabul and Baghdad, and who will no doubt cheer and dance once more should Iran or Syria be bombed next. Soldiers shoot with their guns; they with their pens. They are hegemony's apologists. Without them the emperor stands naked.[25]

While it is true that abuses of women's rights, and human rights more generally, are sometimes invoked for cynical purposes in support of a military intervention (though hardly ever as the principal justification), it is ludicrous to suggest that all human rights activism in the west, or even a large part of it, is driven by some grand hegemonic plan. Joseph Massad of Columbia University – who is of Palestinian-Christian descent – makes a similar argument in relation to gay rights, accusing what he calls the "Gay International" of reserving "a special place for the Muslim countries in its discourse", which he attributes to orientalist and colonialist impulses. On what Massad bases this claim is unclear but, judging by the websites of Human Rights Watch and Amnesty International, there is no evidence that either organisation focuses disproportionately on Muslim countries in its gay and lesbian rights activity. In fact, the country most targeted by Human Rights Watch in its gay/lesbian press releases is the United States.[26] Interestingly, although homosexuality is often regarded in the Middle East as a foreign (ie western) import, despite ample historical and contemporary evidence to the contrary, gay rights cannot readily be portrayed as an arm of US foreign policy. Gay rights figured nowhere in the "forward strategy of freedom" for the Middle East announced by President Bush in 2003 and only rarely does the US intervene officially on gay issues at an international level; one of the few occasions involving an Arab country was in 2005 when the State Department spoke out against compulsory hormone injections for a group of men arrested at an allegedly gay party in Abu Dhabi.[27]

Resisting challenges and innovative ideas from outside on the grounds that they are foreign and must therefore have some destructive neo-colonial motive behind them is a form of self-deception which, as Amartya Sen, the Indian-born Nobel laureate, points out, creates barriers to progress:

> The misdiagnosis that globalisation of ideas and practices has to be resisted because it entails dreaded westernisation has played quite a regressive part in the colonial and postcolonial world. This assumption incites parochial tendencies and undermines the possibility of objectivity in science and knowledge. It is not only counterproductive in itself; given the global interactions throughout history, it can also cause non-western societies to shoot themselves in the foot – even in their precious cultural foot ...
>
> To see globalisation as merely western imperialism of ideas and beliefs (as the rhetoric often suggests) would be a serious and costly error ... Of course, there are issues related to globalisation that do connect with imperialism (the history of conquests, colonialism, and alien rule remains relevant today in many ways), and a postcolonial understanding of the world has its merits. But it would be a great mistake to see globalisation primarily as a feature of imperialism. It is much bigger – much greater – than that.[28]

Setting aside the political and cultural sensitivities, Benjamin Barber, an American political theorist, describes globalisation as having "four imperatives": a market imperative; a resource imperative; an information technology imperative; and an ecological imperative.[29]

The market imperative transcends national boundaries and, to some extent, national sovereignty too:

> All national economies are now vulnerable to the inroads of larger, transnational markets within which trade is free, currencies are convertible, access to banking is open, and contracts are enforceable under law. In Europe, Asia, Africa, the South Pacific, and the Americas such markets are eroding national sovereignty and giving rise to entities – international banks, trade associations, transnational lobbies like Opec and Greenpeace, world news services like CNN and the BBC, and multinational corporations that increasingly lack a meaningful national identity – that neither reflect nor respect nationhood as an organising or regulative principle.[30]

The resource imperative, basically, means that no country is self-sufficient and all countries must rely on others to fulfil at least some of their needs. The ancient Athenians, Barber notes, tried for a while to create a way of life simple and austere enough to make them genuinely self-sufficient. The Athenians were unable to do so and the complexity of modern life makes the dream of self-sufficiency ever more elusive. Some countries still try to mitigate the effects of interdependence. Saudi Arabia, for example, seeks to reduce its dependence on foreign guest-workers through its "Saudisation" policy and there are hugely expensive schemes to grow wheat in the desert, but these are piecemeal initiatives. The only real solution is to accept the inevitability of interdependence.

The information technology imperative needs little explanation. "The pursuit of science and technology asks for, even compels, open societies," Barber says. "Satellite footprints do not respect national borders; telephone wires penetrate the most closed societies. With photocopying and then fax machines having infiltrated Soviet universities and *samizdat* literary circles in the eighties, and computer modems having multiplied like rabbits in communism's bureaucratic warrens thereafter, *glasnost* could not be far behind. In their social requisites, secrecy and science are enemies."

The ecological imperative also cuts across national boundaries. We inhabit a shared planet and what happens in one part of the globe – industrial pollution or the destruction of rainforests, for instance – can have an environmental impact thousands of miles away. One example in the Middle East is the Euphrates river, which rises in the Kurdish mountains of eastern Turkey and meanders for more than 1,700 miles through Syria and Iraq into the Gulf. Whatever use one country makes of its waters is bound to have an impact on the others further downstream.[31]

It is not difficult to see that these four imperatives have major implications for governments everywhere and particularly those where national sovereignty is treated as a sacred principle. The age of post-colonial independence is giving way to an age of interdependence as globalisation erodes sovereignty, transferring power from national governments upwards and outwards to supranational and transnational bodies and organisations, but also – no less importantly – downwards to ordinary citizens.

This may not mean the end of nation-states as such, but probably the end of nation-states as Arab regimes would like them to be. The ability of national governments to make decisions in isolation, uninfluenced by the decisions of other governments, is being steadily diminished. Barber writes:

> In the context of common markets, international law ceases
> to be a vision of justice and becomes a workaday framework
> for getting things done – enforcing contracts, ensuring that

governments abide by deals, regulating trade and currency relations, and so forth.[32]

For most of the Arab countries, establishing this "workaday framework" is more easily said than done. Meeting international standards requires adequate mechanisms within the country – among other things, laws and regulations that are properly implemented, an independent judiciary and clear, transparent systems of administration that are not continuously circumvented by corruption or favouritism. Without that machinery they risk being left behind. At the same time, it is becoming more difficult for Arab governments to control what happens within their own borders. Evolving information-technology makes physical barriers and censorship less and less effective in keeping foreign influences at bay. It is also more difficult to prevent information leaving the country, with the result that repressive actions by governments are more likely to be noticed – and complained about – abroad.

For regimes that derive a large part of their legitimacy from nationalist or traditionalist sentiment, the diminution of national sovereignty caused by globalisation is a very sensitive issue. Sovereignty is one western political concept that Arab leaders have had no hesitation in adopting and making sacrosanct. It originated in Europe during the sixteenth and seventeenth centuries when the emerging nation states were looking for a secular basis for their authority. The Arab preoccupation (some might say obsession) with national sovereignty is a result of struggles for independence. In the immediate post-imperial era, it was natural for new states to guard their sovereignty jealously – and woe betide anyone who tried to interfere. This created a sense of insularity that even the dreams of pan-Arabism largely failed to dislodge.

The dismal performance of the Arab League is a case in point, especially when contrasted with the development of the European Union. Back in 1945 Egypt, Iraq, Lebanon, Saudi Arabia, Syria, Jordan and Yemen got together to form the Arab League, as a first step towards Arab unity. About the same time, European leaders were developing similar ideas: in 1946 Winston Churchill called for a "United States of Europe" – though it was not until 1957 that the Treaty of Rome formally established the European Economic Community (later to become the EU). Today, the EU has a single market with freedom of movement for goods, services, capital and people. Many laws have become standardised across its member states and it has developed common policies, both internally (agriculture and fisheries, for example) and, increasingly, externally in its dealings with other countries. Increasingly, too, EU bodies are able to make decisions without the agreement of all their members. None of that could have been achieved without members being willing to sacrifice some of their sovereignty. How much to sacrifice is still a contentious issue (barely half of the twenty-seven states have so far adopted the Euro as their common currency) but gradually people are recognising the benefits of doing so and, step by step, the original idea of a United States of Europe is coming closer.

In the meantime, the Arab League – despite having grown to include twenty-two countries and a population of more than 200 million – has barely got beyond the starting blocks. To see why, we need look no further than the league's charter, drafted in 1945, which talks about strengthening "the close relations and numerous ties which bind the Arab states" and "cementing and reinforcing of these bonds" while simultaneously consolidating their separate independence and national sovereignty.[33] The nub of the problem lies in Article VII of the charter which begins by stating, rather oddly, that unanimous decisions are binding on all member states (there is no reason for them not to be binding if everyone is in favour), then adds that majority decisions are binding only on those states that have accepted them (again, it would not be surprising if the countries that were in favour of a decision were happy to be bound by it). Article VII ends by saying that in both cases – whether unanimous or not – decisions shall be implemented in each country "according to its basic rules".[34] This amounts to a licence for each country to ignore or implement decisions in whatever way it chooses, with no mechanism for reconciling differences of interpretation.

The league's charter also requires members to "respect the systems of government established in the other member states and regard them as exclusive concerns of those states". So, for instance, if one Arab country complains about human rights violations in another, it could be in breach of the charter.[35] The insistence on respecting each other's systems of government was probably intended to defuse conflicts between Arab republics and monarchies. Whereas in the EU republics and monarchies do not differ radically in the way they are actually governed, the same cannot be said of the Arab countries, where there has been a great deal of tension and hostility over the years between the two. In the past these differences seemed as irreconcilable, in many ways, as the differences between capitalism and communism in Europe.

Though it might be argued that at the time the Arab League was formed these nationalistic attitudes served a purpose in helping to consolidate the newly independent states, today "sovereignty" has become an obstacle to progress and a reactionary force. It is often nothing more than a smokescreen for the "right" of Arab regimes to misgovern – as, for example, in 2005 when the Egyptian regime rejected international election observers on the grounds that this would infringe national sovereignty.[36]

Whether they like it or not, most Arab regimes do recognise that in order to reap the benefits of globalisation they must sacrifice a measure of sovereignty, but they try to cherry-pick. In the economic sphere, compliance with international standards is generally acceptable and uncontroversial (at least, in principle). In the social-cultural-political sphere, however, the moment international standards are mentioned issues of sovereignty and cultural distinctiveness raise their head. This can lead to some bizarre arguments, as seen early in 2008 when a quarrel broke out between the EU and the Mubarak regime in Egypt. It began with a resolution from the European parliament criticising human rights abuses. In particular, the resolution called on the Egyptian government to end its harassment of journalists and human rights defenders, lift the twenty-six-year-old state of emergency, investigate suspected cases of torture and guarantee the independence of the judiciary.[37] Compared to what might have been said, this was pretty mild stuff and, as Bahieddin Hassan, director of the Cairo Institute for Human Rights Studies, later remarked, its content was "too true to be refuted".[38]

The response from Mubarak's National Democratic party, however, was one of unmitigated fury. "The age of capitulation is over and Egypt no longer accepts the language of foreign dictates," Fathi Sorour, the parliamentary speaker, fumed. Threatening to cut all ties with the European parliament, he announced he would be raising the issue at a meeting of the Union of Muslim Parliaments, which would focus on "Islamophobia in Europe" and "western hostility against Islamic values".[39] Other NDP representatives blamed Israel for the European resolution. Abdel-Ahad Gamaleddin, the ruling party's parliamentary spokesman, said he suspected Israel of trying to kill two birds with one stone – embarrass Egypt and distract international attention from Israeli atrocities in Gaza.

Presumably these verbal fireworks were meant for domestic consumption. Despite its efforts to portray the criticisms as unwarranted meddling in the country's internal affairs, the Egyptian government was not only aware that the EU was monitoring its human rights performance but had voluntarily agreed to it in exchange for trade privileges.

In 1995 Egypt was one of a dozen non-EU countries – along with fifteen EU countries – that voluntarily signed up to the Barcelona Declaration, which aims to develop security, stability, trade and cultural cooperation in the Mediterranean region, and also to promote democracy, good governance and human rights. Egypt was receiving €30 million ($44 million) a year under the Barcelona process,[40] supposedly for the purpose of developing human rights and good governance – so it could hardly complain if other signatories questioned what was being achieved with the money. Since 2004 Egypt and the EU have also had an association agreement[41] – one of a series involving Mediterranean countries. These agreements provide important economic benefits but they are not purely about trade; they encompass cooperation in many areas, including "political dialogue" and "respect for human rights and democracy". Again, this was something that the Egyptian government signed of its own accord, no doubt for the economic benefits, but it could scarcely plead ignorance about the other aspects since they were spelled out in the agreement itself[42] and the EU has always made clear that "respect for human rights is a fundamental value" of such agreements. At a joint meeting with Egypt in 2006 the EU explained this in more detail:

> The EU seeks to work with each partner [in Association Agreements] individually, at the appropriate pace, to achieve a significant degree of economic integration as

well as deepening of political cooperation and achieve the objectives of a privileged relationship based on mutual commitment to human rights, including the rights of women and rights of persons belonging to minorities, and to shared values, principally within the fields of the rule of law, good governance and democracy ... The relationship will be shaped by the degree of commitment to these common values and principles ...[43]

As part of this process, eight joint committees were set up, including a political committee described as the official vehicle for EU–Egyptian dialogue "on concrete human rights issues". It was in preparation for a meeting of the political committee that the European parliament issued its resolution about the state of human rights in Egypt.

International agreements such as UN conventions involving human rights present Arab states (and the Islamic countries more generally) with a dilemma. On one hand they are reluctant to accept the principle of universality, arguing for exceptions to be made on cultural or religious grounds, while on the other they feel a need to demonstrate that Islam respects human rights by signing up to UN conventions [see table on p. 280]. This, basically, is a case of having the cake and eating it. Becoming a party to the various human rights conventions bestows an aura of respectability without necessarily creating any serious obligations in terms of compliance – firstly because the conventions themselves lack effective enforcement mechanisms and secondly because the parties to a UN convention can often choose to ignore parts of it simply by registering their "reservations". In some cases these reservations can be so sweeping as to negate the essential substance of the agreement. Liesbeth Lijnzaad, in her book, *Reservations to UN Human Rights Treaties: Ratify and Ruin?* sums up the problem thus:

> By making reservations to human rights treaties, states frequently undermine essential rules, and indeed essential human rights guarantees ... The impression is that many states, when ratifying, at the same time ruin the treaty. Reservations restrict the potential domestic effect of the human rights treaty, and a large number of reservations made by a great many states will turn a human rights instrument into a moth-eaten guarantee.[44]

In theory, reservations which are "incompatible with the object and purpose" of a UN convention are not allowed but in practice they can be difficult to prevent. When North Yemen acceded to the International Convention on the Elimination of All Forms of Racial Discrimination (CERD) in 1989 it declared reservations "in respect of article 5 (c) and article 5 (d) (iv), (vi) and (vii)". In effect, it was claiming the right to discriminate on racial grounds with regard to political rights, marriage rights, inheritance rights and the right to freedom of thought, conscience and religion.[45] This was obviously incompatible with the aims of the convention and Australia, Belgium, Canada, Denmark, Finland, France, Germany, Italy, Mexico, the Netherlands, New Zealand, Norway, Sweden and the United Kingdom all lodged formal objections. However, their numbers fell well short of the two-thirds of states-parties required to block the Yemeni reservations,[46] and there was little that could be done about it except patiently cajole: seventeen years later, the UN Committee on the Elimination of Racial Discrimination was continuing to repeat its "recommendation" that Yemen should "consider withdrawing its reservation".[47]

Arab ratification of UN human rights conventions

	CESCR	CCPR	CERD	CEDAW	CAT	CRC	MWC
Algeria	+	+	+	+	+	+	+
Bahrain	+	+	+	+	+	+	
Comoros			+	+		+	
Djibouti	+	+		+	+	+	
Egypt	+	+	+	+	+	+	+
Iraq	+	+	+	+		+	
Jordan	+	+	+	+	+	+	
Kuwait	+	+	+	+	+	+	
Lebanon	+	+	+	+	+	+	
Libya	+	+	+	+	+	+	+
Mauritania			+	+	+	+	+
Morocco	+	+	+	+	+	+	+
Oman			+	+		+	
Qatar			+		+	+	
S. Arabia			+	+	+	+	
Somalia	+	+	+		+		
Sudan	+	+	+			+	
Syria	+	+	+	+	+	+	+
Tunisia	+	+	+	+	+	+	
UAE			+	+		+	
Yemen	+	+	+	+	+	+	

+ Indicates ratification, blank cells indicate non-ratification
CESCR: International Covenant on Economic, Social and Cultural Rights; CCPR:
International Covenant on Civil and Political Rights; CERD: International Convention
on the Elimination of All Forms of Racial Discrimination, CEDAW; Convention on
the Elimination of All Forms of Discrimination against Women; CAT: Convention
against Torture and Other Cruel, Inhuman or Degrading Treatment or Punishment;

CRC: Convention on the Rights of the Child; MWC: International Convention on the Protection of the Rights of All Migrant Workers and Members of Their Families

Note: CESCR and CCPR are particularly important because, together with the Universal Declaration of Human Rights, they form the International Bill of Rights. It is notable that several Gulf states – Oman, Qatar, Saudi Arabi and the UAE have not signed these.

Meanwhile Saudi Arabia, despite operating what is probably the world's most comprehensive system of institutionalised discrimination against women, is a party – together with seventeen other Arab states – to the Convention on the Elimination of All Forms of Discrimination against Women (CEDAW). The kingdom rationalises this seemingly irreconcilable position, after a fashion, by saying it does not consider itself bound by any part of the convention that conflicts with "the norms of Islamic law".[48] Among the other Arab countries, Bahrain, Egypt, Iraq, Kuwait, Libya, Mauritania, Morocco, Oman, Syria and the UAE have also lodged reservations based on Islamic law.

Citing "Islamic law" in the context of international treaties is especially problematic because no one can be sure what it means. The shari'a is not formally codified, there are various methods of interpretation and scholars can sometimes reach wildly differing conclusions. As Denmark noted in its objection to Saudi Arabia's reservations, the references to the provisions of Islamic law were "of unlimited scope and undefined character".[49]

The key point, though, is that religious principles are a convenient vehicle for excusing all manner of abuse. In reality, the abuses usually have more to do with local customs and practice than religious doctrine but invoking religion removes any need to account for them or try to justify them. Since religious belief demands respect and tolerance from others, dressing up unsavoury practices in religious garb becomes a way of silencing critics. The overall effect of dragging

Islamic law into human rights debates, then, is to lower standards rather than raise them, as Ann Elizabeth Mayer demonstrates in her book, *Islam and Human Rights – Tradition and Politics*. "Distinctive Islamic criteria have consistently been used to cut back on the rights and freedoms guaranteed by international law, as if the latter were deemed excessive," she writes. "The literature arguing that Muslims may have human rights, but only according to Islamic principles, provides the theoretical rationales for many recent government policies that have been harmful for rights."[50] Although there are many points of contention between the concept of universal rights and Islamic law (as variously conceived), the principal ones are in the areas of women's rights, freedom of religion, and the treatment of non-Muslims.

This is not to suggest that Islam is incapable of accommodating modern concepts of universal human rights. Individual freedoms are a relatively undeveloped area of Islamic law and Mayer suggests this is largely for historical reasons:

> Since the pious Muslim was only supposed to understand and obey the divine law, which entailed abiding by the limits that God had decreed, demands for individual freedoms could sound distinctly subversive to the orthodox mind ...
>
> The aim of Islamic law was generally conceived to be ensuring the wellbeing of the Islamic community, or *umma*, as a whole, in a situation where both the ruler and the ruled were presumed to be motivated to follow the law in order to win divine favour and avoid punishment in Hell. In consequence, shari'a doctrines remained highly idealistic and were not elaborated with a view to providing institutional mechanisms to deal with actual situations where governments disregarded Islamic law and oppressed and exploited their subjects.
>
> Scholars of Islamic law did not traditionally address issues

like what institutions and procedures were needed to constrain
the ruler and curb oppression; rather, they tended to think
of the relationship between ruler and ruled solely in terms
of this idealised scheme, in which rulers were conceived of as
pious Muslims eager to follow God's mandate.[51]

Arguments about universality versus cultural relativism lie at the
heart of the globalisation debate but they are also, in many cases,
a red herring – a part of the political game. It would be wrong to
assume that the Arab states, with all their bluster about "the norms
of Islamic law", stand firmly and consistently on the side of cultural
relativism. On the whole they do not, except when it suits them, and
in this they are no less hypocritical than the western governments
that claim to uphold universal rights but champion them more
strongly among enemies than allies. The Arab states, through their
membership of the UN and other bodies, are willing members of the
international community; they accept the principle of international
law and, along with other countries, play a part in formulating it.
They are also among the first to complain about human rights abuses
and infringements of international law where Israel is concerned.

In partially exempting themselves from international standards,
the Arab states are not so much arguing for cultural relativism as
for a form of *cultural selectivity* – and a very particular one at that.
What they are actually seeking to protect is not the sum-total of
authentic local tradition but an imagined, officially approved version
of it which in some cases has to be imposed on reluctant citizens –
for example, through the policing of dress codes and the closure of
shops at prayer time. The Islamic "norms" that Saudi Arabia waves
in international forums are not those of the country as a whole but
those of the Wahhabi sect, which happens to have become dominant
through its political alliance with the royal family.

The other problem with cultural relativism arguments in connection with the Arab countries is that they are also invoked selectively. They are used as a defence against external influences (the unwelcome ones, at any rate) and especially in dealings with the west. But if Arab governments really believed in cultural relativism as a principle they would surely also apply it within their own countries by insisting on respect for the different norms and traditions of whatever distinctive religious, ethnic or regional groups may be found within their own borders. Mostly they do not.

ARAB RESISTANCE TO globalisation comes mainly from two directions: nationalist and religious. In 2007, when Jordan finally ratified the international Convention on the Elimination of all Forms of Discrimination Against Women (fifteen years after originally signing it), the reaction from the Islamic Action Front was thoroughly predictable: it denounced the move as an "American and Zionist" attempt to strip the nation of its "identity and values", to steer people away from religion and to destroy "the Muslim family".[52] In Saudi Arabia, true to stereotype, Saud al-Funaysan, a professor of Islamic law at Imam Mohammed bin Saud University, described globalisation as "a new western heresy that limits the entity of the Arab nation, weakens its soul, sucks it material wealth and breaks its social ties". He told a Saudi interviewer:

> It is a real fact and an unavoidable evil. Before discussing its negative repercussions, we have to warn that the precursor to globalisation, that is, modernity with its intellectual and social meaning, paved the way for globalisation's appearance and dissemination. Modernity, with its comprehensive meaning, knocked on our doors, and we welcomed it, thinking naively that it was just western technology. But it entered carrying the west's culture of ideology and thought.

Views of this sort are not hard to find, but one only has to look at the plethora of modern Islamic gadgetry on sale to see that many ordinary Muslims take globalisation more easily in their stride: digital Qur'ans, watches that provide an alert at prayer times, online *qibla* calculators,[53] even a Muslim Barbie doll complete with hijab and prayer mat.[54] Islamic organisations of various types were quick to recognise the importance of the internet and to make use of it – in some cases with Islamic scholars providing online fatwas in response to emails sent to them.[55] Tarabichi suggests that many Islamists do not reject the concept of globalisation itself "because a primary theoretical pillar of their discourse is the internationalisation of the Islamic mission".[56] This is certainly the view adopted by IslamOnline, a vast English/Arabic website which describes itself as "a unique, global Islamic web portal" aimed at both Muslims and non-Muslims.[57] When it was launched in 1999 Yusuf al-Qaradawi, the prominent Qatar-based scholar, had no hesitation in calling for the internet to be used to spread Islam's message:

> It is our duty to carry this religion to all people around the world until they understand it, become interested in it, look for it, and enter it in surges as God would like ... The people of the 20th century must be spoken to in the language they understand, and not in the language of past centuries. We must use the tools needed to achieve that. We used print, radio, and television. Today, there is a new medium known as the internet. All religions have used it to call to their religions and sects. It is the duty of the Muslims to use this tool to call to their great religion ... [58]

On the negative side, al-Qa'ida owes its existence to globalisation. It has become the first truly globalised terror network, selecting targets and recruiting operatives in many parts of the world. Though often harking back to the early days of Islam, it has also embraced some of the most obvious features of globalisation – air travel, satellite TV and the internet – without which it could never have caused as much trouble as it has. Nor has al-Qaʻida been immune to "alien" influences, as Jason Burke, an expert on the terror network pointed out:

> In any clutch of speeches by Bin Laden or Ayman al-Zawahiri you will find an extraordinary selection of old anti-colonial political slogans, Third Worldism, new anti-Americanism and anti-capitalism, Arab chauvinism, quotes from medieval and contemporary Islamic scholars, new political Islamist thinkers, the Koran, barely disguised influences from hardline leftist thought, etc. As a result, al-Qaʻida-ism is as much an alien import as any other "globalised" idea parachuted in from elsewhere.[59]

Overall then, with the exception of the most traditionalist elements, Muslims are more receptive to globalisation than might be imagined. As elsewhere, there is some concern and confusion but also recognition that it brings advantages as well as disadvantages. Eagerness to adopt the technology of globalisation is coupled with attempts to separate the technology from what are seen as the negative values of globalisation: "It could be Satan's weapon, but it can also be Satan's weapon redirected against him."[60]

Though Arab Muslims still have to grapple with the paradox of authenticity versus modernity, Tarabichi suggests that Islamists are more likely to see potential benefits in globalisation than the Arab nationalists or Marxists.[61] Dr Hoda Gamal Abdel Nasser, as her name might suggest, is the eldest daughter of the late Egyptian president and still carries a torch for pan-Arab nationalism. In a speech to Arab-American graduates at Georgetown university, she said:

The first problem which the Arab World must contend with in the face of globalisation is how to protect Arab national identity and Arab culture. The US is seeking to project American culture as a model for a global culture that should be disseminated over international communications networks, with no restrictions whatsoever.

But the Arab world faces a second dilemma – the encroachment of the forces of globalisation on the authority of the nation-state ... The state in the Arab world is extremely important as a symbol of national identity. Not only does it have the task to steer the country towards domestic economic and social equilibrium, it also takes the lead in the expression of national culture. The deliberate weakening of the forces of the nation-state may well give rise to chaos and domestic strife and further the spread of extremism.

Unsurprisingly, her solution was remarkably similar to the one favoured by her father:

The Arab countries must move quickly to organise a regional bloc ... I believe that the Arab World has a distinct advantage in this regard as any steps we take toward Arab unification will serve to enhance Arab nationalism ... The key to overcoming the obstacles that hinder the creation of such an Arab bloc lies in each Arab country developing the conviction that, on its own, it is too weak to stand up against the forces of globalisation. Unfortunately, time is not on our side. We must move quickly ...[62]

Regrettably or not, that is no more likely to succeed than it was in the 1950s and 1960s, but Dr Nasser's analysis also rests on several highly questionable assumptions: that Arab culture and national identity must be protected, that the expression of national culture should be led by the state, and that the reduced power of nation-states as a result of globalisation will lead to chaos.

This stems from a basic misconception about the nature of cultures – one which is very prevalent in the Arab countries and lies at the root of their globalisation fears. A culture, in its broadest sense, is simply "the way we do things here". It is organic. It serves the needs of the people who happen to belong to it and it changes with their needs. In the past the changes may have been so slow as to be barely perceptible but with globalisation they happen more quickly and dramatically, hence the alarm. But resisting these changes – in effect, trying to freeze a culture in time – serves no useful purpose: it simply makes the culture less relevant to people's actual needs and builds up frustration and resentment, particularly among the young.

Equally, there is no such thing as a "pure" culture, totally uninfluenced by the world outside. A culture which is confident of its own strengths does not worry about protecting itself: it looks at what is on offer elsewhere, borrows what it likes and if necessary adapts it to local conditions. Music is one obvious example. What passes today for western music has absorbed ideas from all sorts of places. The same when it transfers to an Arab culture: just a few lines from a Moroccan rapper will show what happens: yes, it's rap, but it's also distinctively Moroccan. External influences, and the multiple ways they can be adapted and incorporated, are what give a culture vibrancy; they only become a threat when the indigenous culture is losing its relevance – a point that Arab regimes might fruitfully ponder.

When Arab critics of globalisation talk about protecting their culture, they are primarily thinking in geographical and national terms – of the elements that distinguish Arab countries from others. That is how cultural diversity has traditionally been perceived, and they are probably correct in assuming that globalisation will eventually make all countries more similar to each other. However, this ignores another crucial feature of globalisation: that it greatly increases people's choice, no matter where they happen to be. So, although there is likely to be less diversity *between* countries in the future, there will be more diversity *within* them. As the American economist, Tyler Cowen, puts it:

> Individuals are liberated [by globalisation] from the tyranny of place more than ever before. Growing up in an out-of-the-way locale limits an individual's access to the world's treasures and opportunities less than ever before. This change represents one of the most significant increases in freedom in human history.[63]

It is not merely a question of having a wider range of goods, services and entertainment to choose from; we are also witnessing the creation of a free market for ideas. Ideas – regardless of where they originate – are no longer tied by national or cultural boundaries; their geographical origins matter less and less. If Arab critics of globalisation were genuinely concerned with diversity they would welcome this, but instead they perceive it as undermining their own particular view of what Arab societies ought to be or ought not to be. On that score, they are right to be fearful, because in the long run a free market for ideas poses the greatest threat imaginable to the stultifying monoculture that they have striven for so long to develop and preserve.

9   Escape from history

PREVIOUS CHAPTERS HAVE alluded to the influence of east–west politics without discussing its impact on the Arab countries in detail – not because it is unimportant but because it can so easily overshadow everything else. Arabs, with good reason, have come to regard themselves as prisoners of history. During the past century in particular, in the face of international machinations, they have grown accustomed to the role of victim, at times almost to the point of relishing it. It has become a commonplace to blame foreign meddling for the region's ills, either to the exclusion of other factors or as an excuse to delay confronting the many internal problems. This tendency to blame others, justified as it may be in many cases, has now become a problem in itself, allowing Arabs to absolve themselves from responsibility. In order to gain more control over their own destiny they have to escape from their historical straitjacket.

Unlike Africa, Australia or the Americas, the Middle East is not a clearly defined land mass and its exact boundaries, even today, are still largely a matter of opinion. The Middle East is not so much a geographical entity as a geopolitical concept – invented, just over 100 years ago, by the British and the Americans:

> The term was clearly conceived in the framework of European/ western geopolitical and strategic considerations, delineating the region as a realm of actual or potential political, military, and economic rivalry and spheres of influence among European/western imperial powers.[1]

Surprising as it may seem today, the term "Middle East" did not appear in print until 1900 – in an article by General Sir Thomas Gordon, a British intelligence officer and director of the Imperial Bank of Persia. Gordon, who was concerned mainly with protecting British-ruled India from Russian threats, located the Middle East in Persia (present-day Iran) and Afghanistan.[2] Two years later, an American naval historian, Captain Alfred Mahan, referred to "the Middle East" in an article entitled "The Persian Gulf and International Relations". As an enthusiast of sea power, Mahan centred his Middle East around the waters of the Gulf.[3] Shortly after that, the term gained wider currency in Britain through a series of articles published in *The Times* in 1902 and 1903, under the title "The Middle Eastern Question". Written by Valentine Chirol, head of the newspaper's foreign department, the articles expanded Mahan's concept of the Middle East to include all land and sea approaches to India: Persia, the Persian Gulf, Iraq, the east coast of Saudi Arabia, Afghanistan and Tibet.

Before the discovery of oil British interest in the region was focused mainly on protecting India, the jewel in its imperial crown. To that end, in 1839, Britain had taken possession of Aden on the southern tip of the Arabian peninsula, which thereafter served as a refuelling post on the route east and as a base from which to protect shipping. Until 1937 Aden continued to be ruled as part of British India.

> The issue of the security of the Indies route also entailed control of the Persian Gulf, a bolt-hole for pirates plying the Indian Ocean. Rather than direct rule, the British navy opted for the protectorate system, initially imposing a treaty on the shaikhs of the region, which turned the Pirate coast into the Trucial coast, now the United Arab Emirates. The

> same approach was used in 1899 with the shaikh of the little
> known town of Kuwait ... and the Sultanate of Muscat [in
> modern Oman].[4]

This set a pattern which continues to the present day, with the
notional boundaries of "the Middle East" defined and occasionally
readjusted according to the political and strategic interests of
foreigners rather than those of its inhabitants. The changing concerns
of foreigners over time are also reflected in the way "Near East" has
gradually been subsumed into "Middle East". Initially the word
"middle" served to distinguish between the "far" east (India and
beyond) and the "near" east (the lands of the eastern Mediterranean
sometimes also known as the Levant). By the end of the First World
War, however, the distinction between "near" and "middle" was
becoming blurred, at least in the minds of British policymakers.
The war had brought the collapse of the Ottoman Empire and the
beginnings of Arab nationalism. Britain had gained control over
Palestine, Transjordan, Iraq, Syria and Lebanon and its strategic
interests were changing. Protecting the route to India was still a vital
concern, but there was also growing awareness of the importance of
oil. In London, the Royal Geographical Society proposed extending
the Middle East westwards to include all the Arabic-speaking lands,
plus Turkey – an idea that was readily adopted in Britain.

The US, meanwhile, had settled on "Near East" as its preferred
term but during the Second World War British and American
concepts of the region began to converge, mainly for military
reasons.[5] Although US presidents from Eisenhower onwards have
generally talked in public about "the Middle East", internally the
US government has been slower to accept the term. The State
Department still has its Near Eastern Affairs bureau (NEA), covering
everything from Morocco to Iran (though Turkey was switched

from the Near East to the European Affairs bureau in the 1970s for administrative convenience during the Greek-Turkish conflict over Cyprus). For all practical purposes, though, there is no difference in American parlance nowadays between "Near" and "Middle" East: they are interchangeable even if different arms of the US government view the boundaries differently. The US Defence Department, for instance, favours "Near East" but, unlike the State Department, extends it to include Bangladesh, Sri Lanka and Nepal.[6] This, in turn, is different from the area covered by Centcom, the relevant section of the US military, which excludes Libya, Tunisia, Algeria and Morocco in the west but stretches east beyond the Arabian peninsula to include Afghanistan, Iran, Kazakhstan, Kyrgyzstan, Pakistan, Tajikistan, Turkmenistan and Uzbekistan.[7]

The picture has been further complicated by sometimes adding the word "greater" to the "Middle East" – again, in the context of specific western concerns. Originally coined towards the end of the 1990s,[8] the term "Greater Middle East" was adopted by the administration of George W Bush in its push for reform, democratisation – and, of course, security: "We will challenge the enemies of reform, confront the allies of terror," Bush said in his 2004 state of the union address.[9] However, Washington – perhaps wary of stepping too blatantly into Russia's traditional sphere of influence – appeared to exclude the Caspian basin from its concept of a greater Middle East. According to a leaked working paper prepared by the US for the G-8 summit in 2004, the "Greater Middle East" consisted of the Arab countries plus Pakistan, Afghanistan, Iran, Turkey and Israel. The rationale behind these wider definitions is easy to see. The G-8 working paper of 2004, for instance, presented the case for reform in the "Greater Middle East" primarily in terms of self-interest: "So long as the region's pool of politically and economically disenfranchised individuals grows, we will witness an increase in extremism, terrorism, international crime, and illegal migration," it warned, adding that failure to embrace reform would "pose a direct threat to the stability of the region, and to the common interests of the G-8 members".[10]

From the moment of its conception through to the present day, the "Middle East" has been defined by western powers mainly in terms of the problems it might cause for them – problems that are also magnified by their dependence on its most valuable product, oil. Meanwhile the problems of the people who happen to live there – together with their wishes, needs and interests – if considered at all have generally come a distant second. This is not to suggest that the interests of ordinary Arabs and those expressed by the G-8 are necessarily at odds with each other; broadly they are not, at least in terms of the general goals. Few Arabs would disagree, for example, that it is necessary to combat terrorism, extremism, international crime, etc, but differences soon arise over definitions and priorities, and the means to be used. Who, exactly, decides what extremism is? Does combating extremism give the Egyptian government a right to imprison nonviolent supporters of the Muslim Brotherhood in their hundreds? Does it give the Yemeni government a licence to wage war on Zaidi villages in the north of the country?[11]

"Stability" raises similar questions. Stability may be generally desirable but we also have to ask: stability on what terms? When stability becomes a barrier to progress and necessary change, how valuable is it? For a long time, the prevailing view in the west favoured maintaining stability (and hence security of oil supplies) – on the basis that the known was preferable to the unknown. Thus, whatever happened internally was a matter of no great concern so long as those in charge were not ill-disposed towards western powers. "He may be a bastard, but he's *our* bastard" is a quip attributed to various US presidents in connection with several different dictators in various parts of the world, but it certainly applies to the approach adopted over the years towards Arab leaders. Thus, client regimes – supported and sometimes installed by western powers – were allowed to behave more or less as they pleased so long as they posed no threat to western interests. The result, however, was not always the stability that the west hoped for. Public disillusionment with the client regimes meant that leaders who made a point of defying the west and/or Israel – among them Nasser and Saddam Hussein – acquired hero status, particularly outside their own countries where people tended to overlook their other failings and their sometimes reckless behaviour. In 2006, for example, a poll in the UAE asked young Arabs to name a famous person who they "admire or think of as a role model". Conducted just a few weeks after the month-long war between Israel and Hizbullah, it showed the Hizbullah leader, Hassan Nasrallah, as clear favourite – way ahead of any other politician, film star, footballer or even the Prophet Muhammad.[12]

The long-cherished idea of maintaining stability at almost any cost was rejected by the neoconservatives who began to dominate US foreign policy when Bush arrived at the White House in 2001. In Bush's own words:

> Sixty years of western nations excusing and accommodating the lack of freedom in the Middle East did nothing to make us safe – because in the long run, stability cannot be purchased at the expense of liberty. As long as the Middle East remains a place where freedom does not flourish, it will remain a place of stagnation, resentment, and violence ready for export. And with the spread of weapons that can bring catastrophic harm to our country and to our friends, it would be reckless to accept the status quo.[13]

The September 11 attacks, less than a year after Bush came to power, also opened the way to more radically interventionist discourse – especially interventions of the military kind. "We should have no misgivings about our ability to destroy tyrannies," Michael Ledeen, one of the leading neocon ideologues, wrote in the *National Review Online*.[14] "It is what we do best. It comes naturally to us, for we are the one truly revolutionary country in the world, as we have been for more than 200 years. Creative destruction is our middle name." In the same publication Adam Mersereau, a former Marine Corps officer, expounded on the virtues of "total war" in contrast to "limited" war (in which military force is used to achieve a particular objective "without mobilising the entire nation, and while minimising casualties"):

> By "total" war, I mean the kind of warfare that not only destroys the enemy's military forces, but also brings the enemy society to an extremely personal point of decision, so that they are willing to accept a reversal of the cultural trends that spawned the war in the first place. A total-war strategy does not have to include the intentional targeting of civilians, but the sparing of civilian lives cannot be its first priority ... The purpose of total war is to permanently force your will on to another people group. Limited war pits combatants against combatants, while total war pits nation against nation, and even culture against culture.[15]

It was in the midst of such histrionics from the neoconservatives that Bush launched the war to topple Saddam Hussein in Iraq and followed it up with his "forward strategy of freedom" for the Middle East as a whole. These two campaigns were linked by the idea of creating a free market democracy in Iraq that would become a model for the region – "a watershed event in the global democratic revolution," as Bush put it.[16] Iraq, though, with its religious, ethnic and tribal divisions, was one of the least promising candidates for democratisation: it was selected for other reasons. A group of experts, sitting down to consider which of the Arab countries offered the best hope of establishing democracy, would never have suggested Iraq because there were better prospects elsewhere: Egypt, for example, which had a more homogeneous population and a stronger sense of national identity, plus a tradition of competing political parties and civil society organisations, even if they were repressed by the existing regime.

If the neoconservatives made any useful contribution it was in challenging the sacred cow of stability in the Middle East by highlighting the need for change. More questionable, though, was the type of change they envisaged and the means for achieving it, especially their arrogant belief that the US had a mission to deliver it and their fondness for military solutions. Nevertheless, despite the neoconservatives' bold rhetoric, President Bush's efforts to spread democracy in the Arab world ran into the problem of conflicting objectives: claiming to promote freedom and democracy while continuing to support client regimes that often showed little respect for either. Regimes considered hostile to the United States were thus condemned as irredeemably undemocratic while the friendly ones received praise for their often minimal "reforms". The contortions this required could be seen from Bush's speech in 2003, setting out his "forward strategy of freedom". The countries where he claimed to detect "stirrings" of democracy – Morocco, Bahrain, Oman, Qatar, Yemen, Kuwait, Saudi Arabia and Egypt – were all friendly towards the United States. Saudi Arabia, an absolute monarchy with an appalling human rights record (but a valuable US ally) won praise for "taking first steps toward reform". Meanwhile, the president told

Iran its regime "must heed the democratic demands of the Iranian people, or lose its last claim to legitimacy". Iran, in fact – whatever its other faults – had gone further down the democratic path than Saudi Arabia, holding fiercely contested elections regularly since the Islamic revolution.[17]

The selective nature of this campaign for democracy promotion was so transparent that it swept away any hopes of credibility the plan might have had, deepening wariness within the region about America's real intentions. Meanwhile, activists working for change and democracy within the region were liable to find themselves dismissed as tools of American foreign policy. Kenneth Roth, the director of Human Rights Watch, commented later:

> The US government's vigorous criticism of democratic shortcomings tends to be reserved mainly for long-time adversaries or pariahs, such as Syria, Burma or Cuba. Washington has largely exempted such allies as Saudi Arabia, Tunisia, or Ethiopia, while its short-lived pressure on others, such as Egypt or Jordan, has waned. Indeed, the US government is often a major funder of these allied governments despite their repressive practices. This obvious double standard makes the promotion of democracy seem like an act of political convenience rather than a commitment of principle, weakening the pressure for real democratic change.[18]

Perceptions that American democracy promotion was based more on politics than principle were not helped either by Bush's oft-repeated claim that "democracies don't fight each other". Besides being open to challenge on grounds of historical accuracy,[19] this presented a case for democracy in military/security terms rather than as something to be valued in its own right.

Assertions of the freedom principle were further contaminated during the Bush administration by the "war on terror" which provided a smokescreen for repressive measures in the name of combating extremism. The scandal of Abu Ghraib, the US-run prison in Iraq, plus the treatment of detainees in Guantanamo deflected attention from similar abuses by Arab regimes. Describing the Egyptian newspapers' coverage of Abu Ghraib as "nationalist, inflammatory, misinforming and shameless", Hisham Kassem, publisher of the weekly *Cairo Times*, said: "They talk about American monstrosities as if their own governments have never practised anything similar. It's nothing in comparison to what's happening in Arab prisons."[20]

The inevitable result of these conflicting objectives is a lowering of democratic expectations among favoured allies. The Jordanian regime has been one of the beneficiaries of this, Roth noted, "due largely to the US government's fear that Islamists in the country might replicate Hamas's victory in the Occupied Palestinian Territories, but also to Washington's apparent gratitude for Jordan's assistance in fighting terrorism by providing secret detention centres where US-delivered suspects could be tortured." He continued:

> Jordan's municipal elections in July 2007 were reportedly tainted by massive fraud, including soldiers bussed to opposition strongholds to vote for the government, multiple voting, and manipulated voter rolls. Yet both the US ambassador and Congress congratulated Jordanians on the exercise of their democratic rights. Some of these faults were allegedly replicated in parliamentary elections in November, but the US State Department "commend[ed]" the Jordanian government for "ensuring another step has been taken on the country's path of political development." The State Department praised in particular the use of "independent national observers" without noting that, as mentioned, the

government had reneged on its promise to allow them to enter polling places, forcing them to try to observe the proceedings from outside.

The European Union's reaction to the Jordanian elections was no more principled. It issued no known public protest, even though Jordan, as a member of the European Neighbourhood Policy, has signed an Association Agreement with the EU, of which respect for democratic principles and fundamental human rights is supposed to constitute an "essential element" ...

Such unprincipled endorsements suggest that Washington and often the European Union will accept an electoral facade so long as the "victor" is a strategic or commercial ally. The fairness of the vote and the openness of campaign conditions seem to matter less than the political orientation of the democracy pretender.[21]

Another source of conflict between democracy promotion and other aspects of US foreign policy is that free elections do not necessarily bring the happy outcome that the US would like to envisage. Indeed, there is a high probability that they will not: given a free choice for the first time in years, it is scarcely surprising if voters express pent-up resentments against the old regime by voting for radical change. A grim early warning of how this could develop came from the Algerian elections of December 1991 when the Islamic Salvation Front (FIS) won 188 parliamentary seats outright in the first round, and seemed certain to gain an overall majority in the second round. The elections were duly aborted and Algeria then plunged into a long armed conflict which is estimated to have claimed more than 100,000 lives.[22] Saudi Arabia's first tentative foray into electoral politics – with men-only local elections in 2005 – also brought significant victories for Islamist candidates rather than the liberalisers who had been pressing for democracy.[23]

The elections to the Palestinian parliament held in 2006 – the first for ten years – were meant to bolster the position of President Mahmoud Abbas and pave the way for a re-invigorated peace process with Israel. In the event, Abbas's Fatah movement won only 45 of the 132 seats, while the Islamic Resistance Movement, Hamas, unexpectedly secured an absolute majority with 74 seats.[24] The electoral process that delivered this victory to Hamas met international standards – "conducted in a well-organised and democratic fashion, better than seen in some Council of Europe member states," according to one European observer team[25] – but for Israel, the US, the EU and numerous other countries, the outcome was simply unacceptable. A few weeks later, the *New York Times* reported:

> The United States and Israel are discussing ways to destabilise the Palestinian government so that newly-elected Hamas officials will fail and elections will be called again, according to Israeli officials and western diplomats.
>
> The intention is to starve the Palestinian Authority of money and international connections to the point where, some months from now, its president, Mahmoud Abbas, is compelled to call a new election. The hope is that Palestinians will be so unhappy with life under Hamas that they will return to office a reformed and chastened Fatah movement ...
>
> [Officials] say Hamas will be given a choice: recognise Israel's right to exist, forswear violence and accept previous Palestinian-Israeli agreements – as called for by the United Nations and the west – or face isolation and collapse.[26]

More generally, fears of an Islamist takeover play into the hands of autocratic rulers. "Savvy dictators have learned to use a me-or-them logic to justify continued rule," Roth notes. "If an Egyptian seeks an alternative to Mubarak and his ruling National Democratic Party, the Muslim Brotherhood appears to be the only real game in town. That serves Mubarak well, because western acquiescence in his electoral manipulations is more likely ... US pressure for democratisation largely ended with the strong Muslim Brotherhood showing [in the parliamentary elections] of 2005." Although the Brotherhood does have genuine popular support, the solidity of its support is more difficult to judge: suppression of secular opposition by the Mubarak regime (and the Sadat regime before it), plus the difficulty of attacking mosque-based movements that claim to be pious servants of God, has given the Brotherhood an advantage – but one that could prove transient. In any case, it is doubtful whether the Brotherhood could win outright in a free and fair election. In 2005 candidates backed by the Brotherhood won 20 per cent of the parliamentary seats – most of those they contested. However, as John Bradley points out, no more than 25 per cent of the electorate voted, making it almost impossible to gauge the party's overall level of support by extrapolating.[27] Bradley also comments that there is ...

> ... plenty of anecdotal evidence suggesting that many – perhaps the majority – of those who vote for the Islamists do so not because they have any great love for what they stand for ... but in protest at the corruption and brutality of a military regime that has succeeded in crushing all secular alternatives.[28]

Whatever the voters' real motivations, it is possible that elections will bring Islamist parties into government in some Arab countries. This is especially likely if long-standing political constraints are lifted suddenly or where political rights and activities are focused mainly on elections and lack real depth. The need here, Roth suggests, is to ensure that voters "face a meaningful range of political options before marking their ballot", and to "prioritise respect for an array of essential political rights over the balloting itself".[29] Nevertheless, if western powers genuinely want to see democracy established in the region they have no choice but to accept Islamist parties as part of the region's political mix. A report published by the American RAND Corporation said:

> Accepting and engaging Islamist parties (at least those that adhere to nonviolent practices) may not be ideal, given that many hold positions contrary to US interests. But the dominance of Islamist movements in the region, if only because authoritarian governments have not allowed any other alternatives to develop, is a reality in the region that US policy cannot wish away.
>
> Over time, Islamist popularity may erode if they also fail to deliver and respond to basic needs in society, but, at the moment, such movements fill a gap not provided by existing leaderships. To enhance the legitimacy of reform processes in the region, the United States must recognise the role Islamists play and engage such actors.[30]

Aside from the drastic step of invading Iraq, western efforts to promote democracy in the Arab countries at a practical level have generally been more low-key but no less problematic. The Middle East Partnership Initiative (MEPI) was established at the end of 2002 as the "primary diplomatic policy and development programmatic tool" to support President Bush's "forward strategy of freedom"[31] and in apparent homage to the venerable Middle Eastern tradition of nepotism, was initially headed by Vice-President Cheney's daughter, Liz. In the words of the State Department's website, "MEPI is at the forefront of US efforts to advance democratic reform and vibrant, prosperous societies in the Middle East and North Africa. An integral part of US policy, MEPI provides coordinated, tangible support and public commitment to indigenous efforts in the areas of women's empowerment, educational advancement, economic development and political participation." [32]

Although MEPI has funded some worthy projects (and others of more dubious value), its actual contribution towards democracy is at best questionable, and some regard it as fatally ill-conceived. A congressional research report in 2005 commented:

> Critics suggest that MEPI will have little effect in both encouraging political change and countering anti-Americanism in the region. Observers note that MEPI's underlining strategy of funding small-scale projects has proven ineffective in the past when faced with the challenge of reforming closed economies and entrenched state bureaucracies. Other sceptics even suggest that MEPI will only encourage opponents of US policy in the region, who may perceive the programme as an exercise in US imperialism or an imposition of democracy from the west. Some critics of US policy assert that there is an inherent contradiction in US foreign policy in the Middle East, in which the United States advocates liberalisation in the region, while bolstering ties with autocratic regimes with similar strategic interests. Others suggest that no amount of public diplomacy can overcome the Arab perception that the United States is too closely aligned with Israel. [33]

A further problem, according to Thomas Carothers of the Carnegie Endowment for International Peace, was that MEPI had been set up without properly understanding the nature of its task:

> Most US democracy promotion efforts of recent decades that

have been directed at friendly governments ... have taken place in countries where fundamental political change away from dictatorial rule was already under way. In such situations, external democracy promoters seek to facilitate the advance of existing change, not to create it from scratch. This was the case with most of the large wave of democracy-building support to Latin America starting in the 1980s, Eastern Europe after 1989, sub-Saharan Africa from the early 1990s on, and elsewhere. In the Middle East, the United States is not pushing on an open political door. Although some Arab governments have undertaken modest political reforms in recent years, these measures are part of a defensive strategy to defuse pressure from within and abroad for more fundamental change. Pushing on a closed door is much harder.[34]

Despite MEPI's declared intention of supporting Arab civil society groups, a review by the Brookings Institution found that most of its funding in the first two years of operation had gone to the governments it was supposedly trying to change. "More than 70% of MEPI's first $103 million in grants was distributed to programmes that either directly benefited Arab government agencies (in activities ranging from translating documents to computerising schools) or provided training programmes and seminars for Arab government officials (including ministry bureaucrats, parliamentarians, and judges)," the report said.[35] Regardless of its source and its intended purpose, this was money that Arab governments were only too happy to receive. The report continued:

Most Arab leaders recognise that their stagnant social environments and state-dominated economies cannot meet the expectations of their young and increasingly restless populations. Yet most also seek to reform in ways that improve governmental and economic performance without changing the distribution of political power. While a few forward-leaning regimes have placed limited power in the hands of their peoples through constitutional and electoral reforms, many others are trying to create just enough sense of forward motion and participation without power to alleviate the building public pressure for change at the top.

The trouble with this approach, in the words of the Brookings report, is that it can easily end up stifling political change by subsidising Arab governments' efforts "to build a kinder, gentler autocracy". It is not just a problem confined to MEPI; it bedevils all schemes to promote "good governance" in countries where there has not already been significant progress towards genuine democracy.

The amounts disbursed by MEPI are tiny in comparison with the $9 billion a year[36] allocated worldwide through USAID (primarily for economic development and humanitarian relief) and the even greater amounts in military aid. Egypt – a classic "friendly autocracy" – provides an interesting (and expensive) example of aid used for conflicting purposes. After Israel, Egypt was the second-largest recipient of American aid until both were overtaken by Iraq following the removal of Saddam Hussein. Since 1975 Egypt has received well over $50 billion from US taxpayers – money which is "seen as bolstering Egypt's stability, support for US policies in the region, US access to the Suez Canal, and peace with Israel", according to the *Christian Science Monitor*.[37] American aid to Egypt was dramatically increased following the peace treaty with Israel in 1979 and is normally around two-thirds of what Israel receives. This includes $1.3 billion a year in military aid[38] and payments under USAID which totalled $23.4 billion between 1975 and 2006 – the bulk of it ($14.8 billion) under the heading "strengthening the economy".[39] There is reportedly $200 million a year of USAID in cash handouts which the Egyptian government uses more or less as it pleases – though the money is "theoretically conditional upon economic reforms in problem areas such as deregulation, privatisation, and free trade".[40]

Most of this money was intended to promote stability rather than change and, in the short term at least, it has done exactly that; it has cushioned the regime against the greatest domestic threat – the frustrations of the Egyptian people – and has bottled up problems for a later date, without resolving them. Although more than a billion dollars of the aid money was supposedly earmarked for "democracy and governance", it is difficult to see what this has achieved. In the meantime, USAID also helped to fund new presses – the most modern in the country – for the semi-official *al-Ahram* newspaper. As *The Arabist* blog put it: "American taxpayers, you financed the Egyptian *Pravda*!"[41]

"Aid offers an easy way out for Egypt to avoid reform," Edward Walker, a former US ambassador to Cairo told the *Christian Science Monitor*.[42] "They use the money to support antiquated programmes and to resist reforms." In testimony to Congress he also complained that it was unclear what USAID was trying to achieve:

> Frankly ... I don't know what the US objective is. Are we trying to alleviate poverty? Are we trying to build the middle class? Are we fostering upward mobility? Are we trying to improve our image? Are we trying to create jobs, any jobs, or are we trying to create jobs that fulfil expectations? Is our objective 100% literacy and if so why, in a largely subsistence economy? When I look at the aid programme ... I see a Chinese Menu – a little of this and a little of that. I don't see a focused programme and I surely don't see priorities that could make a substantial difference. We should not forget, that what happens in Egypt with about 23% of the total Arab

population in the region, has a profound effect on other Arab countries. If Egypt sincerely embraces reform, it becomes far easier for others to follow in its wake.[43]

GIVEN THE HISTORY of western powers' involvement in the Middle East, it is not surprising that many Arabs view everything the west does with deep suspicion, and that the usual – nationalist and anti-imperialist – response is to say "hands off!" Equally, there are many in the west who cling to old attitudes and assume that "we" must "do something" about the Middle East. Not only is this often counter-productive – intervention can easily have the opposite effect to what was intended – but it also helps to perpetuate the culture of dependence and helplessness among Arabs. It is time for westerners, too, to break free from their history in this respect. Both Arabs and westerners would then have a chance to set their relationship on a more productive footing.

Up to a point the nationalist and anti-imperialist arguments are right: Arabs' problems are mainly Arabs' problems. But they are not exclusively Arabs' problems. In an increasingly interdependent world, as the importance of national sovereignty declines, everyone – to a greater or lesser degree – becomes a stakeholder in their solution: people as well as governments. However, there is a crucial difference between being a stakeholder and dictating the shape of the outcome: western countries can be facilitators for freedom, but they should not try to be its deliverers as well. A good starting point, therefore, is to recognise that the ability of westerners (and especially western governments) to effect positive change in the Middle East is limited and that ill-considered interventions can make matters worse.

In principle Bush was right to highlight freedom, or lack of it, as central to the Middle East's problems, though he overlooked his own country's role in suppressing freedom through proxies. His "forward strategy of freedom" was sadly misdirected too, seeking quick and superficial results – mainly in the form of regime change and free elections but with little regard for the social and political institutions needed to give them solid foundations. Blaming autocratic regimes and talking of sweeping them away also held out the prospect of simple solutions when, in reality, such regimes are as much a symptom of the problem as its cause. Of course, Arab regimes do systematically deny people their rights, imprison people unjustly and torture them, but most of the abuses of rights in the Middle East – at least in terms of the numbers affected and their impact on everyday life – are inflicted by ordinary people upon each other. Discrimination, whether it is based on ethnicity, religion, gender, sexuality or family background, is rife almost everywhere.

The need, therefore, is to assist the development of freedom in depth – personal liberties, respect for human rights, equality of opportunity and so on – which can underpin political and social change as well as helping to drive it forward. Focusing on rights rather than regimes, if done in an even-handed way, is also less likely to be perceived as furthering a foreign political agenda. The key point about human rights is that they apply to everyone, everywhere, without distinction. As fellow members of the human race, we all have a stake in protecting these rights – and that includes doing what we can to support people who are deprived of them, regardless of national boundaries and irrespective of religion or culture.

Considering the difficulty of addressing sensitive issues within the Arab countries themselves, external pressures can, at the very least, play a useful role by highlighting areas where change is needed. Again, this is not a matter for governments alone. Non-governmental organisations and individuals have a role too: grassroots support and solidarity is an important component of creating an untainted transnational impetus for change. One example of this was the sense of east–west solidarity, at a people-to-people level, that became apparent in Arab countries as a result of western protests against the invasion of Iraq.[44]

In order to have credibility, though, efforts to promote freedom in depth must pass the sincerity test, and so western countries have to be seen upholding the values they preach. Among other things, that means no more Guantánamos, no more Abu Ghraibs – and Barack Obama's decision, as one of the first acts of his presidency, to close Guantánamo was certainly a step in the right direction. Perhaps even more significantly for the long term, Obama's election, as an African-American, was a powerful message in itself to people in all those countries where such things seem impossible. Could a Kurd ever become president of Syria, or a Christian president of Egypt? Obama's description of the United States, in his victory speech, as "a place where all things are possible" invited the question: why not the Middle East too?

Passing the sincerity test also requires a balanced approach that does not discriminate between friendly and unfriendly regimes in terms of their political practices or disrespect for human rights and does not make capital out of their abuses in pursuit of other objectives. This means abandoning the old patron–client relationships and replacing them with something more appropriate for an age of interdependence. It is not by any means an easy change to make or one that can be made swiftly but until it happens western efforts to help Arabs achieve their freedom will continue to be undermined by accusations of neo-colonialism and cultural imperialism. People will tend to focus on the messenger and the messenger's history rather than the message itself.

In the meantime, one way to reduce the appearance of singling out friends for special treatment is to look at progress towards democracy, human rights, etc, comparatively – by considering where each country stands in relation to others. This already happens to some extent with the "freedom" ratings produced by Freedom House[45] and Transparency International's Corruption Perceptions Index. A similar example at a governmental level is the US State Department's classification system for human trafficking which divides countries into three categories. In the top tier are those that fully comply with minimum standards for the elimination of trafficking. In the second tier are those that do not fully comply but "are making significant efforts to bring themselves into compliance" and the bottom tier is for those that "neither satisfy the minimum standards nor demonstrate a significant effort to come into compliance". The second tier also includes a watch list of countries "requiring special scrutiny". Countries in the bottom tier may be subjected to certain kinds of sanctions.[46]

Inevitably, league tables of this kind are subjective to some extent because they involve assessment rather than scientific measurement but if the methodology is reasonably transparent and the same benchmarks are used for all countries, they can help to reduce the influence of broader foreign policy considerations. The fourteen countries in the State Department's bottom tier for human trafficking in 2008 (half of them Arab countries) included a number of long-standing allies as well as foes: Algeria, Burma, Cuba, Fiji, Iran, Kuwait, Moldova, North Korea, Oman, Papua New Guinea, Qatar, Saudi Arabia, Sudan and Syria.[47] One benefit of league tables is that they make discrimination by western powers more difficult, since it is easier to see if one country is being let off the hook while another is being victimised for extraneous reasons. There is also some evidence that a poor ranking can induce some countries to improve their performance, especially those that are sensitive about their international image. Qatar, for example, started work on a new law against human trafficking[48] while Saudi Arabia launched an anti-corruption campaign after Transparency International's index showed the kingdom was perceived as far more corrupt than its Gulf neighbours.

In terms of specific things that western governments might do, working harder to achieve an equitable and comprehensive resolution of the Arab–Israeli conflict stands out as the one that could do most to open the doors to progress throughout the Arab world. For more than sixty years this issue has blighted the region and overshadowed the political discourse. It has spawned militant and terrorist groups of almost every hue, from nationalist to Islamist. It has impeded peaceful change and modernisation and has helped to keep authoritarian regimes in power by diverting the attention of Arabs from their internal problems and providing an excuse for failed leaders to survive well beyond their sell-by date.

Without a resolution of the Arab–Israeli conflict, "there will be little chance of dealing with other problems in the Middle East," the European Council noted in its security strategy document.[49] Similarly, the UN-appointed High-Level Group for the Alliance of Civilisations described the Israeli–Palestinian conflict as "a major factor in the widening rift between Muslim and western societies":

> In this regard, it is our duty to express our collective opinion that without a just, dignified, and democratic solution based on the will of all peoples involved in this conflict, all efforts ... to bridge this gap and counter the hostilities among societies are likely to meet with only limited success. Our emphasis on the Israeli–Palestinian conflict is not meant to imply

that it is the overt cause of all tensions between Muslim and western societies. Other factors also create resentment and mistrust ... Nevertheless, it is our view that the Israeli-Palestinian issue has taken on a symbolic value that colours cross-cultural and political relations among adherents of all three major monotheistic faiths well beyond its limited geographic scope.[50]

To anyone who is reasonably familiar with the Arab world and has no particular axe to grind, these are statements of the obvious. It is not just the occupation of the Palestinian territories but the wider effects too: perpetuation of the conflict undoubtedly makes reform in the Arab countries more difficult.

THE ARAB "freedom deficit", as previous chapters have shown, manifests itself in many different ways and many places: from homes, schools and universities to business and politics. The problems of patriarchy, autocracy, intolerance, discrimination, corruption and the suppression of free speech are all linked in that they involve a denial of rights – and denial of *equal* rights in particular. As a first step towards positive change Arabs must recognise that rights are an entitlement, not a privilege to be granted or removed on the whim of a ruler. The second step is to embrace the principle of equal rights. Though much abused in practice, equality is nevertheless widely recognised as desirable and is espoused, in a rather abstract way, by most Arab constitutions. The problem, therefore, is not so much the concept as how to internalise and apply it – which at least provides a starting point for activists to build on. Unlike calls for democracy, demands for equal rights are less tainted by association with the west and are difficult to oppose by rational argument, though some object on religious and traditionalist grounds. Focusing on equal rights thus forces rejectionists on to weak ground, defending the indefensible.

Achieving equal rights is likely to be a piecemeal process that moves forward by addressing specific abuses rather than the generalities. Winning acceptance of the equality principle in one area, even a small one, has a knock-on effect which, over time, becomes cumulative and begins to change attitudes and practices more generally. Tackling the issue of human trafficking, for example, raises questions about how to prevent it – thus also focusing attention on the need for effective laws – as well as questions about other unfair employment practices.

Equal rights cannot exist without freedom of religion. In the Arab countries this is probably the biggest single obstacle to positive change, because religious teaching is so often invoked to justify abuses that cannot be justified by rational argument. Freedom of religion requires a state which is religiously neutral, not only permitting citizens to practise their faith (or not to practise any) according to their own beliefs, but guaranteeing their right to do so. Separation of religion and state is therefore essential to any serious agenda for reform but also, in the short term, very difficult to achieve. The assumption that Arab states have religious responsibilities is so strong that full-scale separation is more likely to be the culmination of other changes rather than their precursor.

One significant chink in the armour of states that claim to protect or promote "Islam" is the diversity of Islamic thought through the ages. What these states actually promote is not "Islam" as such, but a particular interpretation of its teaching – and they can only maintain that position by denying the possibility of alternative interpretations. Thus, the more diversity of opinion within Islam can be highlighted, the weaker their case becomes. At the same time, it is important to distinguish between religious and social traditions – especially forms of abuse practised by people who happen to be Muslims, under the cover of a religious smokescreen.

The influence of religion in Arab countries is undoubtedly strengthened by political repression and poor standards of education. In a less repressive atmosphere, and with a better quality of education, it is likely that people would turn to more enlightened forms of Islam where reason triumphs. In most Arab countries, though, at present and for the foreseeable future, the influence of religion (and particularly dogmatic forms of it) is inescapable – which raises the question of how to respond.

In many societies discussion of social and political change relies mainly on secular arguments. Human rights activists and feminists in most parts of the world have usually shown little interest in religious debate, judging – correctly in most cases – that abuses are social or cultural in origin, even when religion is invoked to justify them. Some are also reluctant to engage in religious argument for fear of bolstering the status of religion at the expense of secular movements and institutions. This broadly applies to the Arab countries too, where the first generation of human rights activists in the 1980s came mainly from a nationalist or leftist background and approached the problem from a secular viewpoint. Similarly, it is noticeable that the four Arab Human Development Reports – produced by reform-minded Arabs under UN auspices – present a wide-ranging critique of the region's problems with little more than a passing nod towards the influence of religion.

In societies where religion is so pervasive at a daily level, however, making a purely secular case for human rights or for social and political change is not a practical option; if such arguments are to carry any weight the religious dimension cannot be ignored, as Kecia Ali has pointed out:

> For the vast majority of Muslims worldwide – not only extremists or conservatives, but also those who consider themselves moderate or progressive – determining whether a particular belief or practice is acceptable largely hinges on deciding whether or not it is legitimately "Islamic". Even many of those who do not base their personal conduct or ideals on normative Islam believe, as a matter of strategy, that in order for social changes to achieve wide acceptance among Muslims they must be convincingly presented as compatible with Islam.

Following the September 11 attacks, the need to engage with religion became more widely recognised, but in ways that were often misguided. Various western leaders sought, as Amartya Sen puts it, to "present a superficially nobler vision" that would woo terrorists away from violence by defining Islam as a religion of peace and tolerance.[51] Sen continues:

> The denial of the necessity of a confrontational reading of Islam is certainly appropriate and extremely important today, and Tony Blair in particular deserves much applause for what he has done in this respect. But in the context of Blair's frequent invoking of "the moderate and true voice of Islam",[52] we have to ask whether it is at all possible – or necessary – to define a "true Muslim" in terms of political and social beliefs about confrontation and tolerance, on which different Muslims have historically taken ... very different positions.[53]

Just as it is futile to counter religious arguments with secular ones and hope that people will be persuaded, so too with statements that lay claim to the "true voice" of Islam. Islamists and religious traditionalists do this all the time. When scholars begin a sentence with the words "Islam says ...", it is a sure sign that some particularly dogmatic statement is about to follow. The point of doing this is to claim a monopoly on rectitude: by asserting that the speaker's view is the correct one and that anyone who disputes it cannot be a good Muslim. Such claims seek to shut down debate rather than open it up. Western anti-Muslim polemics take a similar approach, picking up the most extreme statements – on jihad, for example – and presenting them as representative of Islam as a whole, in order to more easily argue their case. On the other side, liberal Muslims sometimes fall into the same trap, claiming that "real" Islam supports their arguments. In one fairly typical example, a prominent Swedish Muslim, Shaikh Omar Ahmed, announced to an international conference on female circumcision:

> I as Imam would like, with my colleagues, to turn to the Islamic world, particularly in Africa, and inform people that female genital mutilation is prohibited ... It is a matter of abuse and violation of the female body and is quite clearly forbidden according to Islam.[54]

As with many statements of this kind, part of the shaikh's intention, besides condemning the practice, was probably to counter negative stereotypes of Muslims. Kecia Ali comments that although this was undoubtedly well meant, the problem is that the shaikh's claim "to present the definitive Islamic view on what he terms 'female genital mutilation' fits into patterns of modern legal [shari'a] authoritarianism". Claims and counter-claims where scholars declare a practice "Islamic" or "un-Islamic" and expect believers to accept it on the basis of their status within the community do not lead to productive debate but simply reinforce the authoritarian tendencies of current religious teaching.

The question this raises is: who decides whether a particular practice is Islamic or not, and on what basis?

> Is it God, via the literal words of the Qur'an? The Prophet and, secondarily, his Companions, as their statements and actions have been recorded in books of hadith? Should such determinations be based on the judgment of the religiously trained scholars, the *'ulama*, who interpret these sources in works of exegesis and jurisprudence? Or perhaps what is Islamic might be better identified with the actual practice of Muslims rather than any normative ideal. In that case, what happens when practices vary dramatically among Muslims, or when what Muslims do contravenes the authoritative texts? When views have shifted over time, do earlier ideals or practices have more weight or does the contemporary state of affairs take precedence?[55]

Female genital cutting (FGC) – also known as female circumcision and female genital mutilation (FGM) – is one example among many that illustrates the dilemma. It is widely practised in some Muslim countries but not in others; it predates Islam and is also practised by non-Muslims, especially in Africa. It is not mentioned in the Qur'an but is referred to in the hadith. Some scholars say it is obligatory, some say it is forbidden, while others shift the decision away from religion by suggesting it may be carried out for medical reasons (of which there are none). There are disputes too, among those who approve of it, about the amount of cutting that may be permitted or required.

Given all these divergent and often diametrically opposing views, the insistence that Islam forbids FGC, Ali says, "is not so much false as meaningless: it depends entirely on what one intends by the term 'Islam.'" She continues:

> There are solid reasons for Muslims to reject female genital cutting without making grandiose claims about its "un-Islamic" nature, but such an approach requires a willingness to treat not only jurisprudence but also sunnah and hadith as products of their time, with limited currency as formal rules for contemporary application. Thorough and honest discussions of controversial practices such as female genital cutting must move beyond simplistic binaries of "Islamic" and "un-Islamic" or lawful/prohibited to a more complex scheme of ethical and moral valuation.[56]

Clerics can denounce FGC and governments can outlaw it (as some have indeed done) but all that is likely to be futile unless there is a change of public opinion in communities where such practices are the norm. To make any progress in that, religious language has to be employed but the need is not to *refute* religious objections to change as to *challenge* them and ultimately to *neutralise* them; not to counter one supposedly definitive ruling with another saying the opposite but to highlight the diversity of opinion among believing Muslims and the scope for a variety of interpretations. In that way a space is created where people can confront the underlying moral issues and feel free enough to make their own choices.

One Arab human rights organisation that has begun engaging with religion in this way is the Egyptian Initiative for Personal Rights. Its director, Hossam Bahgat, acknowledges that the policy is highly controversial. "Many colleagues in the human rights movement think we're being irresponsible and short-sighted by agreeing to engage with the Islamists on religious ground and that we are contributing to the increase in religious dosage in the public sphere, and giving even more space to the Islamists," he said. "Our experience shows that it is quite the opposite. We don't think it's a luxury, we think it's the only way, especially where the sole argument is a religious one. By ignoring it you are basically forfeiting the fight." He continued:

> We decided to stop ignoring religion and pretending that it doesn't exist, and decided to actively engage with the shari'a arguments that are sometimes brought as justification for certain human rights abuses, in particular with regard to issues of religious freedom, religious discrimination, issues of sexuality and the death penalty – issues where the heart of the opposing argument, or the justification for the abuse, is Islamic law. We realised that we can no longer afford to look the other way and ignore the Islamic law argument supporting the abuse by just stressing the universality of human rights and the principles of equality, justice and freedom.
>
> We needed to do our homework and study shari'a and to argue back when the government or other conservative forces in society quote shari'a arguments against us, and we realised that in some instances we can win.[57]

The EIPR used this approach in its campaign for official recognition of the Baha'i faith in Egypt. "One scholar after another, one government official after another, would insist that under Islam only three religions are allowed – Islam, Christianity and Judaism," Bahgat recalled, "but when we started doing research we realised there is no basis in the Qur'an or the Sunna to support their claim that Muslims may only coexist with 'people of the book' – and we started saying so." The aim, he explained, was to "neutralise religion" by forcing those who used religious arguments to "come clean on what is really behind the abuse, because in many cases religion is brought up only to cover the real reasons behind discrimination

– and the real reasons are usually just bigotry that you can see across religions and across cultures." He continued:

> I was once in a televised debate with the former president of al-Azhar university who was one of the chief jurists of the Islamic Religious Council and we were talking about the Baha'i faith. He started stating the usual position that Islam only allows adherents to the three Abrahamic religions. So I challenged him on this and said: "What's your evidence?"
>
> I think he was stunned. He never expected a human rights activist to start questioning his shari'a argument. He hadn't even bothered to prepare a shari'a argument. I was prepared, so cited all the arguments from shari'a – all the evidence about how the Prophet Muhammad in Madina never discriminated between people of the Book and others who adhered to other faiths – like the Zoroastrians, for example. I cited them one after the other and he couldn't argue with my evidence because my evidence came not from fringe opinions but from major books that are selectively avoided by scholars because they don't give them the cover they want for their bigotry.[58]
>
> So immediately he shifted. He said: "Yes, but they [the Baha'is] have their headquarters in Haifa in Israel and they work against the fabric of our society, their presence is against national unity," etc. The point here is that this senior scholar immediately moved to secular arguments – which is what we want, because they are easier to deal with.

FREEDOM IN DEPTH requires a society of engaged citizens, a society that is confident enough in its own strengths to examine its failings openly and honestly, a society that not only respects equal rights regardless of ethnicity, religion, gender, sexuality or family background, but treasures its diversity, a society where new ideas can be explored without censure or recrimination and opportunities are not stifled by privilege or corruption. No society meets all those requirements all of the time but Arab societies are further from that goal than many. Viewed from where they stand now the task looks daunting, though perhaps more so in Riyadh and Baghdad than in Beirut and Rabat.

This often leads to speculation that something in the nature of Arab societies makes them peculiarly resistant to change. There are clearly many obstacles but the problems themselves are by no means unique: they have all existed at one time or another elsewhere in the world and there are many societies that have succeeded in overcoming them. It is worth remembering that western societies were once patriarchal too and that others, such as India and China, are gradually transforming as modernisation dissolves and dilutes the old ways. The Arab countries are not immune. Seeds of change – even if they are still microscopic in places – are visible almost everywhere, from the disaffected young who dream only of emigrating to the fearful governments that hope against hope to control the internet.

Despite resistance from traditionalists and regression here and there, Arab society is less male-dominated than it was a couple of generations ago; more Arab women are educated and go out to work; an increasing numbers of the urban young value individuality, particularly among the middle classes, while others seek to achieve a more "modern" balance between the demands of the family and the individual. The overall direction of the trend is clear, even if there is still a long way to go. In the midst of this changing reality which has begun to undermine older concepts of the Arab family, efforts to re-embrace social conservatism can be seen as a rearguard action. But it is too late for that: the genie is out of the bottle.

One further indication it that there is certainly more talk of change among Arabs now than there was just a decade ago. Talking of change is not the same as doing it but talk can have a cumulative effect. Underlying that, however, more fundamental processes are at work. Trade, travel and global communications are weakening the influence of nation-states and the power of governments to control what happens within their borders. At the same time, ordinary people are exposed to ideas and ways of doing things that they never knew of before – not because of some imperialist conspiracy to promote them but because they exist and are increasingly accessible. The Arab countries cannot survive in a shell, protected from the rest of the world; even imagining they might do so is futile. Faced with all this, change appears not so much difficult or impossible, but inevitable: the Arab countries cannot carry on as they are, simply because the status quo has become unsustainable.

The question, really, is not *whether* change will occur but *how long* it will take. Years? Decades? Centuries? Given a choice, there is little doubt that most Arabs would prefer to do it slowly, with as little upheaval and turmoil as possible. The Saudis in particular seem set on that but it is not the only scenario, nor is it necessarily the most likely one. Developments elsewhere in the world may force the pace, and change, even if it starts gradually, has a tendency to gather momentum, which could lead to a comparatively rapid paradigm shift. For those with a vested interest in the status quo, a reform here and a reform there, carried out at leisure, may seem the more attractive proposition, but it is difficult to isolate reforms, one from another, because the principles they are based on – fairness, equality and so forth – are often the same. The key lies in winning acceptance for these basic principles. The west's own experience shows that the most enduring change comes from within – from the disaffected masses or visionary individuals who inspire others to see a different future. The Arab world is no exception and needs to find its own way, albeit with a little help from its friends.

Notes

Introduction

1. Doha Debates: 'This House believes that Arab governments are not interested in genuine reform'. 13 October 2004. http://www.thedohadebates.com/debates/debate.asp?d=31&s=1&mode=transcript.
2. Kassir, Samir: *Being Arab.* London: Verso, 2006. p. 4.
3. *Nakba* ("catastrophe") is the term used by Arabs for the displacement and dispossession of Palestinians when Israel was created.
4. Statement by Condoleezza Rice to the Senate Foreign Relations Committee, 18 January 2005. http://foreign.senate.gov/testimony/2005/RiceTestimony050118.pdf.

Chapter 1

1. Author's interview in Cairo, June 2008. Mounir is not his real name.
2. Author's interview in Cairo, 26 April 2008.
3. Arab Human Development Report (AHDR) 2003: 'Building a knowledge society.' New York: United Nations Development Programme, 2003. p. 3.
4. AHDR 2003. pp. 53–54.
5. Arab Human Development Report (AHDR) 2004: 'Towards freedom in the Arab world.' New York: United Nations Development Programme, 2005. p. 147.
6. *The Road Not Traveled: Education Reform in the Middle East and North Africa.* Washington: International Bank for Reconstruction and Development / The World Bank, 2008. p. 88. http://siteresources.worldbank.org/INTMENA/Resources/EDU_Flagship_Full_ENG.pdf.
7. Valverde, G, *et al:* 'An exploratory analysis of the content and expectations for student performance in selected mathematics and biology school-leaving examinations from the Middle East and North Africa.' Paper prepared for the World Bank, 1995.

8. *The Road Not Traveled.* p. 89.
9. This problem was was described to me by a senior education official in Egypt.
10. Author's interview in Paris, 1 February 2009. For a report of the suicide see: 'Suicide d'une femme à Mohammedia avec ces trois filles' Casafree.com, 20 November 2008 (in French). http://www.casafree.com/modules/newbb/ viewtopic.php?topic_id=30266&forum=13. Morocco had recently introduced a new law intended to discourage polygamy which required husbands to obtain permission from their first wife before marrying another, and this case highlighted the limited effectiveness of the law. See: 'New law limits polygamy, says expert.' Adnkronos International. 27 May, 2008. http://europenews.dk/en/node/10519.
11. Arab Human Development Report (AHDR) 2002: 'Creating opportunities for future generations.' New York: United Nations Development Programme, 2002. p. 3.
12. 'Education for girls.' Saudi Ministry of Education website. Retrieved 16 November 2008. http://www.moe.gov.sa/openshare/englishcon/ About-Saud/Education6.htm_cvt.html#Table.
13. AHDR 2002. p. 94.
14. *The Road Not Traveled.* p. 138.
15. Collelo, Thomas (ed.): *Syria: A Country Study.* Washington: Library of Congress, 1987. http://countrystudies.us/syria/37.htm.
16. Basic Law, 1992. Article 13. http://www.servat.unibe.ch/law/icl/ sa00000_.html.
17. AHDR 2003. p. 53.
18. Miller, Gerald: 'Classroom 19: A study in behaviour in a classroom of a Moroccan primary school,' in Brown, Carl and Itkowitz, Norman (eds): *Psychological Dimensions of Near Eastern Studies.* Princeton, NJ: Darwin Press, 1977. pp. 142–153. Cited by Pollack, Kenneth: 'Arab culture and Arab military performance: tracing the transmission mechanism.' Paper presented at the Ideas, Culture and Political Analysis Workshop, Princeton University, May 15–16 1998. http://www.ciaonet.org/conf/ ssro1/ssro1af.html.
19. Author's interview in Cairo, 27 June 2008.
20. Metz, Helen Chapin (ed.): *Saudi Arabia: A Country Study.* Washington: Library of Congress, 1992. http://countrystudies.us/saudi-arabia/31. htm.
21. Abdulkareem, Saleh al-: 'Education development in Saudi Arabia.'

Retrieved 17 November 2008. http://faculty.ksu.edu.sa/25384/ Researches%20and%20Studies%20in%20English/Summary%20of%20 Education%20Development%20in%20Saudi%20Arabia-Historical%20 Project.doc.

22. 'Kuwait disowns Bin Laden aide.' BBC website, 14 October, 2001. http:// news.bbc.co.uk/1/hi/world/middle_east/1599088.stm.

23. Author's interview with Bishara and Mubarak, Kuwait, March 2002.

24. Landis, Joshua: 'Islamic education in Syria: undoing secularism.' Paper prepared for 'Constructs of Inclusion and Exclusion: Religion and Identity Formation in Middle Eastern School Curricula.' Watson Institute for International Studies, Brown University, November 2003. http:// faculty-staff.ou.edu/L/Joshua.M.Landis-1/Islamic%20Education%20 in%20Syria.htm.

25. *International Religious Freedom Report 2008: Syria.* US State Department Bureau of Democracy, Human Rights, and Labor, 2008. http://www. state.gov/g/drl/rls/irf/2008/108493.htm.

26. 'Islamic education' grade 12 textbook, p. 149. Cited by Landis, *op. cit.*

27. 'Islamic education' grade 12 textbook, p. 150. Cited by Landis, *op. cit.*

28. Landis comments: "To Syria's credit, it must be stated, that no other Arab country, as far as I can tell, expressly states in its Islamic classes that Christians will go to heaven. Saudi Arabia, by contrast, condemns Christians to damnation and categorises them as unbelievers (kuffar)."

29. 'Islamic education' grade 9 textbook, pp. 66–67. It is likely that these views of Jews are coloured to some extent by the political situation. Recovering the Golan Heights, occupied by Israel since 1967, is one of the main planks of the regime's policy. The two countries are still notionally at war and this undoubtedly has some bearing on the way Jews are presented in school textbooks. Landis points out that although some Syrians are careful to draw a distinction between Zionism and Jews, this is not a distinction made in Syria's school texts. For example, the tenth-grade textbook says: "The Jews took advantage of Muhammad's forgiveness in the old days. They exploited his forgiveness in order to deceive the Muslims and this is a characteristic of traitors and betrayers in every time and place. This is an indication of the evil enemy characteristics that are imbedded in the personality of the Jews. This confirms that it is dangerous to live with or near them. This danger threatens the existence of the Arab and Islamic world with destruction and disappearance." (Grade 10, p. 78) However, Landis notes that the fifth grade textbook, newly written in

2001, "discusses the Jews, their prophets, and the Torah in a respectful manner (Grade 5, p. 20). It contains three chapters on the prophet Moses, which describe how he helped his people (banu Isra'il) escape from Pharaoh's Egypt and which stress how Muslims must have faith in all the prophets equally without discriminating between them (Grade 5, p. 59)." Interestingly, though the Jews are portrayed as an oppressed people, the book does not mention that Moses was delivering them to the "Promised Land".

30. *The Road Not Traveled.* pp. 84–85.

31. AHDR 2003. p. 163.

32. AHDR 2003. p. 70.

33. AHDR 2003. pp. 70–71.

34. McGann, James: 'The global "go-to think tanks".' Think Tanks and Civil Societies Programme, Foreign Policy Research Institute, Philadelphia. 2007. http://fpri.org/research/thinktanks/mcgann.globalgotothinktanks. pdf. As part of this study, a large panel of experts identified 228 "leading" think tanks from around the world, of which twelve were in Arab countries: Al-Ahram Centre for Political and Strategic Studies (Egypt), Arab Reform Forum at the Bibliotheca Alexandrina (Egypt), Centre d'Etudes et de Recherches en Sciences Sociales (Morocco), Centre for Strategic and Future Studies (Kuwait), Centre for Strategic Studies (Jordan), Centre for Sudanese Studies (Sudan), Emirates Centre for Strategic Studies and Research (UAE), Gulf Research Centre (UAE), Gulf Strategic Studies Institute (UAE), King Faisal Centre for Research and Islamic Studies (Saudi Arabia), Palestinian Centre for Policy and Survey Research (West Bank), The Lebanese Centre for Policy Studies (Lebanon).

35. Based on McGann 2007, with population figures as in the table of internet use in Chapter 4 of this book.

36. AHDR 2003. p. 56.

37. AHDR 2003. Table 3.2, p. 73.

38. Levy, Frank, and Murnane Richard: *The New Division of Labor: How Computers Are Creating the Next Job Market.* Princeton: Princeton University Press and the Russell Sage Foundation. 2004. Cited in *The Road Not Traveled.* pp. 86–87.

39. *The Road Not Traveled.* p. 87. This is not to suggest that the need for routine tasks will disappear but that businesses which manage knowledge

well will be generally more productive, with consequent benefits for the whole workforce.

40. *'Man Nahnu'* ('Who we are'). Capmas website in Arabic, retrieved 26 November 2008. http://www.msrintranet.capmas.gov.eg/pls/fdl/frm202?lang=1&lname=0.

41. 'About Us.' Capmas website in English. Retrieved 26 November 2008. http://www.msrintranet.capmas.gov.eg/pls/fdl/frm_capmse?lang=0&lname=.

42. *Reading between the 'red lines': the repression of academic freedom in Egyptian universities.* Human Rights Watch, June 2005. http://www.hrw.org/en/reports/2005/06/08/reading-between-red-lines-repression-academic-freedom-egyptian-universities.

43. Ibid.

44. Whitaker, Brian: 'Polls apart.' *Guardian* website, 4 March 2002. http://www.guardian.co.uk/Archive/Article/0,4273,4367628,00.html.

45. *Muqaddima li Dirasat al-Mujtama al-Arabi,* published in 1975.

46. Author's interview in Amman, 6 July 2008.

47. AHDR 2003. p. 74.

48. AHDR 2003. p. 75.

49. *The Effect of Islamic Legislation on Crime Prevention in Saudi Arabia.* Proceedings of the symposium held in Riyadh, 16–21 Shawal 1396 AH. Crime Prevention Research Centre, Ministry of Interior, 1980. pp. 531–535.

50. Quoted by Iqbal, Muzaffar: *Science and Islam.* Westport, CT: Greenwood Publishing, 2007. p. 157.

51. Ziadat, Adel: *Western Science in the Arab World: The Impact of Darwinism, 1860–1930.* London: Macmillan, 1986, p. 94 Quoted in 'Muslim Responses to Darwinism.' *Islam Herald* website. Retrieved 27 November 2008. http://www.islamherald.com/asp/curious/evolution/muz/muz-part3.asp.

52. 'Darwin's theory of evolution in Sudan.' Undated web page, retrieved 27 November 2008. http://www.thefileroom.org/documents/dyn/DisplayCase.cfm/id/189.

53. Shanavas, T O: *Evolution and/or Creation: An Islamic Perspective.* Philadelphia: Xlibris Corporation, 2005.

54. Majid, Abdul: 'The Muslim responses to evolution.' Islamic Research Foundation International. Retrieved 27 November 2008. http://www.irfi.org/articles/articles_151_200/muslim_responses_to_evolution.htm.

55. At the beginning of 2009 IslamOnline's internet traffic placed it among the top 200 sites in Yemen, Sudan, Algeria, Jordan, Morocco, Egypt and Saudi Arabia. It was among the top 400 sites in Qatar, Libya, Oman, Syria, Kuwait, the UAE and Iraq. http://www.alexa.com/data/details/traffic_details/islamonline.net.

56. 'Darwinism from an Islamic perspective.' IslamOnline. Retrieved 27 November 2008. http://www.islamonline.net/servlet/Satellite?pagename=IslamOnline-English-Ask_Scholar/FatwaE/FatwaE&cid=1119503543966.

57. 'Darwin's theory of evolution in Sudan.' Undated web page, retrieved 27 November 2008. http://www.thefileroom.org/documents/dyn/DisplayCase.cfm/id/189.

58. Campbell, Duncan: 'Academics fight rise of creationism at universities.' *Guardian*, 21 February 2006. http://www.guardian.co.uk/world/2006/feb/21/religion.highereducation.

59. Birch, Nicholas: 'Turkey: scientists face off against creationists.' Eurasianet.org, 24 May 2007. http://www.eurasianet.org/departments/insight/articles/eav052407.shtml.

60. *Atlas of Creation.* Available online at: http://www.harunyahya.com/books/darwinism/atlas_creation/atlas_creation_01.php.

61. For example, in 2004 a group of Muslim students in biomedical sciences at the Vrije Universiteit in Amsterdam were reported to have uncritically copied text from "Islamic creationist" websites for an essay assignment on "Man and evolution". See: Koning, Danielle: 'Anti-evolutionism among Muslim students.' *ISIM Review,* Autumn 2006. http://www.isim.nl/files/Review_18/Review_18-48.pdf.

62. Edis, Taner: 'Cloning Creationism in Turkey.' Reports of the National Center for Science Education, vol. 19, no. 6, pp. 30–35, Nov–Dec 1999.

63. See, for example, Rafiq, Amjad: 'The Qur'an and modern science.' Islam 101 website. Retrieved 27 November 2008. http://www.islam101.com/science/qur'an_sc_tv.html.

64. Qur'an 18:90, Al-Kahf (Pickthall's translation): "Till, when he reached the rising-place of the sun, he found it rising on a people for whom We had appointed no shelter therefrom." See also Salmawi, Ashraf: 'Life on Earth.' Submission.org website. Retrieved 27 November 2008. http://www.submission.org/life.html.

65. Qur'an 21:30, Al-Anbiya (Pickthall's translation): "Have not those who disbelieve known that the heavens and the earth were of one piece, then

We parted them, and we made every living thing of water? Will they not then believe?"

66. Qur'an 6:2, Al-Anaam (Pickthall's translation): "He it is Who hath created you from clay, and hath decreed a term for you. A term is fixed with Him. Yet still ye doubt!"

67. Qur'an 71:14, Nuh (Pickthall's translation): "When He created you by (divers) stages?"

68. Charfi, Farida Faouzia: 'When Galileo meets Allah.' *New Perspectives Quarterly,* Winter 2002. http://www.digitalnpq.org/archive/2002_winter/charfi.html.

69. Koning. *op. cit.*

70. Hassab-Elnaby, Mansour: 'A new astronomical Qur'anic method for the determination of the greatest speed C.' IslamiCity website. http://www.islamicity.com/Science/960703A.SHTML. Retrieved 26 Janaury 2009.

71. Charfi, *op. cit.*

Chapter 2

1. Barakat, Halim: *The Arab World: Society, Culture and State.* Berkeley and Los Angeles: University of California Press, 1993. p. 118.

2. Email correspondence with the author.

3. Aisha is a pseudonym. Author's interview, May 2008.

4. Whitaker, Brian: 'Censor sensibility.' *Guardian,* 19 May 2003. http://www.guardian.co.uk/technology/2003/may/19/comment.worlddispatch.

5. Hofheinz, Albrecht: 'Arab internet use: popular trends and public impact', in Sakr, Naomi (ed): *Arab Media and Political Renewal.* London: I B Tauris, 2007. p. 57.

6. Barakat, *op. cit.* pp. 100–101.

7. AHDR 2004. p.146.

8. Barakat, *op. cit.* pp. 101–102.

9. Author's interview in Cairo, 26 June 2008.

10. Barakat, *op. cit.* p. 117. An interesting case of the God/ruler imagery is the Moroccan "trinity" where stones are laid out on hillsides to spell "*Allah, al-watan, al-malik*" (God, homeland, king) in a triangular shape with God at the apex.

11. Sharabi, Hisham: *Neopatriarchy: A Theory of Distorted Change in Arab Society.* Oxford: Oxford University Press, 1988. p. 7.

12. Cunningham, Robert and Sarayrah, Yasin: *Wasta: The Hidden Force in Middle Eastern Society*. Westport, Connecticut: Praeger, 1993. p. 2.

13. Author's interview, 14 May 2008. Salam Pax came to international attention with his chronicle of life in Baghdad before, during and immediately after the overthrow of Saddam Hussein. His blog was later published in book form: *The Baghdad Blog*. London: Atlantic Books, 2003. Also published in the US as *The Clandestine Diary of an Ordinary Iraqi*. New York: Grove Press, 2003.

14. Author's interview in Paris, 1 February 2009.

15. For a comparative discussion of care of the elderly in Arab and western countries see Malik, Nesrine: 'What shall we do with grandad?' Comment Is Free, 19 November 2008. http://www.guardian.co.uk/commentisfree/2008/nov/19/socialcare-family.

16. 'Naturally, She's an Extension of Myself!' Question and answer, IslamOnline. http://www.islamonline.net/servlet/Satellite?cid=1175008866280&pagename=IslamOnline-English-Parent_Counsel%2FParentCounselE%2FPrintParentCounselE.

17. See, for example, 'Live Dialogue'. IslamOnline, 25 June 2005. http://www.islamonline.net/LiveDialogue/English/Browse.asp?hGuestID=190glN#.

18. Barakat, *op. cit.* p. 24.

19. Allen, Mark: *Arabs*. London and New York: Continuum, 2006. pp. 44–45.

20. Sharabi, op. cit. pp. 30–31.

21. Sharabi identifies five kinship categories: nuclear family (usrah), extended family (a'ilah), clan or lineage (hamulah), subtribe (ashira) and tribe (qabilah). Sharabi, *op. cit.* p. 31.

22. Ahmed is a pseudonym, Author's interview, February 2008.

23. Allen, *op. cit.* pp. 46–47.

24. Peteet, Julie: 'Male gender and rituals of resistance in the Palestinian intifada: a cultural politics of violence.' In Ghoussoub, Mai and Emma Sinclair-Webb: *Imagined Masculinities: Male Identity and Culture in the Modern Middle East*. London, Saqi Books: 2000. pp. 109–110.

25. Having a family member who is known to be gay can also affect the marriage prospects of siblings. A young man from a prosperous and respectable Palestinian family who has lived in the United States for many years described to me his problem: "Of course, my family can see that I'm not macho like my younger brother. They know that I'm

sensitive, that I'm effeminate and I don't like sport. They accept all that, but I cannot tell them that I'm gay. If I did, my sisters would never be able to marry, because we would not be a respectable family any more." Whitaker, Brian: *Unspeakable Love: Gay and Lesbian Life in the Middle East*. London: Saqi Books, 2006. p. 27.

26.   Comment by 'Ieuan' (No. 991686) in 'Party time', Comment Is Free, 14 December 2007. http://www.guardian.co.uk/commentisfree/2007/dec/14/partytime?commentid=0fb85645-d270-4c68-be3b-69ea5461d488.

27.   Bahgat, Hossam and Afifi, Wesal: 'Sexuality Politics in Egypt', in Parker, R, Petchesky, R and Sember, R (eds): *SexPolitics – Reports from the Front Lines* (e-book). Sexuality Policy Watch, 2007. http://www.sxpolitics. org/frontlines/book/pdf/capitulo2_egypt.pdf.

28.   Sharp, Heather: 'Cairo youth break sex taboos.' BBC, 25 December 2005. http://news.bbc.co.uk/1/hi/world/middle_east/4708461.stm.

29.   Kandela, P: 'Egypt's trade in hymen repair.' *Lancet*, vol. 347, issue 9015, June 1996. p. 1615.

30.   Sharp, *op. cit.*

31.   Shahine, Gihan: 'Illegitimate, illegal or just ill-advised?' *Al-Ahram Weekly*, issue 417, 18–24 February 1999. http://weekly.ahram.org.eg/1999/417/li1.htm.

32.   Ibid.

33.   Lutfi, L: 'Atfaal bila Wujood ... wa-Nisaa Yahmilna al-Sakhr' (Children with no presence ... and women carrying heavy weights). *New Woman Publication*, no. 16, December 2005, pp. 18–19. Cited by Bahgat and Afifi, *op. cit.*

34.   Bahgat and Afifi. *op. cit.*

35.   Rashad, Hoda *et al*: 'Marriage in the Arab world.' Washington: Population Reference Bureau, 2005. http://www.prb.org/pdf05/MarriageInArabWorld_Eng.pdf.

36.   Complaints of brides' families demanding excessive dowries are common, particularly in the more traditional Arab societies. In 2008 a $50,000 dowry was reported in Yemen. See: Kholidy, Majed Thabet al-: 'Do you believe a $50,000 dowry?' *Yemen Times*, 28 February 2008. http://www.yementimes.com/article.shtml?i=1133&p=community&a=3.

37.   Diane Singerman and Barbara Ibrahim, 'The cost of marriage in Egypt: A hidden variable in the new Arab demography,' in the *New Arab Family*,

Cairo Papers in Social Science 24 (2001). Cairo: American University in Cairo Press, 2003, p. 106.

38. 'Why should I marry?' http://www.inter-islam.org/Lifestyle/marry. htm#Mastb.

39. Whitaker, Brian: 'Making sure the young can marry.' *Guardian* website, 8 September 2000. http://www.guardian.co.uk/Archive/ Article/0,4273,4061057,00.html.

40. 'Young Saudis beat inflation via group weddings.' Reut-ers, 25 June 2008. http://economictimes.indiatimes.com/Young_Saudis_beat_ inflation_via_group_weddings/articleshow/3165091.cms.

41. In 2006 the Jeddah-based Islamic Fiqh Academy, an affiliate of the Organisation of the Islamic Conference, issued a *fatwa* declaring *misyar* marriages valid. See: Hakeem, Mariam al-: '*Misyar* marriages gain popularity among Saudis.' *Gulf News*, 25 May 2006. http://archive. gulfnews.com/articles/06/05/25/10042261.html. In the opinion of Yusuf al-Qaradawi, the prominent Qatar-based scholar, *misyar* marriages are "Islamically valid" but their social acceptability is questionable. See: 'Misyar marriage.' IslamOnline fatwa bank, 6 July 2006. http://www. islamonline.net/servlet/Satellite?pagename=IslamOnline-English-Ask_ Scholar/FatwaE/FatwaE&cid=1119503544160. In Shi'i Islam, *mut'ah* marriage has a similar social function to *misyar*, though the nature of the contract is different. *Mut'ah* is essentially a fixed-term marriage which is automatically dissolved when the time limit expires, without the need for divorce.

42. Jabarti, Somayya: 'Misyar marriage – a marvel or misery?' *Arab News*, 5 June 2005. http://www.arabnews.com/?page=9&section=0&article= 64891.

43. Rashad, Hoda, *et al., op. cit.*

44. Ibid.

45. Jabar, Faleh and Dawod, Hosham (eds): *Tribes and Power: Nationalism and Ethnicity in the Middle East.* London: Saqi, 2003. pp. 7–8.

46. Author's interview, 14 May 2008.

47. Khatib, Jamal: *'Ala Madhbah al-Hukm.* Amman: Dar Majdalawi, 2008.

48. The Quraysh were the dominant tribe of Mecca at the time of the Prophet's birth, and included numerous clans.

49. Author's interview in Amman, 6 July 2008.

50. AHDR 2004. pp. 145–146.

51. AHDR 2004. p. 17.
52. AHDR 2004. pp. 145–146.

Chapter 3

1. Author's interview in Beirut, 17 July 2008.
2. Author's interview, 26 April 2008.
3. AHDR 2004. p. 129.
4. The Moroccan king, for instance, is officially described as "the protector of the rights and liberties of the citizens"; he "guarantees the independence of the nation and the territorial integrity of the kingdom". See: 'Le Roi.' Official website (in French). http://www.royal-maroc.net/index.php?/famille/informations/le-roi/id-menu-38.cfm.
5. The current king, Abdullah, has made a particular point of this, preferring to be addressed by his religious title rather than "your majesty". See: Whitaker, Brian: 'Straightforward is the word most often used to describe him, but it is not always meant as a compliment.' *Guardian*, 24 March 2006. http://www.guardian.co.uk/world/2006/mar/24/saudiarabia.brianwhitaker.
6. 'King Abdullah.' Royal Hashemite Court website. http://www.kingabdullah.jo/main.php?main_page=0&lang_hmka1=1.
7. Saudi Basic Law, article 5(b). http://www.servat.unibe.ch/icl/sa00000_.html
8. See: Herb, Michael: *All in the Family: Absolutism, Revolution, and Democracy in the Middle Eastern Monarchies*. Albany: State University of New York, 1999.
9. Constitution of Oman, 1996. Article 6. http://www.servat.unibe.ch/law/icl/mu00000_.html
10. For an English translation of the letter see http://www.al-bab.com/arab/docs/jordan/hussein99.htm.
11. Constitution of Morocco (1996), Article 20. http://www.al-bab.com/maroc/gov/con96.htm.
12. Saudi Basic Law, article 6. http://www.servat.unibe.ch/icl/sa00000_.html.
13. Herb, *op. cit.*
14. Herb, *op. cit.* pp. 36–37.
15. Whitaker, Brian: 'Kuwait mourns after emir dies.' *Guardian*, 16 January

2006. http://www.guardian.co.uk/world/2006/jan/16/brianwhitaker. mainsection.

16. Whitaker, Brian: 'Kuwaiti paper calls for ruler to step down.' *Guardian*, 21 January, 2006. http://www.guardian.co.uk/world/2006/jan/21/ brianwhitaker.mainsection.

17. He died just over two years later, on 13 May 2008.

18. Constitution of Kuwait, article 60. http://www.servat.unibe.ch/law/ icl/ku00000_.html.

19. Whitaker, Brian: 'Royal hush.' *Guardian*, 23 January 2006. http://www. guardian.co.uk/world/2006/jan/23/worlddispatch.brianwhitaker.

20. Whitaker, Brian: 'Kuwaiti MPs declare emir unfit for office.' *Guardian*, 25 January 2006. http://www.guardian.co.uk/world/2006/jan/25/ brianwhitaker.mainsection.

21. Sturcke, James: 'New "Bin Laden" tape posted on website.' *Guardian*, 16 December 2004. http://www.guardian.co.uk/world/2004/dec/16/ alqaida.saudiarabia1.

22. Zambelis, Chris: 'Morocco cracks down on Islamist opposition group JSA.' *Terrorism Focus*, Vol. 3, 22 (June 2006). http://www.jamestown. org/single/?no_cache=1&tx_ttnews%5Btt_news%5D=811.

23. Author's interview in Riyadh, December 2005.

24. AHDR 2004. p. 129.

25. Kuran, Timur: 'The vulnerability of the Arab State.' *The Independent Review*, vol. III, no. 1, Summer 1998, pp. 111–123. http://www.independent. org/pdf/tir/tir_03_1_kuran.pdf.

26. Lebanon is the most notable exception because of the power-sharing system established after the civil war.

27. I have often heard this said of both Saddam Hussein and Hosni Mubarak. Saddam was widely admired for standing up to the Americans. Mubarak was a bomber pilot who rose to become an Air Chief Marshal.

28. Concise Oxford Dictionary.

29. Adams, Julia: 'The rule of the father: patriarchy and patrimonialism in early modern Europe,' pp. 237–266. In Camic C, Gorski PS and Trubek DM (eds): *Max Weber's Economy and Society: A Critical Companion*. Stanford, California: Stanford University Press, 2005. http://research. yale.edu/sociology/faculty/docs/adams/adams_ruleFather.pdf.

30. Ibid.

31. 'Chiefs of State and Cabinet Members of Foreign Governments.' CIA

online directory. https://www.cia.gov/library/publications/world-leaders-1/. Retrieved 27 January 2009.

32. Schlumberger, Oliver: 'Statehood and governance: Challenges in the Middle East and North Africa.' Briefing Paper 4/2007. Bonn: German Development Institute (Deutsches Institut für Entwicklungspolitik), 2007. http://www.die-gdi.de/CMS-Homepage/openwebcms3_e.nsf/(ynDK_contentByKey)/ADMR-7BMJHX/$FILE/4%202007%20EN.pdf.

33. Novak, Jane: 'Ali Abdullah Saleh family in Yemen govt and business.' *Armies of Liberation* blog, 8 April 2006. http://armiesofliberation.com/archives/2006/04/08/ali-abdullah-saleh-family-in-yemen-govt-and-business/.

34. Adams, *op. cit.*

35. Quoted by Jonathon Gatehouse: 'Syria's next trick: a bargain for power.' *Macleans* magazine, 3 August 2006. http://www.macleans.ca/world/global/article.jsp?content=20060814_131615_131615.

36. Quimpo, Nathan Gilbert: 'Trapo parties and corruption', *KASAMA* vol. 21, no. 1, January–February–March 2007. http://cpcabrisbane.org/Kasama/2007/V21n1/TrapoPartiesAndCorruption.htm.

37. Quoted in 'The unlovable Saudis'. Undated article on *Guardian* website. http://www.guardian.co.uk/baefiles/page/0,,2095803,00.html. Two pages of the document are reproduced at: http://image.guardian.co.uk/sys-files/Guardian/documents/2007/05/29/ch04doc01.pdf.

38. Author's interview in Damascus, October 2003. See: Whitaker, Brian: 'Syrian whispers'. Guardian Unlimited, 28 October, 2003. http://www.guardian.co.uk/world/2003/oct/28/syria.worlddispatch.

39. 'Rami Makhluf designated for benefiting from Syrian corruption.' US Treasury statement HP-834, 21 February 2008. http://www.treas.gov/press/releases/hp834.htm.

40. Author's interview in Cairo, 30 June 2008.

41. Blanford, Nicholas: *Killing Mr Lebanon*. London: I B Tauris, 2006. pp. 60–61.

42. Ibid. p. 61.

43. Ibid. p. 44.

44. For details of these, and other criticisms, see: Ohrstrom, Lysandra: 'Solidere: "Vigilantism under color of law".' *Daily Star*, 6 August 2007. http://www.dailystar.com.lb/article.asp?edition_id=1&categ_id=25&article_id=84354.

45. AHDR 2004. p. 152. The AHDR's figures for European taxation appear to be wrong. See: 'Taxation trends in the EU'. Eurostat news release 89/2007. http://epp.eurostat.ec.europa.eu/pls/portal/docs/page/pgp_prd_cat_prerel/pge_cat_prerel_year_2007/pge_cat_prerel_year_2007_month_06/2-26062007-en-ap.pdf.

46. Arab Monetary Fund: *Al-Taqrir al-Iqtisadi al-'Arabi al-Muwahhad* (Joint Arab Economic Report 2007). Chapter 6, appendix 2. In Arabic. http://www.amf.org.ae/amf/website/Weblisher/Storage/Uploads/Docs/ECONOMIC%20DEPT/JOINT%20REPORT%202007/CHPTR-6.pdf.

47. Ibid.

48. AHDR 2004. pp. 152–3.

49. The Qatar Foundation is a non-profit educational organisation founded by the emir and chaired by his wife, Sheikha Mozah. http://www.qf.org.qa/.

50. Doha Debate: 'This House believes that oil has been more of a curse than a blessing for the Middle East.' 15 November 2005. http://www.thedohadebates.com/debates/debate.asp?d=23&s=2&mode=transcript.

51. For a detailed study of rentier states in an Arab context see Beblawi, Hazem: *The Rentier State in the Arab World*. London, Routledge 1987 and Berkeley: University of California Press, 1990.

52. Smith, Benjamin: 'Oil wealth and regime survival in the developing world: 1960–1999.' *American Journal of Political Science,* 48:2 (2004), pp. 232–246.

53. For a more sceptical view of the negative connection between rents and democracy see Herb, Michael: 'No representation without taxation? Rents, development and democracy.' Georgia State University, 2003. http://www2.gsu.edu/~polmfh/herb_rentier_state.pdf.

54. Smith, *op. cit.*

55. Burkeman, Oliver: 'America signals withdrawal of troops from Saudi Arabia.' *Guardian*, 30 April 2003. http://www.guardian.co.uk/world/2003/apr/30/usa.iraq.

56. Whitaker, Brian: 'Saudis tiptoe to democracy.' *Middle East International*, 18 February 2005. http://www.al-bab.com/yemen/artic/mei108.htm.

57. 'National Dialogue chief says no boundaries in forums.' Saudi-US Relations Information Service, 26 April, 2007. http://www.saudi-us-relations.org/articles/2007/ioi/070426-national-dialogue.html.

58. http://www.al-bab.com/arab/docs/reform/alex2004.htm.

59. http://www.al-bab.com/arab/docs/reform/sanaa2004.htm.

60. http://www.al-bab.com/arab/docs/reform/doha2004.htm.

61. http://www.weforum.org/pdf/ABC/ABC_R1.pdf.

62. 'Muslim Brotherhood submits own initiative for reform.' IslamOnline, 4 March 2004. http://www.islamonline.net/English/News/2004-03/04/article04.shtml.

63. Opening speech by President Hosni Mubarak to the Arab reform conference in Alexandria, Egypt, 12 March 2004. http://www.al-bab.com/arab/docs/reform/mubarak2004.htm.

64. Yacoubian, Mona: 'Promoting Middle East Democracy II, Arab Initiatives.' *Special Report 136*, United States Institute of Peace, May 2005. http://www.usip.org/pubs/specialreports/sr136.html. The USIP is a non-partisan American organisation funded by Congress.

65. Ibid.

66. Speech by President George Bush to mark the twentieth anniversary of the National Endowment for Democracy, in Washington on 6 November 2003. http://www.al-bab.com/arab/docs/reform/bush2003.htm.

67. Lush, Julian: 'Emerging Democracies Forum.' *British Yemeni Society Journal*, 1999. http://www.al-bab.com/bys/articles/lush99.htm.

68. Roth, Kenneth: 'Despots masquerading as democrats.' Human Rights Watch 2008. http://hrw.org/wr2k8/introduction/index.htm.

69. Kuran, Timur: 'The vulnerability of the Arab state.' *The Independent Review*, vol. III, no. 1, Summer 1998, pp. 111–123. http://www.independent.org/pdf/tir/tir_03_1_kuran.pdf.

70. Resende, Madalena and Kraetzschmar, Hendrik: 'Parties of power as roadblocks to democracy – The cases of Ukraine and Egypt.' Centre for European Policy Studies, Policy Brief no. 81/August 2005. http://aei.pitt.edu/6624/01/1258_81.pdf

71. Kuran, *op. cit.*

Chapter 4

1. Author's interview in Cairo, 28 June 2008. According to the traditions of the Prophet, a group of men from the 'Ukl tribe came to the Prophet and embraced Islam. The climate of Medina did not suit them and they became ill. The Prophet ordered them drink the milk and urine of camels – after which they recovered. A number of Muslim websites

make extraordinary claims about camel urine's medicinal properties. It is also said to be good for the hair. See, for example: 'Yemen: Camel urine trade flourishing.' AKI news agency, 11 July 2008. http://www. adnkronos.com/AKI/English/CultureAndMedia/?id=1.0.233033413 2

2. In Alexa's list of the most popular Arabic-language websites, the ranking of Islamway is 18, Islamweb 23 and IslamOnline 60. From a worldwide perspective, this is unusual. No religious sites appear among the top 100 websites in English or most other languages. http://www.alexa.com/site/ ds/top_sites?ts_mode=lang&lang=ar (retrieved 3 October 2008). Note: Alexa's system appears not to distinguish between Arabic and Farsi; the list includes at least two Farsi websites.

3. Author's interview, February 2008.

4. Author's interview, 26 April 2008.

5. Qur'an 13: 11, Al-Rad (Pickthall's translation). For repeated use of this verse see, for example, Amr Khaled's message 'To the Youth of the Muslim Omma'. http://english.islamway.com/bindex. php?section=article&id=263.

6. Author's interview in Cairo, 30 June 2008.

7. Author's interview in Paris, 1 February 2009.

8. The report accompanying the poll did not attempt to explain its findings in Lebanon and Egypt. However, Lebanon has a large Christian population and is also highly sectarian. Lebanese Muslims tend to identify themselves by sect rather than simply as "Muslim". Egypt also has a substantial number of Christians and popular awareness of its long pre-Islamic history dating back to the Pharoahs may mean that the sense of nationhood is stronger in Egypt than in other Arab states.

9. 'Arab Attitudes Towards Political and Social Issues, Foreign Policy and the Media.' Poll conducted jointly by the Anwar Sadat Chair for Peace and Development at the University of Maryland and Zogby International, May 2004.

10. Whitaker, Brian: 'Cartoons herald return of cinema to Saudi Arabia'. *Guardian,* 19 October 2005. The availability of videos was one factor mentioned by the chargé d'affaires in 2005 following the announcement of the first public film screening in the kingdom for 20 years – a one-hour programme of cartoons for an audience of women and children. http:// www.guardian.co.uk/world/2005/oct/19/film.saudiarabia.

11. Mutaqqun Online: 'Male hijab according to Qur'an and Sunnah'. http://www.muttaqun.com/malehijab.html.

12. Mutaqqun Online: 'Beard according to Qur'an and Sunnah'. http://muttaqun.com/beard.html.

13. IslamOnline: 'Men wearing silver chains'. http://www.islamonline.net/servlet/Satellite?pagename=IslamOnline-English-Ask_Scholar/FatwaE/FatwaE&cid=1119503548602.

14. 'Malaysian conf. probes how Muslim astronauts pray', *Turkish Weekly*, 20 April 2006. Reproduced at http://www.islamonline.net/English/News/2006-04/19/article04.shtml.

15. 'Malaysia issues guidebook for Muslims in space.' Reuters, 6 October 2007. http://www.reuters.com/article/scienceNews/idUSKLR33337720071006.

16. Worth, Robert: 'A haircut in Iraq can be the death of the barber', *New York Times*, 18 March 2005. http://www.nytimes.com/2005/03/18/international/middleeast/18barber.html?ex=1268802000&en=898f35fbd97d012c&ei=5090&partner=rssuserland.

17. 'Al-Qa'eda in Iraq alienated by cucumber laws and brutality.' *Daily Telegraph*, 11 Aug 2008. http://www.telegraph.co.uk/news/worldnews/middleeast/iraq/2538545/Al-Qaeda-in-Iraq-alienated-by-cucumber-laws-and-brutality.html. Impositions such as this were said to be a major reason for al-Qa'ida's declining support among Iraqi Sunnis.

18. Soage, Ana Belén: 'Faraj Fawda, or the cost of freedom of expression'. *Middle East Review of International Affairs*, vol. 11, no. 2, June 2007. http://meria.idc.ac.il/journal/2007/issue2/jv11no2a3.html.

19. Johnson-Davies, Denys: 'Naguib Mahfouz' (obituary). *Guardian*, 31 August 2006. http://www.guardian.co.uk/obituaries/story/0,,1861412,00.html.

20. Diab, Khaled: 'A banquet for conservative', *Diabolic Digest,* June 2000. http://www.diabolicdigest.net/Egypt/banquet_conservatives.htm.

21. 'From confiscation to charges of apostasy'. Center for Human Rights Legal Aid, September 1996. http://www.wluml.org/english/pubsfulltxt.shtml?cmd%5B87%5D=i-87-2619.

22. Weaver, Mary Anne: 'Revolution by stealth'. *New Yorker* magazine, 8 June 1998. Reproduced at http://www.dhushara.com/book/zulu/islamp/egy.htm.

23. Abou El-Magd, Nadia: 'When the professor can't teach'. *Al-Ahram Weekly*,

issue 496, 15-21 June 2000. http://weekly.ahram.org.eg/2000/486/eg6.htm.

24. Ibid.

25. Author's interview in Leiden, 25 April 2008.

26. See: Abootalebi, Ali: 'Islam, Islamists, and democracy.' *MERIA Journal*, vol. 3, no. 1, March 1999. http://meria.biu.ac.il/journal/1999/issue1/jv3n1a2.html.

27. Mabruk, Muhammad Ibrahim: *al-'Almaniyyun* (The Secularists). Cairo, 1990, pp. 148–9. Cited by Najjar, Fauzi: 'The debate on Islam and secularism in Egypt.' *Arab Studies Quarterly,* Spring 1996.

28. For the discussion of Arab constitutions in this chapter the following sources are used: Algeria (1996): http://www.servat.unibe.ch/law/icl/ag00000_.html; Bahrain (2002): http://www.servat.unibe.ch/law/icl/ba00000_.html; Comoros (2001): http://www.chr.up.ac.za/hr_docs/constitutions/docs/ComorosC%20(english%20summary)(rev).doc; Djibouti (1992): http://www.pogar.org/publications/other/constitutions/dj-constitution-92-e.pdf; Egypt (1980, with amendments): http://www.misr.gov.eg/english/laws/constitution/default.aspx; Iraq (Interim Constitution, 2004): http://www.washingtonpost.com/wp-dyn/content/article/2005/10/12/AR2005101201450.html; Jordan (1952): http://www.kinghussein.gov.jo/constitution_jo.html; Kuwait (1962): http://www.servat.unibe.ch/law/icl/ku00000_.html; Lebanon (1990): http://www.servat.unibe.ch/law/icl/le00000_.html; Libya (1992): http://www.servat.unibe.ch/law/icl/ly00000_.html; Mauritania (1991): http://www.servat.unibe.ch/law/icl/mr00000_.html; Morocco (1996): http://www.al-bab.com/maroc/gov/con96.htm; Oman (1996): http://www.servat.unibe.ch/law/icl/mu00000_.html; Palestine (Draft Palestine Constitution, 2003): http://www.mideastweb.org/palconstitution.htm; Qatar (2003): http://www.servat.unibe.ch/law/icl/qa00000_.html; Saudi Arabia (Basic law, 1992): http://www.servat.unibe.ch/law/icl/sa00000_.html; Sudan (1998): http://www.sudan.net/government/constitution/english.html; Syria (1973): http://www.servat.unibe.ch/law/icl/sy00000_.html; Tunisia (1991): http://www.servat.unibe.ch/law/icl/ts00000_.html; United Arab Emirates (1996): http://www.helplinelaw.com/law/uae/constitution/constitution01.php; Yemen (1994): http://www.al-bab.com/yemen/gov/con94.htm. Somalia is omitted because at the time of writing it had no effective government.

29. Algeria: Article 178; Morocco: Article 106.

30. Article 5.

31. Preamble to the Fundamental Law (2001).

32. Syrian constitution, Article 35.

33. Djibouti: Articles 1 and 3; UAE: Article 25.

34. *CIA World Factbook*. https://www.cia.gov/library/publications/the-world-factbook/geos/su.html#People.

35. Article 16.

36. Yemen: Article 3; Egypt: Article 2; Oman: Article 2.

37. Bahrain: Article 2; Kuwait: Article 2; Syria: Article 3; Qatar: Article 1.

38. Article 2.

39. Syria is one of the more secular Arab states, though its regime is dominated by adherents of the minority Alawi sect. According to Joshua Landis, "In 1973 Hafiz al-Asad was forced to give Islam an integral place in the new Syrian constitution. Pressured by widespread popular protests, the government included the controversial article that the president of the republic had to be a Muslim. Hafiz al-Asad conceded to the majority demand ... but he did so while pursuing an aggressive policy of redefining the Alawites legally and socially as Muslims. In essence, Alawis have sacrificed their religion, or perhaps more correctly, they have converted to mainstream Islam as the price for political power and full inclusion in the nation." Landis, *op. cit.*

40. The relevant articles in the constitutions are: Algeria 71(1); Mauritania 23; Syria 3(1); Tunisia 38; Yemen 106.

41. Jordan (article 28e): "No person shall ascend the Throne unless he is a Muslim, mentally sound and born by a legitimate wife and of Muslim parents." Kuwait (article 4.5): "The Heir Apparent shall have attained his majority, be of sound mind, and a legitimate son of Muslim parents." Oman (article 5): "It is a condition that the male who is chosen to rule should be an adult Muslim of sound mind and a legitimate son of Omani Muslim parents." Qatar (article 9): "The Heir Apparent must be a Muslim of a Qatari Muslim mother."

42. Whitaker, Brian: 'War on witches.' *Comment Is Free,* 5 November 2007. http://www.guardian.co.uk/commentisfree/2007/nov/05/waronwitches.

43. 'Saudi executes Egyptian for practising "witchcraft".' Reuters, 2 November 2007. http://www.westernresistance.com/blog/archives/003981.html.

44. 'Saudi unrest blamed on "sorcerer".' BBC website, 25 April 2000. http://

news.bbc.co.uk/1/hi/world/middle_east/725597.stm. For a more detailed discussion of the treatment of Ismailis of Najran and the accusations of 'sorcery' see: *The Ismailis of Najran*. Human Rights Watch, September 2008. http://www.hrw.org/en/node/75197/section/1.

45. For the text of the Act see: http://www.hulford.co.uk/act1736.html.

46. 'Virtue Commission's special wing fights charlatans.' *Arab News*, 27 October 2007. http://www.arabnews.com/?page=1&section=0&article=10288 9&d=27&m=10&y=2007&pix=kingdom.jpg&category=Kingdom.

47. Qusti, Raid: 'Virtue Commission Members Are Not Above Law: Al-Ghaith.' *Arab News*, 25 March 2007. http://www.arabnews.com/?page =1&section=0&article=94140&d=25&m=3&y=2007.

48. 'Black magic: Rulings & remedy.' *IslamOnline,* fatwa bank. http:// www.islamonline.net/servlet/Satellite?pagename=IslamOnline-English-Ask_Scholar/FatwaE/FatwaE&cid=1119503543818

49. Najjar, *op. cit.*

50. Tamimi, Azzam: 'Democracy in Islamic political thought.' Paper based on a lecture given at the Belfast Mosque in October 1997. Tamimi is a Palestinian-born academic with close connections to Hamas. http:// www.iol.ie/~afifi/Articles/democracy.htm.

51. Esposito, John (ed.): *The Oxford History of Islam*. Oxford: Oxford University Press, 1999, p. 300.

52. Discussing the etymology of *'almaniyya*, Najjar says: "According to the Arabic Language Academy in Cairo, the term is derived from 'alam (world), and not from 'ilm (science), as some think, thus giving the wrong impression that science is opposed to religion. Some writers suggest the Arabic term 'alamaniyya in order to avoid the confusion. Others prefer dunyawiyya (worldly) in contrast to dini (religious)." Najjar, *op. cit.*

53. Najjar, *op. cit.*

54. De Ley, Herman: 'Humanists and Muslims in Belgian secular society.' Centrum Voor Islam in Europa (CIE) 2000. De Ley appears to be referring mainly to North Africa or perhaps those areas that came under French influence. http://www.flwi.ugent.be/cie/CIE/deley10.htm.

55. Binder, Leonard: *Islamic Liberalism: A Critique of Development Ideologies*. Chicago: University of Chicago Press, 1988. p. 129. For a detailed discussion of 'Abd al-Raziq's book, see Chapter 4: 'Ali Abd al-Raziq and Islamic liberalism: The rejected alternative'.

56. Binder, *op. cit.* p. 131.

57. Binder, *op. cit.* p. 132.

58. Binder, *op. cit.* p. 129.

59. Tamimi, *op. cit.*

60. Binder, *op. cit.* p. 131.

61. The Madina document, often described as a constitution, provided a means for coexistence among the various tribes, including Muslims, Christians, Jews and pagans. The original document has not survived but several versions exist from early Muslim sources. See: http://en.wikisource.org/wiki/Medina_Charter.

62. Author's interview in Leiden, 25 April, 2008.

63. An-Na'im, Abdullahi Ahmed: *Islam and the Secular State – Negotiating the Future of Shari'a.* Cambridge, Mass: Harvard University Press, 2008. pp. 53–54.

64. An-Na'im, *op. cit.* p. 53.

65. Author's interview in Leiden, 25 April 2008.

66. Qur'an 9:29. Yusuf Ali's translation.

67. Dawoud, Khaled. *Al-Ahram Weekly*, 17–23 April 2007. Not available in the paper's online archive but cited by several online sources, including: https://www.strategicnetwork.org/index.php?loc=kb&view=v&id=777&fto=594&.

68. Morqos, Samir: 'Bridging the divide.' *Al-Ahram Weekly*, 10–16 November 2005. http://weekly.ahram.org.eg/2005/768/op11.htm.

69. An article in the *New York Times* magazine describes some of the Brotherhood's other compromises. Among other things, it quotes Magdy Ashour, a member of the Brotherhood's parliamentary bloc, as apparently accepting the sale of alcohol in hotels on the grounds that "there is a concept in shari'a that if you commit the sin in private it's different from committing it in public". See: Traub, James 'Islamic Democrats?' *New York Times* magazine, 29 April 2007. http://www.nytimes.com/2007/04/29/magazine/29Brotherhood.t.html?_r=3&pagewanted=all.

70. An-Na'im, *op. cit.* p. 4.

71. An-Na'im, *op. cit.* p. 1.

72. Packer, George: 'The moderate martyr.' *New Yorker*, 11 September 2006. http://www.newyorker.com/archive/2006/09/11/060911fa_fact1. See also: Tangenes, Gisle: 'The Islamic Gandhi.' Bitsofnews.com, 11 September 2006. http://www.bitsofnews.com/content/view/3856/42.

73. An-Na'im, *op. cit.* p. 4.

74. An-Na'im, *op. cit.* p. 10.

75. An-Na'im, *op. cit.* pp. 29–30.

76.   An-Na'im, *op. cit.* pp. 38.

Chapter 5

1.   http://www.youtube.com/user/TarSniper.

2.   http://www.youtube.com/watch?v=Z8RgWRmRtUc. The incident can be seen approximately 2min 9sec into the clip.

3.   'Morocco's "video sniper" sparks a new trend.' menassat.com, 12 November 2007. http://www.menassat.com/?q=en/news-articles/2107-moroccos-video-sniper-sparks-new-trend. What happened to the Targuist Sniper is unclear. He stopped publishing videos and there were rumours that he had been arrested. According to *TelQuel*, several young men, including the Sniper, were interrogated by the police who said they were treating them as witnesses. The MAP news agency quoted an official source saying that "the authors of the videos denouncing acts of corruption have been identified and have been invited to make a statement. They will appear as witnesses in the judicial procedure."

4.   Loum44 (in French): "Vous vous acharner sur des petit gendarmes qui prennent des 20 dh car la vie est dure ce qu'il faudrait c'est des sniper pour les gros voleur qui prennent le gros pactole sans se faire sniper voila ce qu'il faut." http://gratis.download-de-videos.com/video/pzieMrb4Smc/gendarmes.html.

5.   Author's interview in Cairo, 30 June 2008.

6.   Confidential letter to David Owen from the British embassy in Jeddah, ECO/121/3(E), 3 May 1977. http://image.guardian.co.uk/sys-files/Guardian/documents/2007/05/28/ch04doc04.pdf.

7.   Leigh, David and Evans, Rob: 'The unlovable Saudis.' *Guardian,* 8 June 2007. http://www.guardian.co.uk/world/2007/jun/08/bae46

8.   AMX 30. http://en.wikipedia.org/wiki/AMX_30#History.

9.   Leigh, David and Evans, Rob 'Ali Reza.' *Guardian,* 8 June 2007. http://www.guardian.co.uk/world/2007/jun/08/bae19.

10.   Letter from Antony Acland, Arabian Department, to Sam Falle, British Ambassador, 11 June 1970. British National Archives, WO S2/20748. http://image.guardian.co.uk/sys-files/Guardian/documents/2007/05/29/ch04doc18.pdf.

11.   'Briefing for the prime minister's meeting with Prince Sultan'. Ministry of Defence, 25 September 1985. http://image.guardian.co.uk/sys-files/Politics/documents/2006/10/27/PJ5_39BriefforThatcherSept85.pdf.

12. Leigh, David and Evans, Rob: 'BAE accused of secretly paying £1bn to Saudi prince.' *Guardian*, 7 June 2007. http://www.guardian.co.uk/world/2007/jun/07/bae1.

13. Robinson, Michael: 'BBC lifts the lid on secret BAE slush fund.' BBC website, 5 October 2004. http://news.bbc.co.uk/1/hi/business/3712770.stm. Leigh, David and Evans, Rob: 'BAE chief linked to slush fund.' *Guardian*, 5 October 2004. http://www.guardian.co.uk/uk/2004/oct/05/saudiarabia.armstrade.

14. Leigh, David and Evans, Rob: 'BAE accused of secretly paying £1bn to Saudi prince.'

15. 'Saudi prince "received arms cash".' BBC website, 7 June 2007. http://news.bbc.co.uk/1/hi/business/6728773.stm.

16. AHDR 2004. p. 137.

17. The survey was published in March 2000 by a non-governmental organisation, Kulluna Massoul ("We Are All Responsible"). See: Blanford, *op. cit.* p. 60.

18. Corruption Perceptions Index 2008. The Palestinian territories were not included. http://www.transparency.org/policy_research/surveys_indices/cpi/2008.

19. Transparency International: 'Frequently Asked Questions'. http://www.transparency.org/policy_research/surveys_indices/cpi/2007/faq. For a critique of the index's methodology see Thompson, Theresa and Shah, Anwar: 'Transparency International's corruption perceptions index: whose perceptions are they anyway?' World Bank, March 2005. http://siteresources.worldbank.org/INTWBIGOVANTCOR/Resources/TransparencyInternationalCorruptionIndex.pdf.

20. For the data see: http://info.worldbank.org/governance/wgi2007/.

21. AHDR 2004. pp. 140–141. For detailed figures see p. 214.

22. Transparency International: 'Report on the Transparency International Global Corruption Barometer 2007'. Berlin, Transparency International 2007. p. 13. http://www.transparency.org/content/download/27256/410704/file/GCB_2007_report_en_02-12-2007.pdf.

23. 'Most important news.' Local news summary issued by the US embassy, Damascus, June 2006. http://damascus.usembassy.gov/uploads/images/zQPAAizRteCrjYg8Qlocnw/Monthly_Report_-_June_06.pdf.

24. Author's interview, 27 June 2008.

25. 'Egypt school exam cheats jailed.' BBC website, 9 September 2008. http://news.bbc.co.uk/1/hi/world/middle_east/7606062.stm.

26. Nkrumah, Gamal: 'Tricksters go academic.' *Al-Ahram Weekly*, 902, 19–25 June 2008. http://weekly.ahram.org.eg/2008/902/eg7.htm.

27. Frisch, Dieter: 'The effects of corruption on development.' *The Courier ACP-EU*, No 158, July–August 1996. pp. 68–70. http://www.euforic. org/courier/158e_fri.htm.

28. 'Honesty in financial dealings.' IslamOnline, 23 June 2004. http://www. islamonline.com/news/newsfull.php?newid=740.

29. Qur'an: 4.29. 'An-Nisa'. http://www.usc.edu/dept/MSA/qur'an/004. qmt.html.

30. Naomani, Moulana Manzoor: 'Honesty in monetary dealings.' Islam For Today website. http://www.islamfortoday.com/honesty.htm.

31. Ninteenth Islamic Conference of Foreign Ministers, Session of Peace, Interdependence and Development. Cairo, 31 July–5 August 1990. Cited by Pope, Jeremy: *TI Source Book 2000 – Confronting Corruption: The Elements of a National Integrity System.* Berlin: Transparency International (TI), 2000. p. 6. http://www.transparency.org/publications/ sourcebook.

32. AHDR 2004. p. 136.

33. Author's interview, 6 July 2008.

34. Author's interview, 26 April 2008.

35. Author's interview, 26 June 2008.

36. This is the definition now adopted by Transparency International (TI) and others. A more traditional definition is "the misuse of public power for private profit" but TI considers this too narrow. "Entrusted power" includes the private sector as well as public and "private benefit" extends beyond the person misusing the power to include his or her family and friends. See Pope, *op. cit.* pp. 1–2 and relevant footnotes.

37. Secretdubai: 'The wonders of wasta.' *Aqoul* blog, 9 July 2005. http:// www.aqoul.com/archives/2005/07/the_wonders_of.php. In Arabic it is referred to as "*fitamin waw*" – *waw* being the name for the letter W.

38. Author's interview, 14 May 2008.

39. A survey in Jordan by the Arab Archives Institute in 2000 found that 66 per cent said they would use *wasta* for "anyone who asks"; 27 per cent said they would use it for relatives and 17% for friends (question 22). Full results were published in Sakijha, Basem and Kilani, Sa'eda (eds): *Towards Transparency in Jordan.* Amman: Arab Archives Institute, 2000.

pp. 103–114. The authors state that the survey used a stratified random sample covering various parts of Jordan. Four hundred questionnaires were distributed and the results were based on replies from 360 of them.

40. *Al-Ra'i*, 17 February, 1992, cited by Cunningham, Robert and Sarayrah, Yasin: *Wasta: The Hidden Force in Middle Eastern Society*. Westport, Connecticut: Praeger, 1993. p. 7.

41. Kilani, Sa'eda and Sakijha, Basem: *Wasta, The Declared Secret: A Study on Nepotism and Favouritism in Jordan*. Amman: Arab Archives Institute, 2002. Electronic edition, page 21. http://www.alarcheef.com/studies/wasta.asp.

42. *Al-Ra'i*, 23 January, 2001. Cited by Kilani and Sakijha, *op. cit.*, p. 21.

43. The two studies were: Cunningham and Sarayrah, *op. cit.*, and Kilani and Sakijha.

44. *Al-Rai*, 16 January, 2001. Cited by Cited by Kilani and Sakijha *op. cit.*, p. 7.

45. Ibid., p. 10.

46. Ibid., pp. 10–11.

47. *Al-Hadath*, 6 August, 2001. Cited by Kilani and Sakijha, *op. cit.*, p. 52.

48. Kilani and Sakijha *op. cit.*, p. 11.

49. Sa'ad Eddin, Nadia: 'Cronyism, nepotism and wasta.' *Al-Aswaq*, 10 July 1999. Cited by Kilani and Sakijha, *op. cit.* p.42.

50. Kilani and Sakijha (2002), p. 41.

51. *Al-Arab al-Yawm*, 28 October, 2000. Cited by Kilani and Sakijha, *op. cit.*, p. 42.

52. Cunningham and Sarayrah, *op. cit.* p. 155.

53. Kilani and Sakijha, *op. cit.*, p. 12.

54. Sakijha and Kilani, *op. cit.*, pp. 104–114. The authors state that the survey used a stratified random sample covering various parts of Jordan. Four hundred questionnaires were distributed and the results were based on replies from 360 of them.

55. It is sometimes suggested that people may use *wasta* because dealing directly with a bureaucracy can be humiliating or involve a loss of face – important factors in Arab society. However, the small number of people citing "social standing" in this survey as their reason for using *wasta* implies that it is a relatively minor element.

56. *Ad-dustour*, June 20, 2000. Cited by Kilani and Sakijha, *op. cit.*, p. 27.

57. Author's interview, 5 July 2008.

58. For the list of signatories, see the website of the UN Office on Drugs and Crime. http://www.unodc.org/unodc/en/treaties/CAC/signatories. html. For the full text of the convention see http://www.unodc.org/ unodc/en/treaties/CAC/index.html#textofthe.

59. For a discussion of the convention's provisions, see Schultz, Jessica: *The United Nations Convention against Corruption – A Primer for Development Practitioners*. Bergen: Anti-Corruption Resource Centre, 2007. http:// www.u4.no/themes/uncac/introduction.cfm.

60. 'Former Syrian PM commits suicide.' BBC website, 22 May 2000. http:// news.bbc.co.uk/1/hi/world/middle_east/757960.stm.

61. *Al-Quds al-Arabi*, 12 May 2000. Cited by Gambill, Gary: 'Syria's night of long knives.' *Middle East Intelligence Bulletin*, vol. 2, no. 5, June 2000. http://www.meib.org/articles/0006_s1.htm. The article notes: "This was only the third time that a high-ranking member of the Ba'ath party had been publicly disgraced in such a fashion (the only precedents being Rifaat Assad in 1998 and former deputy prime minister Muhammad Haidar in 1999)."

62. The suicide explanation was greeted with scepticism in some quarters. In 2005 the Syrian interior minister allegedly shot himself in a similar manner. See: Whitaker, Brian: 'Syrian state inquiry finds minister killed himself.' *Guardian*, 14 October 2005. http://www.guardian.co.uk/world/2005/oct/14/syria.brianwhitaker.

63. 'Syrian official "arrested for corruption".' BBC website, 25 June 2000. http://news.bbc.co.uk/1/hi/world/middle_east/804759.stm.

64. 'Two former ministers convicted, imprisoned on corruption charges.' *Middle East Intelligence Bulletin,* vol. 3, no. 11, November 2001. http:// www.meib.org/articles/0112_sb.htm.

65. For a discussion of this case and other corruption allegations involving Airbus, see: 'Airbus's secret past.' *Economist,* 12 June 2003. http://www. transparency.org.au/documents/Economist12.6.pdf.

66. Gambill, *op. cit.*

67. 'Three Syrian MPs to be tried for stealing public funds.' *Middle East Intelligence Bulletin*, vol. 2, no 6, July 2000. http://www.meib.org/ articles/0007_sb.htm.

68. Corruption Perceptions Index 2008. http://www.transparency.org/ policy_research/surveys_indices/cpi/2008.

69. The other members of the GCC are Bahrain, Kuwait, Oman, Qatar, and

the United Arab Emirates. Corruption Perceptions Index 2007. http://
www.transparency.org/policy_research/surveys_indices/cpi/2007.

70. Glass, Amy: 'Saudi bribery cases surge, despite crackdown.' *Arabian
Business*, 20 February 2008. http://www.arabianbusiness.com/511762-
saudi-bribery-cases-surge-despite-govt-crackdown-?ln=en.

71. Abdul Ghafour, PK: 'Eight health officials accused of graft.' *Arab News*, 30
July 2008. http://www.arabnews.com/?page=1&section=0&article=112
252&d=30&m=7&y=2008&pix=kingdom.jpg&category=Kingdom.

72. Al-Hakeem, Mariam: 'Saudi health ministry exposes bribery
attempt.' *Gulf News*, 13 August, 2008. http://archive.gulfnews.com/
articles/08/08/14/10236963.html.

73. The transfers were recounted by Prof Aida Saif al-Dawla during an
interview in Cairo (30 June 2008). For details of the blood bags affair
see Maged, Ahmed: 'Contaminated blood bags implicate member of
parliament.' *Daily Star Egypt*, 10 January 2007. http://www.dailystaregypt.
com/article.aspx?ArticleID=4892 and Shalabi, Ahmed: 'Public
prosecutor files a notice of appeal against acquittal of Hani Surour in
the case of contaminated blood bags.' *Al-Masri al-Youm,* 11 June 2008.
http://www.almasry-alyoum.com/article2.aspx?ArticleID=108839. The
court proceedings were unresolved at the time of writing.

74. Author's interview, 1 July, 2008.

75. Author's interview, 5 July 2008.

Chapter 6

1. Kassem, Hisham: 'How the Cairo Times came to be published out of
Cyprus.' Chapter in World Bank: *The Right to Tell: The Role of Mass
Media in Economic Development.* Washington: World Bank Publications,
2003.

2. The English-language *Cairo Times* was published for seven years and
established a reputation for tackling stories that other papers were
reluctant to touch. In 2004, after its closure, Kassem established the
Arabic-language daily, *al-Masri al-Youm*.

3. Author's interview by telephone, 1 October 2008. The website of the
International Center for Not-for-Profit Law is http://www.icnl.org/.

4. In January 2003 Crown Prince Abdullah had held an unprecedented three-
hour audience with thirty-four Saudi critics of the regime. The group

was drawn from 103 signatories of a "national reform document" which called for "basic rights in justice, equality, and equal opportunity".

5. Whitaker, Brian: 'Saudi king agrees to human rights panel.' *Guardian,* 8 May 2003. http://www.guardian.co.uk/world/2003/may/08/saudiarabia. brianwhitaker.

6. 'Free detained advocates of reform.' Human Rights Watch press release, 8 February 2007. http://hrw.org/english/docs/2007/02/08/saudia15287. htm.

7. Malo, Hoshyar Salam: 'The future of civil society in Iraq.' *The International Journal of Not-for-Profit Law*, Vol. 10, Issue 4, August 2008. http://www. icnl.org/knowledge/ijnl/vol10iss4/special_1.htm.

8. 'What is civil society?' Centre for Civil Society, London School of Economics, 1 March 2004. http://www.lse.ac.uk/collections/CCS/ what_is_civil_society.htm. Some definitions also regard political parties as part of civil society. In the Middle East, tribes and clans are usually considered as "family" and therefore excluded.

9. http://www.annd.org/.

10. Abdel Samad, Ziad: 'Civil society in the Arab region: Its necessary role and the obstacles to fulfillment.' *The International Journal of Not-for-Profit Law*, vol. 9, issue 2, April 2007. http://www.icnl.org/knowledge/ijnl/ vol9iss2/special_1.htm.

11. 'Guidelines for Laws Affecting Civic Organizations.' New York: Open Society Institute, 2004, p9. www.soros.org/resources/articles_ publications/publications/lawguide_20040215/osi_lawguide.pdf.

12. Reasons for this weakness are discussed by Abdel Samad, *op. cit.*

13. Ibid.

14. http://www.presidency.gov.eg/html/the_first_lady.html.

15. http://en.wikipedia.org/wiki/Asma_Assad and http://www. syrianembassy.us/first_lady_of_syria.htm.

16. http://www.queenrania.jo/default.aspx.

17. http://www.mozahbintnasser.qa/output/page1.asp.

18. 'Country Reports on Human Rights Practices – 2007'. US State Department, Bureau of Democracy, Human Rights, and Labor. 11 March, 2008. http://www.state.gov/g/drl/rls/hrrpt/2007/. See section on UAE: 'Freedom of association'. Unregistered organisations do exist, depending partly on the nature of the organisations and how strictly the law is enforced. Kuwait, for example, has numerous unlicensed civic groups,

clubs, and unofficial NGOs. The law is also applied loosely in parts of the Emirates.

19. Abdel Samad, *op. cit.*

20. A number of laws relating to Arab NGOs and other not-for-profit organisations can be found on the ICNL website: http://www.icnl.org/knowledge/library/index.php.

21. 'Country Reports on Human Rights Practices – 2007.' See relevant country sections.

22. http://www.helem.net.

23. Author's interview with Georges Azzi of Helem in Beirut, 4 July 2008.

24. 'Country Reports on Human Rights Practices – 2007.' See section on Tunisia, 'Freedom of association': http://www.state.gov/g/drl/rls/hrrpt/2007/100607.htm.

25. Bahrain: Decree No. 21 (1989): Law of Associations, Social and Cultural Clubs, Special Committees Working in the Field of Youth and Sports and Private Institutions. Article 11. Oman: Sultani Decree No. 14/2000: Issuing the Civil Associations Law. Article 11

26. 'Country Reports on Human Rights Practices – 2007.' See section on Qatar: http://www.state.gov/g/drl/rls/hrrpt/2007/100604.htm.

27. *Law No 84/2002 on Non-Governmental Societies and Organisations.* Cairo: Middle East Library of Economic Services. www.egyptlaws.com.

28. *Egypt: Margins of Repression – State Limits on Nongovernmental Organisation Activism.* Human Rights Watch, July 2005. http://hrw.org/reports/2005/egypt0705/.

29. Hossam Bahgat, Egyptian Initiative for Personal Rights (EIPR). Quoted in *Egypt: Margins of Repression.*

30. Ibid.

31. Author's interview by telephone, 1 October 2008.

32. Law on Societies 2008. For English text see: http://www.icnl.org/knowledge/library/browseSearchResults.php?countrytosearch=Jordan&languagetosearch=English&subCategory=4.

33. *Shutting out the critics: restrictive laws used to repress civil society in Jordan.* Human Rights Watch, December 2007. http://hrw.org/reports/2007/jordan1207/.

34. 'The legal reality for non-profit companies – penned by Dr Mahmud 'Ababina.' *al-Ra'i* newspaper (in Arabic), 12 February 2006. http://www.alrai.com/pages.php?news_id=80412. Quoted in *Shutting out the critics.*

35. Whitaker, Brian: 'Cartoonist gives Syria a new line in freedom.' *Guardian*, 3 April 2001.

36. *World Press Freedom Review 2003*. International Press Institute. http://www.freemedia.at/cms/ipi/freedom_detail.html?country=/KW0001/KW0004/KW0105/&year=2003.

37. Country reports 2007: Qatar. Freedom House. http://www.freedomhouse.org/template.cfm?page=251&country=7256&year=2007.

38. The situation with terrestrial broadcasting is more complicated because the number of available frequencies is finite and a means has to be found to allocate them to broadcasters so that they do not cause interference with each other.

39. For more information see Harrison, Stanley: *Poor Men's Guardians: A Record of the Struggles for a Democratic Newspaper Press, 1793–1973.* London: Lawrence and Wishart, 1974. For a briefer summary see: 'Taxes on knowledge'. http://www.spartacus.schoolnet.co.uk/PRknowledge.htm.

40. Press and Publications Law 1990, Article 103. http://www.al-bab.com/yemen/gov/off4.htm.

41. Country reports 2007: Kuwait. Freedom House. http://www.freedomhouse.org/template.cfm?page=251&country=7209&year=2007.

42. 'Qui utilise l'avion de la présidence de la République Tunisienne?' Astrubal's blog (in French), 29 August 2007. http://astrubal.nawaat.org/2007/08/29/tunisie-avion-presidentiel/.

43. Gharbia, Sami ben: 'Ta'ira al-ra'asa al-Tunusiyya: man yast'amalha?' *Fikra* blog (in Arabic), 30 August 2007. http://www.kitab.nl/2007/08/30/tn-president-plane/

44. See: 'Caught in the net: Tunisia's first lady.' *Foreign Policy Magazine.* January–February 2008. p. 104. http://www.foreignpolicy.com/users/login.php?story_id=4090&URL=http://www.foreignpolicy.com/story/cms.php?story_id=4090.

45. Author's interview in Cairo, 27 June 2008.

46. Wael Abbas's blog is Misr Digital, also known in Arabic as *Al-Wa'i al-Masri* ('Egyptian Consciousness') http://misrdigital.blogspirit.com/. He is also on YouTube (http://www.youtube.com/user/waelabbas) and Twitter (http://twitter.com/waelabbas).

47. 'Sexual harassment laws weak, say activists.' Reuters, 9 November 2006.

http://www.alertnet.org/thenews/newsdesk/IRIN/24325c62bf2e603
7a957768ef3df9165.htm

48. Sandels, Alexandra: 'Policemen sentenced to three-year prison terms in high-profile torture case.' *Daily News* (Egypt), 5 November 2007. http://www.thedailynewsegypt.com/article.aspx?ArticleID=10130.

49. Author's interview in Cairo, 29 June 2008. The Arabic Network for Human Rights Information's website is http://anhri.net/.

50. AHDR 2004. p. 131.

51. Registration of Political Parties Act 1998. http://www.opsi.gov.uk/acts/acts1998/ukpga_19980048_en_1.

52. Law No. 66 (1991) Governing Parties and Political Organisations. Article 8. http://www.al-bab.com/yemen/gov/off3.htm.

53. Ibid.

54. Law 177/2005, article 4.2-3.

55. 'Monopolising power: Egypt's political parties law.' Human Rights Watch, January 2007. http://hrw.org/backgrounder/mena/egypt0107/index.htm.

56. Ibid.

57. Ayubi, Nazih: *Over-stating the Arab State: Politics and Society in the Middle East*. London: IB Tauris, 1995. p. 447.

58. Ayubi, *op. cit*. p. 450.

59. See: 'Anger at Egyptian ferry verdict.' BBC website, 27 July 2008. http://news.bbc.co.uk/1/hi/world/middle_east/7527652.stm and Nasr, Octavia: 'Grief and outrage in Egypt.' CNN website, 31 July 2008. http://edition.cnn.com/CNNI/Programs/middle.east/blog/2008/07/grief-and-outrage-in-egypt.html.

60. Ayubi, *op. cit*. p. 449.

61. Ayubi also referred to a third category: the "fierce" state which "is so opposed to society that it can only deal with it via coercion and raw force". Iraq under Saddam Hussein would rank mostly as a "fierce" state, and probably Syria under the late Hafiz al-Asad too.

62. MacFarquhar, Neil: 'Cairo Journal: Egyptians tighten a seat-belt law till it hurts.' *New York Times,* 26 January 2001. http://query.nytimes.com/gst/fullpage.html?res=9A00E2DF143FF935A15752C0A9679C8B63.

63. Author's interview in Cairo, 1 July 2008.

64. Harding, Luke: 'Iraq extends al-Jazeera ban and raids offices.' *Guardian*, 6 September 2004. http://www.guardian.co.uk/media/2004/sep/06/iraq.broadcasting.

65. Author's interview with Jihad Ballout in Doha, January 2003.

66. I observed one of the debates from the control room during a visit to al-Jazeera in January 2003.

67. Author's interview with Faisal al-Qassem in Doha, January 2003.

68. Whitaker, Brian: 'Old guard faces crisis as heat turns on Syria.' *Guardian,* 18 April 2003. http://www.guardian.co.uk/Archive/Article/0,4273,4650792,00.html.

69. Whitaker, Brian: 'Weakening grip.' *Guardian Unlimited,* 1 July 2005. http://www.guardian.co.uk/world/2005/jul/01/worlddispatch.egypt.

70. 'This House believes that the Arab media need no lessons in journalism from the West.' Doha Debate, 31 January 2006. http://www.thedohadebates.com/debates/debate.asp?d=21&s=2&mode=transcript#109.

71. Karam, Imad: 'Satellite television: a breathing space for Arab youth?' In Sakr, Naomi (ed.): *Arab Media and Political Renewal.* London: IB Tauris, 2007. p. 83.

72. Ibid.

73. 'Internet in 2007.' Reporters Without Borders. http://www.rsf.org/article.php3?id_article=20844.

74. 'Internet usage statistics.' Internet World Stats, retrieved 30 October 2008. http://www.internetworldstats.com/stats.htm.

75. *The internet in the Arab world: a new space of repression?* Cairo: Arabic Network for Human Rights Information, 2004. http://www.anhri.net/en/reports/net2004/index.shtml.

76. Ibid.

77. Ibid.

78. 'Saudi internet rules, 2001.' Council of ministers resolution, 12 February 2001. http://www.al-bab.com/media/docs/saudi.htm.

79. http://www.isu.net.sa/.

80. Lee, Jennifer: 'Companies compete to provide internet veil for the Saudis.' *New York Times,* 19 November 2001. http://query.nytimes.com/gst/fullpage.html?res=990DEFDC103BF93AA25752C1A9679C8B63.

81. 'Introduction to content filtering.' Internet Services Unit website. http://www.isu.net.sa/saudi-internet/contenet-filtring/filtring.htm. Retrieved 2 November 2008.

82. Qur'an 12: 33-34, Al-Rad (Pickthall's translation).

83. Lee, *op. cit.*

84. Miller, Robin: 'Meet Saudi Arabia's most famous computer expert.' Linux. com, 14 January 2004. http://www.linux.com/articles/33695.

85. *Internet Filtering in Saudi Arabia in 2004.* OpenNet Initiative, 2004. http://opennet.net/studies/saudi.

86. Ibid.

87. Ba-Isa, Molouk: 'No common sense in censorship bid.' *Arab News,* 12 August 2008. http://www.arabnews.com/?page=11&section=0&article=112734&d=12&m=8&y=2008.

88. *Internet Filtering in Saudi Arabia in 2004.*

89. 'The old User Survey results.' http://www.isu.net.sa/surveys-&-statistics/user-survey.htm.

90. 'User's survey: internet performance.' ISU website, undated. http://www.isu.net.sa/surveys-&-statistics/new-user-survey-results-4.htm. Retrieved 4 November 2008.

91. Qusti, Raid: 'Most of kingdom's internet users aim for the forbidden.' *Arab News,* 2 October 2005. http://www.arabnews.com/?page=1&section=0&article=71012&d=2&m=10&y=2005.

92. Miller, *op. cit.*

93. Balawi, Jameel al-: 'Hackers for hire.' *Arab News,* 3 November 2001. http://www.arabnews.com/?page=1&section=0&article=10277&d=3&m=11&y=2001

94. Various techniques for accessing forbidden websites are explained in 'Everyone's guide to by-passing internet censorship.' The Citizen Lab, University of Toronto. September 2007. http://www.nartv.org/mirror/circ_guide.pdf.

95. *Internet Filtering in Saudi Arabia in 2004.*

96. Noman, Helmi and Zarwan, Elijah: 'Middle East and North Africa.' OpenNet Initiative. http://opennet.net/research/regions/mena. Retrieved 2 November 2008. Elsewhere in the Middle East, Iran also filters broadly and Israel not at all.

97. Miller, *op. cit.*

98. Zittrain, Jonathan and Palfrey, John: 'Internet filtering: The politics and mechanisms of control,' in: Deibert Ronald, *et al* (eds): *Access Denied: The Practice and Policy of Global Internet Filtering.* Cambridge: MIT Press, 2008.

99. 'United Arab Emirates.' OpenNet Initiative, 9 May 2007. http://opennet.net/research/profiles/uae.

100. Author's interview in Cairo, 27 June 2008. Hamalawy's blog is at http://arabist.net/arabawy/.

101. http://tortureinegypt.net/.

102. 'Egypt blogger jailed for "insult".' BBC website, 22 February 2007. http://news.bbc.co.uk/1/hi/world/middle_east/6385849.stm. For more background see: 'Condemn the four-year sentence of Egyptian blogger Karim Amer.' Amnesty International, USA. http://www.amnestyusa.org/all-countries/egypt/background-condemn-the-four-year-sentence-of-egyptian-blogger-karim-amer/page.do?id=1041113.

103. 'Campaign for release of Saudi blogger.' BBC website, 2 January 2008. http://news.bbc.co.uk/1/hi/world/middle_east/7167936.stm; 'Saudi blogger released from jail.' BBC website, 27 April 2008. http://news.bbc.co.uk/1/hi/world/middle_east/7369768.stm.

104. Whitaker, Brian: 'Where comment is not free.' *Comment Is Free,* 9 June, 2006. http://www.guardian.co.uk/commentisfree/2006/jun/09/wherecommentisnotfree.

105. Williams, Daniel: 'Wary of dissent, Tunisia makes war on the web.' *Washington Post*, 22 December, 2005. http://www.washingtonpost.com/wp-dyn/content/article/2005/12/21/AR2005122101981_pf.html.

106. The group was called "6 April". http://www.facebook.com/group.php?gid=22033161578. Retrieved 1 December 2008.

107. 'What to make of the "general strike".' *Arabist* blog, 7 April 2008. http://arabist.net/archives/2008/04/07/what-to-make-of-the-general-strike/.

108. 'Egyptians ignore Facebook strike call.' Associated Press, 4 May 2008. http://www.iht.com/articles/ap/2008/05/04/news/Egypt-Strike.php.

Chapter 7

1. Author's interview, 12 May 2008.

2. Doha Debates: 'This House believes that Arab governments are not interested in genuine reform'. 13 October 2004. http://www.thedohadebates.com/debates/debate.asp?d=31&s=1&mode=transcript.

3. Author's interview in Beirut, 15 July 2008.

4. www.helem.net.

5. Author's interview in Beirut, 11 July 2008.

6. www.eipr.org.

7. Female judges in Egypt are now allowed to sit in family courts, but not criminal courts.

8. Author's interview in Cairo, 29 June 2008.

9. Jureidini, Ray: 'Sexuality and the servant: An exploitation of Arab images of the sexuality of domestic maids living in the household', in Khalaf S and Gagnon J: *Sexuality in the Arab World*. London: Saqi Books, 2006. pp. 130–151.

10. Ibid.

11. Author's interview in Beirut, 15 July 2008.

12. Universal Declaration of Human Rights. UN General Assembly resolution 217 A (III), 10 December 1948. http://www.un.org/Overview/rights. html. The Arab contribution to the document is often overlooked: one of the key figures involved in the drafting process was Charles Malik, a Lebanese Christian.

13. Constitution of Jordan, article 6 (i). http://www.kinghussein.gov.jo/ constitution_jo.html.

14. Constitution of Yemen (1994), article 24. http://www.al-bab.com/ yemen/gov/con94.htm.

15. Abdel Fattah, Moataz: *Democratic Values in the Muslim World*. Cairo: American University in Cairo Press, 2006. p. 46.

16. In the religious area, *fitna* is often applied to the succession struggle over the caliphate which led to the Sunni-Shi'i split.

17. 'Syrian forces clash with Kurds in north'. Reuters, 16 March 2004. See also: Whitaker, Brian: 'All together now'. Guardian Unlimited, 29 March 2004.

18. Lowe, Robert: *The Syrian Kurds: A People Discovered*. Chatham House briefing paper, MEP BP 06/01, January 2006. http://www.chathamhouse. org.uk/files/3297_bpsyriankurds.pdf.

19. Ibid.

20. A report by Amnesty International in 2005 said: "While the authorities do appear to tolerate the circulation of a small number of Kurdish-language publications and music, and, particularly in rural villages, the practice of some Kurdish cultural activities, promoters of and participants in Kurdish cultural and linguistic activities continue to risk harassment, detention, torture and ill-treatment, and imprisonment." The report included details of a number of arrests. See: *Syria: Kurds in the Syrian Arab Republic one year after the March 2004 events*. Amnesty International report MDE

24/002/2005, 10 March 2005. http://www.amnesty.org/en/library/info/MDE24/002/2005.

21. Ibid.

22. *The Silenced Kurds,* Human Rights Watch, vol. 8, no. 4, October 1996. www.hrw.org/reports/1996/Syria.htm.

23. Lowe, *op. cit.*

24. *The Silenced Kurds.*

25. Ibid.

26. Lowe, *op. cit.*

27. Another factor in this was the withdrawal of Syrian support for the PKK's agitation against the Turkish government. See: Brandon, James: 'The PKK and Syria's Kurds'. *Terrorism Monitor* (Jamestown Foundation, Washington), vol 5, issue 3, 2007.

28. 'Syria: Investigate Killing of Kurds'. Human Rights Watch press release, 24 March 2008. http://hrw.org/english/docs/2008/03/24/syria18332.htm.

29. AHDR 2004. p. 91.

30. The government maintains that it needs to know citizens' religious beliefs because Egypt has a faith-based system of family law where different rules apply for different religions. However, human rights organisations have pointed out that there is no need to record this information on ID cards because "a person's religion is maintained with other data in the central Civil Registry and the registry could be consulted, as the need arises, to determine or confirm the proper jurisdiction". See: *Prohibited Identities: State Interference with Religious Freedom.* Human Rights Watch/EIPR, November 2007, p. 7. http://www.hrw.org/en/reports/2007/11/11/prohibited-identities.

31. Report by Abdelfattah Amor, special rapporteur on freedom of religion or belief, to the Commission on Human Rights, 60th session, 16 January 2004. E/CN.4/2004/63, para. 42. http://daccessdds.un.org/doc/UNDOC/GEN/G04/103/43/PDF/G0410343.pdf?OpenElement.

32. 'The Baha'i Faith in Israel.' Baha'i International Community website. http://info.bahai.org/article-1-6-5-1.html.

33. *Prohibited Identities*, p. 18.

34. 'Court overrules Baha'i right to register.' *Egyptian Gazette*, 17 December 2006. http://www.mfa.gov.eg/MFA_Portal/en-GB/Press_and_Media/Economic_Press_Reviews/EP17122006.htm.

35. Hamalawy, Hossam: 'Bigotry and sectarianism par excellence.' *Arabawy*

blog, 16 December 2006. http://arabist.net/arabawy/2006/12/16/anti-bahaais-bigotry-and-sectarianism/.

36. 'Court denies Bahais legal recognition.' *Arabist* blog, 16 December 2006. http://arabist.net/archives/2006/12/16/court-denies-bahais-legal-recognition/.

37. 'Freedom of religion and belief in the first quarter of 2008.' Egyptian Initiative for Personal Rights, April 2008. http://www.eipr.org/en/reports/FRB_quarterly_rep_apr08_en/2904.htm.

38. *Prohibited Identities*, pp. 8–9.

39. Article 46.

40. *Prohibited Identities*, pp. 54–55.

41. *Prohibited Identities*, p. 76.

42. *Prohibited Identities*, p. 78. Yusif Fandi is a pseudonym.

Chapter 8

1. Tarabichi, Georges (Jurj Tarabishi): *Min al-nahdah ila al-riddah: Tamazzuqat al-thaqafah al-Arabiyah fi asr al-awlamah* ('From Arab Renaissance to Apostasy – Arab Culture and its Discontents in the Age of Globalisation'). Beirut: Dar al-Saqi, 2000. Translated extract: http://www.boell-meo.org/download_en/tarabichi.pdf.

2. World Bank: 'What is globalisation?' Briefing paper. PREM Economic Policy Group and Development Economics Group, April 2000. http://web.archive.org/web/20000824105740/www.worldbank.org/html/extdr/pb/globalisation/paper1.htm.

3. World Bank: 'Poverty in an Age of Globalisation'. October 2000. http://www1.worldbank.org/economicpolicy/globalisation/documents/povertyglobalisation.pdf.

4. *ibid.*

5. Tarabichi, *op. cit.* .

6. Za'za', Bassam: 'Arab speakers see threat to culture by globalisation'. *Gulf News*, 21 March 2002. http://www.globalpolicy.org/globaliz/cultural/2002/0321arab.htm.

7. Baroud, Ramzy: 'Arabs and globalisation'. *Al-Ahram Weekly,* Issue 722, 23–29 December 2004. http://weekly.ahram.org.eg/2004/722/op12.htm.

8. Balqaziz, Abdel-Ilah: 'Globalisation and cultural identity,' in *Globalisation*

and the Arabs, Center for Arab Unity Studies, Beirut 1998, p. 24. Quoted by Tarabichi, *op. cit.*

9. Safadi, Mutaa: 'The role of globalisation in the imperialism of the absolute,' *Al-Wifaq al-Arabi,* vol. 1, issue 2, August 1999, p. 24. Quoted by Tarabichi, *op. cit.*

10. Audah, Mohammad: 'Americanisation, not globalisation' at the seminar Anti-Globalisation, in a supplement of *Sutur*, issue 33, August 1999, p. 49. Quoted by Tarabichi, *op. cit.* Although serious questions have been raised about globalisation and the future of the Arabic language, Khawli's claim that the west is intent on destroying the language of "our holy book" seems particularly bizarre coming from an Egyptian. Any Egyptian who used classical Arabic in everyday conversation would be ridiculed.

11. BP Statistical Energy Review 2008. http://www.bp.com/productlanding. do?categoryId=6929&contentId=7044622.

12. For details of Arab investments in Britain see: Mayer, Andrew: 'Who is buying up Britain?' BBC website 31 July 2008. http://news.bbc.co.uk/1/hi/business/7534852.stm and Bill, Peter: 'The $300 billion Arabs are coming.' *Evening Standard* (London), 30 May 2008. http://www.thisislondon.co.uk/standard/article-23488244-details/The+$300+billion+Arabs+are+coming/article.do.

13. Laurance, Ben and Armitstead, Louise: 'Rising power of the sovereign funds.' *Sunday Times,* 28 October 2007. http://business.timesonline.co.uk/tol/business/industry_sectors/banking_and_finance/article2752048.ece.

14. Friedman, Thomas: 'Port controversy could widen racial chasm.' *New York Times* News Service, 24 February 2006. http://deseretnews.com/dn/view/0,1249,635187293,00.html.

15. 'Nuclear reactors top Dubai Ports' cargo list.' NewsMax.com, 23 February 2006. http://archive.newsmax.com/archives/ic/2006/2/23/230611.shtml.

16. King, Neil and Hitt, Gregg: 'Dubai Ports World sells US Assets.' *Wall Street Journal,* 12 December 2006. http://online.wsj.com/article/SB116584567567746444.html. For general background and links to additional sources see: http://en.wikipedia.org/wiki/Dubai_Ports_World_controversy.

17. 'How many Muslims are in the US and the rest of the world.' http://www.religioustolerance.org/isl_numb.htm.

18. Cohn, Barbra: 'Organic spices.' Conscious Choice website, May 1998.

http://www.consciouschoice.com/1995-98/cc113/organicspices1103.html.

19. In September 2005 a Danish newspaper, *Jyllands-Posten*, published a series of critical cartoons depicting the Prophet Muhammad and this caused a furore in a number of Muslim countries. Several years later shops in parts of the Middle East were still refusing to sell Danish products. See: 'Q&A: The Muhammad cartoons row.' BBC website, 7 February 2006. http://news.bbc.co.uk/1/hi/world/4677976.stm.

20. 'Excerpts: Bin Laden video.' BBC website 29 October 2004. http://news.bbc.co.uk/1/hi/world/middle_east/3966817.stm.

21. Ramkumar, KS and Adawi, Hassan: 'Three Die in IKEA Stampede.' *Arab News*, 2 September 2004. http://www.arabnews.com/?page=1&section=0&article=50867&d=2&m=9&y=2004.

22. Athanasiadis, Iason: 'From Asad to Asad: The transfer of power in contemporary Syria.' BA dissertation, St John's College, Oxford, 2000. Khaddam resigned from the vice-presidency in 2005 and went into exile in France. After making various public allegations against the Asad regime he was charged in his absence with treason.

23. Dawoud, Khaled and Whitaker, Brian: 'Sainsbury's on Egyptian boycott list.' *Guardian*, 7 December, 2000. http://www.guardian.co.uk/world/2000/dec/07/israel1.

24. 'Sainsbury's pulls out of Egypt'. BBC website, 9 April, 2001. http://news.bbc.co.uk/1/hi/business/1268099.stm.

25. Ghannoushi, Soumaya: 'Damsels in distress?' *Comment Is Free,* 18 December 2007. http://www.guardian.co.uk/commentisfree/2007/dec/18/damselsindistress.

26. Whitaker, Brian: 'Distorting desire.' al-bab.com, 2007. http://www.al-bab.com/arab/articles/text/massad.htm.

27. Whitaker, Brian: '"Gay party" guests face hormone treatment.' *Guardian*, 30 November 2005.http://www.guardian.co.uk/world/2005/nov/30/gayrights.brianwhitaker.

28. Sen, Amartya: 'How to judge globalism', in Lechner, Frank and Boli, John: *The Globalization Reader*. Oxford: Blackwell Publishing, 2003. p. 17.

29. Barber, Benjamin: 'Jihad vs McWorld.' *Atlantic Monthly,* March 1992. http://www.theatlantic.com/doc/199203/barber.

30. Ibid.

31. For a brief survey of international issues relating to the Euphrates see:

Whitaker, Brian: 'One river's journey through troubled times.' *Guardian*, 23 August 2003. http://www.guardian.co.uk/environment/2003/aug/23/water12.

32. Barber, *op. cit.*

33. 'Al-Mithaq' (The Charter). League of Arab States (in Arabic) http://www.arableagueonline.org/las/arabic/details_ar.jsp?art_id=133&level_id=114. This version omits the preamble quoted here. For an English translation, including the preamble, see: 'Pact of the League of Arab States,' 22 March, 1945. Avalon Project, Yale Law School. http://avalon.law.yale.edu/20th_century/arableag.asp.

34. In the official Arabic version: *wafqan li nudhumiha al-assasiya*.

35. Article VIII.

36. 'Guide to Egypt's election.' BBC, 2 September 2005. http://news.bbc.co.uk/1/hi/world/middle_east/4192438.stm.

37. 'European Parliament resolution of 17 January 2008 on the situation in Egypt' (P6_TA(2008)0023). http://www.europarl.europa.eu/sides/getDoc.do?type=TA&reference=P6-TA-2008-0023&language=EN.

38. Shahine, Gihan: 'Too true to be refuted.' *Al-Ahram Weekly*, NO. 881, 24–30 January 2008. http://weekly.ahram.org.eg/2008/881/eg3.htm.

39. Essam el-Din, Gamal: 'NDP up in arms.' *Al-Ahram Weekly*, no. 881, 24–30 January 2008. http://weekly.ahram.org.eg/2008/881/eg2.htm.

40. Shahine, *op. cit.*

41. European Commission External Relations: 'The EU-Egypt Association Agreements.' http://ec.europa.eu/external_relations/egypt/eu-egypt_agreement/index_en.htm.

42. 'Euro-Mediterranean agreement establishing an association between the European Communities and their member states, of the one part, and the Arab Republic of Egypt, of the other part.' http://ec.europa.eu/external_relations/egypt/aa/06_aaa_en.pdf.

43. Statement by the European Union. Second meeting of the EU-Egypt Association Council, Luxembourg, 13 June 2006. http://ec.europa.eu/external_relations/egypt/aa/eu_dec_0606.pdf.

44. Lijnzaad, Liesbeth: *Reservations to UN Human Rights Treaties: Ratify and Ruin?* Leiden: Martinus Nijhoff, 1995. p. 3.

45. For the full text of the International Convention on the Elimination of All Forms of Racial Discrimination see http://www2.ohchr.org/english/law/cerd.htm.

46. For details of the Yemeni reservations and the objections to them, see:

http://treaties.un.org/Pages/ViewDetails.aspx?src=TREATY&id=319 &chapter=4&lang=en. The reservations remained in place after North Yemen's unification with the south in 1990.

47. Concluding observations of the Committee on the Elimination of Racial Discrimination, 31 July–18 August 2006. http://www2.ohchr.org/english/ bodies/cerd/docs/CERD.C.YEM.CO.16-new.pdf.

48. Reservations to CEDAW. http://www.un.org/womenwatch/daw/cedaw/ reservations-country.htm.

49. Ibid.

50. Mayer, Ann Elizabeth: *Islam and Human Rights – Tradition and Politics.* Boulder, Colorado: Westview Press, 2007. p. 3.

51. Mayer, *op. cit.* pp. 53–54.

52. 'Jordan Islamists slam women's rights convention.' Agence France Presse report in *Khaleej Times,* 5 August 2007. http://www.khaleejtimes. com/DisplayArticleNew.asp?xfile=data/middleeast/2007/August/ middleeast_August54.xml&section=middleeast&col=. The American religious right fulminated in a similar fashion against US ratification of CEDAW. According to one Christian activist, the treaty served a "frivolous and morally corrupt agenda" and it would "legalise prostitution and open the door for the homosexual agenda". See: Goldberg, Michelle: 'Yes to the Bible, no to the treaty.' Salon.com, 22 June 2002. http://dir. salon.com/story/news/feature/2002/06/22/women/index.html.

53. For the puporses of prayer, *qibla* calculators work out the precise direction of Mecca from any point on the globe.

54. Zoepf, Katherine: 'Bestseller in Mideast: Barbie with a prayer mat.' *New York Times,* 22 Sepember 2005. http://www.nytimes.com/2005/09/22/ international/middleeast/22doll.html.

55. Three books by Gary Bunt examine the development of internet use by Muslims: *Virtually Islamic: Computer-Mediated Communication and Cyber Islamic environments*, Cardiff: University of Wales Press, 2000; *Islam in the Digital Age: E-jihad, Online Fatwas and Cyber Islamic Environments*, London & Michigan: Pluto Press, 2003; and *I-Muslims: Rewiring the House of Islam,* London: C Hurst & Co, 2009.

56. Tarabichi, *op. cit.*

57. 'About Us.' http://www.islamonline.net/English/AboutUs.shtml.

58. 'Speech of Shaikh Qaradawi.' http://www.islamonline.net/English/ Qaradawi/index.shtml.

59. Burke, Jason: 'A globalised import.' *Comment Is Free,* 30 November

2007. http://commentisfree.guardian.co.uk/jason_burke/2007/11/a_globalised_import.html.

60. Tarabichi, *op. cit.*

61. Tarabichi, *op. cit.*

62. 'Arabs, Arab-Americans and Globalisation.' Speech to the Association of Arab-American University Graduates' 30th annual convention at Georgetown University, 31 October–2 November, 1997. Reprinted in al-Hewar, Nov/Dec 1997 issue. http://www.alhewar.com/HGANasser.htm.

63. Cowen, Tyler: *Creative Destruction – How Globalisation is Changing the World's Cultures.* Princeton: Princeton University Press, 2002. p. 5.

Chapter 9

1. *Radical History Review* 2003 (86). Editors' introduction, p. 2. http://rhr.dukejournals.org/cgi/reprint/2003/86/1.pdf.

2. Greaves, Rose: 'Gordon, General Sir Thomas Edward.' *Encyclopaedia Iranica* (online edition). http://www.iranica.com/newsite/index.isc?Article=http://www.iranica.com/newsite/articles/v11f2/v11f2031.html.

3. For further information about the emergence of the term "Middle East", see: Roger Adelson, *London and The Invention of the Middle East: Money, Power and War, 1902–1922.* New Haven and London: Yale University Press. 1995.

4. Kassir, *op. cit.* p. 70.

5. Britain had a Middle Eastern command for its wartime North African operations, though it remained unsure about the Middle East's boundaries. Iran was included in 1942, while Eritrea was excluded in 1941, only to be returned to the fold a few months later.

6. When the Pentagon established its Near East and South Asia (NESA) centre in 2000, an official was asked which countries it would cover. "I believe we have 21 what we would call core countries," she replied. "And if you look at the geographic, sort of, piece of real estate that we have included as core countries here, we start from Morocco, we go along north Africa through the Levant and all the way across to Bangladesh, Sri Lanka and Nepal." DoD News Briefing – Alina Romanowski, DASD (Near Eastern & South Asian Affairs), 7 December 2000. http://www.defenselink.mil/transcripts/transcript.aspx?transcriptid=1875.

7. http://www.centcom.mil/en/countries/aor/. Retrieved 23 December 2008.

8   It seems to have originated with the publication of a book: *Allies Divided: Transatlantic Policies for the Greater Middle East* (edited by Robert Blackwill and Michael Sturmer and published in the US in 1997). This extended the Middle East into the Caspian basin and, as the title suggests, viewed the region in terms of US and European policies towards it.

9. State of the Union Address, 20 January 2004. http://georgewbush-whitehouse.archives.gov/news/releases/2004/01/20040120-7.html.

10. http://www.al-bab.com/arab/docs/international/gmep2004.htm.

11. For the origins of this conflict see: *Invisible Civilians: The Challenge of Humanitarian Access in Yemen's Forgotten War.* Human Rights Watch, 19 November 2008. Part III: Background. http://www.hrw.org/en/node/76086/section/5.

12. 'Young Arab opinion.' Poll by Zogby International, September 2006. http://www.businessfordiplomaticaction.org/learn/articles/bdafinalzogbyreport_10106.pdf.

13. Speech by the president marking the twentieth anniversary of the National Endowment for Democracy, 6 November 2003. http://georgewbush-whitehouse.archives.gov/news/releases/2003/11/20031106-2.html.

14. Ledeen, Michael: 'Creative destruction: How to wage a revolutionary war.' *National Review Online*, 20 September 2001.http://www.nationalreview.com/contributors/ledeen092001.shtml.

15. Mersereau Adam: 'Why is our military not being rebuilt? The case for a total war.' *National Review Online,* 24 May 2002. http://www.nationalreview.com/comment/comment-mersereau052402.asp.

16. Speech by the president marking the twentieth anniversary of the National Endowment for Democracy, 6 November 2003. http://georgewbush-whitehouse.archives.gov/news/releases/2003/11/20031106-2.html.

17. *ibid.*

18. Roth, Kenneth: 'Despots masquerading as democrats.' Human Rights Watch 2008. http://hrw.org/wr2k8/introduction/index.htm.

19. The claim that democracies do not fight each other was previously made by President Bill Clinton in 1996. See: Baden, John and Noonan, Douglas: 'Democracies don't fight – except over fish.' *Seattle Times,* 27 November 1996. http://www.free-eco.org/articleDisplay.php?id=242. For further discussion of the claim's accuracy, or otherwise, see: 'Do democracies fight each other?' BBC website, 17 November 2004. http://news.bbc.

co.uk/1/hi/magazine/4017305.stm. Wikipedia has further discussion of the question. http://en.wikipedia.org/wiki/List_of_possible_exceptions_to_the_democratic_peace_theory.

20. Whitaker, Brian and Younge, Gary: 'A scandal, but not a story.' *Guardian*, 10 May 2004. http://www.guardian.co.uk/media/2004/may/10/mondaymediasection2.

21. Roth, *op. cit.*

22. BBC website: 'Timeline: Algeria', 12 December 2007. http://news.bbc.co.uk/1/hi/world/middle_east/811140.stm.

23. Whitaker, Brian: 'Saudis tiptoe to democracy', *Middle East International*, 18 February 2005. http://www.al-bab.com/yemen/artic/mei108.htm. Because political parties were not allowed it is difficult to be specific about the results, though according to the consensus of opinion, Islamists had the upper hand.

24. General Elections Commission – Palestine: 'The final results of the second PLC elections', 29 January 2006. http://www.elections.ps/template.aspx?id=291.

25. Council of Europe: 'Elections for the Palestinian Legislative Council show the level of democratic development of Palestinian society.' Press release, 28 January 2006. https://wcd.coe.int/ViewDoc.jsp?Ref=PR047(2006)&Sector=secDC&Language=lanEnglish&Ver=original&BackColorInternet=F5CA75&BackColorIntranet=F5CA75&BackColorLogged=A9BACE.

26. Erlanger, Steven: 'US and Israelis are said to talk of Hamas ouster.' *New York Times*, 14 February 2006. http://www.nytimes.com/2006/02/14/international/middleeast/14mideast.html?_r=1&ei=5094&en=d28cff5caa1702fa&hp=&ex=1139979600&partner=homepage&pagewanted=print&oref=slogin.

27. Bradley, John: *Inside Egypt: The Land of the Pharoahs on the Brink of a Revolution.* New York: Palgrave Macmillan, 2008. p. 66.

28. Bradley, *op. cit.* p. 67.

29. Roth, *op. cit.*

30. Kaye, Dalia Dassa *et al:* 'More freedom, less terror? Liberalisation and political violence in the Arab world.' Santa Monica, CA: RAND Corporation, 2008. pp. 175–176. http://www.rand.org/pubs/monographs/2008/RAND_MG772.pdf.

31. MEPI Standing Program Announcement, 4 May 2004. http://standing-program-announcement-beginning.idilogic.aidpage.com/standing-

program-announcement-beginning/06-30-2004.htm. Retrieved 9 February 2009.

32. US State Department: 'Mission and goals'. http://mepi.state.gov/c10120. htm.

33. Sharp, Jeremy: 'The Middle East Partnership Initiative: An overview'. CRS Report for Congress, RS21457. February 8, 2005. http://www.italy. usembassy.gov/pdf/other/RS21457.pdf.

34. Carothers, Thomas: 'A better way to support Middle East reform'. Carnegie Endowment for International Peace, February 2005. http:// www.carnegieendowment.org/files/PB33.carothers.FINAL.web.pdf.

35. Yerkes, Sarah and Wittes, Tamara Cofman: 'The Middle East Partnership Initiative: Progress, problems, and prospects'. Brookings Institution, 2004. http://www.brookings.edu/papers/2004/1129middleeast_wittes.aspx.

36. USAID: 'Summary of FY 2007 Budget and Program Overview'. http:// www.usaid.gov/policy/budget/cbj2007/summary.html.

37. Levinson, Charles: '$50 billion later, taking stock of US aid to Egypt'. *Christian Science Monitor*, 12 April 2004. http://www.csmonitor. com/2004/0412/p07s01-wome.html.

38. Levinson, *op. cit.*

39. USAID Egypt: 'Program Overview', http://egypt.usaid.gov/Default. aspx?pageid=367.

40. Levinson, *op. cit.*

41. *Arabist* blog: 'A quick guide to publishing in Egypt', 4 June 2004. http://arabist.net/archives/2005/06/04/a-quick-guide-to-publishing-in-egypt/.

42. Levinson, *op. cit.*

43. Walker, Edward: 'American economic assistance program to Egypt'. Testimony before the House Committee on International Relations, 17 June, 2004. http://www.mideasti.org/transcript/american-economic-assistance-program-egypt.

44. For further discussion of this see Whitaker, Brian: 'Opposition attracts.' *Guardian* website, 10 March 2003. http://www.guardian.co.uk/Archive/ Article/0,4273,4622132,00.html.

45. For the 2008 scores see: http://www.freedomhouse.org/ template.cfm?page=410&year=2008. For methodology see: http://www.freedomhouse.org/template.cfm?page=351&ana_ page=341&year=2008.

46. 'The forms and impact of human trafficking.' US State Department, 12 June 2007. http://www.state.gov/g/tip/rls/tiprpt/2007/82809.htm.

47. *Trafficking in Persons Report, 2008.* US State Department, 4 June 2008. 'Tier Placements' section. http://www.state.gov/g/tip/rls/tiprpt/2008/105383.htm.

48. 'Qatar studies new law to tackle human trafficking.' *Gulf News*, 12 June 2007. http://archive.gulfnews.com/articles/07/06/12/10131776.html.

49. 'A secure Europe in a better world.' Strategy document approved by the European Council, Brussels, 12 December 2003. p. 8. http://www.consilium.europa.eu/uedocs/cmsUpload/78367.pdf.

50. 'Alliance of civilizations.' Report of the High-level Group. New York: United Nations, 13 November 2006. p. 17. http://www.unaoc.org/repository/implementation_plan.pdf.

51. Sen, Amartya: *Identity and Violence: The Illusion of Destiny.* London: Penguin Books, 2007. pp. 13–14.

52. See, for example, Tony Blair's statement to parliament on the London bombings, 11 July 2005. http://www.number10.gov.uk/Page7903.

53. Sen, *op. cit.* p. 77.

54. McLoughlin, Patrick: 'Swedish imam says Islam forbids female circumcision.' Reuters, 10 November 2003. http://www.islamawareness.net/Circumcision/swedish.html. Retrieved 9 December 2008.

55. Ali, Kecia: *Sexual Ethics and Islam.* Oxford: Oneworld Publications, 2006. p. 97.

56. Ali, *op. cit.* pp. 98–99.

57. Author's interview in Cairo, 29 June 2008.

58. Among those Bahgat cited was Abu Abdullah al-Qurtubi (1214–1273).

Bibliography

Abdel Fattah, Moataz: *Democratic Values in the Muslim World*. Cairo: American University in Cairo Press, 2006.

Adelson, Roger: *London and The Invention of the Middle East: Money, Power and War, 1902-1922*. New Haven and London: Yale University Press. 1995.

Ali, Kecia: *Sexual Ethics and Islam*. Oxford: Oneworld Publications. 2006.

Allen, Mark: *Arabs*. London and New York: Continuum, 2006.

An-Na'im, Abdullahi Ahmed: *Islam and the Secular State: Negotiating the Future of Shari'a*. Cambridge, Mass: Harvard University Press, 2008.

Ayubi, Nazih: *Over-stating the Arab State: Politics and Society in the Middle East*. London: IB Tauris, 1995.

Barakat: Halim: *The Arab World: Society, Culture and State*. Berkeley and Los Angeles: University of California Press, 1993.

Beblawi, Hazem: *The Rentier State in the Arab World*. London, Routledge 1987 and Berkeley: University of California Press, 1990.

Binder, Leonard: *Islamic Liberalism: A Critique of Development Ideologies*. Chicago: University of Chicago Press, 1988.

Blanford, Nicholas: *Killing Mr Lebanon*. London: I B Tauris, 2006.

Bradley, John: *Inside Egypt: The Land of the Pharoahs on the Brink of a Revolution*. New York: Palgrave Macmillan, 2008.

Brown, Carl and Itkowitz, Norman (eds): *Psychological Dimensions of Near Eastern Studies*. Princeton, NJ: Darwin Press, 1977.

Bunt, Gary: *I-Muslims: Rewiring the House of Islam*. London: C Hurst & Co, 2009.

Bunt, Gary: *Islam in the Digital Age: E-jihad, Online Fatwas and Cyber Islamic Environments*. London & Michigan: Pluto Press, 2003.

Bunt, Gary: *Virtually Islamic: Computer-Mediated Communication and Cyber Islamic environments*. Cardiff: University of Wales Press, 2000.

Camic C, Gorski PS and Trubek DM (eds): *Max Weber's Economy and Society: A Critical Companion*. Stanford, California: Stanford University Press, 2005.

Cowen, Tyler: *Creative Destruction – How Globalisation is Changing the World's Cultures*. Princeton: Princeton University Press, 2002.

Crime Prevention Research Centre: *The Effect of Islamic Legislation on Crime Prevention in Saudi Arabia*. Proceedings of the symposium held in Riyadh, 16-21 Shawal 1396 AH. Crime Prevention Research Centre, Ministry of Interior, 1980.

Cunningham, Robert and Sarayrah, Yasin: *Wasta: The Hidden Force in Middle Eastern Society*. Westport, Connecticut: Praeger, 1993.

Deibert, Ronald, *et al* (eds): *Access Denied: The Practice and Policy of Global Internet Filtering*. Cambridge: MIT Press, 2008.

Esposito, John (ed.): *The Oxford History of Islam*. Oxford: Oxford University Press, 1999, p300.

Ghoussoub, Mai and Sinclair-Webb, Emma: *Imagined Masculinities: Male Identity and Culture in the Modern Middle East*. Saqi Books, London, 2000.

Herb, Michael: *All in the Family: Absolutism, Revolution, and Democracy in the Middle Eastern Monarchies*. Albany: State University of New York, 1999.

Hopkins, Nicholas (ed.): *The New Arab Family*. Cairo Papers in Social Science 24 (2001). Cairo: American University in Cairo Press, 2003.

Iqbal, Muzaffar: *Science and Islam*. Westport, CT: Greenwood Publishing, 2007.

Jabar, Faleh and Dawod, Hosham (eds): *Tribes and Power: Nationalism and Ethnicity in the Middle East*. London: Saqi Books, 2003.

Kassir, Samir: *Being Arab*. London: Verso, 2006.

Khalaf S and Gagnon J: *Sexuality in the Arab World*. London: Saqi Books, 2006.

Khatib, Jamal: *'Ala Madhbah al-Hukm*. Amman: Dar Majdalawi, 2008.

Khatib, Lina: *Filming the Modern Middle East: Politics in the Cinemas of Hollywood and the Arab World*. London/New York: I B Tauris 2006.

Kilani, Sa'eda and Sakijha, Basem: *Wasta, The Declared Secret: A Study on Nepotism and Favouritism in Jordan*. Amman: Arab Archives Institute, 2002.

Lechner, Frank and Boli, John: *The Globalization Reader*. Oxford: Blackwell Publishing, 2003.

Levy, Frank, and Murnane, Richard: *The New Division of Labor: How Computers Are Creating the Next Job Market*. Princeton: Princeton University Press and the Russell Sage Foundation, 2004.

Lijnzaad, Liesbeth: *Reservations to UN Human Rights Treaties: Ratify and Ruin?* Leiden: Martinus Nijhoff, 1995.

Lynch, Marc: *Voices of the New Arab Public: Iraq, al-Jazeera, and Middle East Politics Today.* New York: Columbia University Press, 2006.

Mayer, Ann Elizabeth: *Islam and Human Rights – Tradition and Politics.* Boulder, Colorado: Westview Press, 2007.

Migdal Joel S: *Strong States and Weak Societies.* New Jersey: Princeton University Press, 1988.

Parker R, Petchesky R and Sember R (eds): *SexPolitics – Reports from the Front Lines* (e-book). Sexuality Policy Watch, 2007.

Pax, Salam: *The Baghdad Blog.* London: Atlantic Books, 2003. Also published in the US as *The Clandestine Diary of an Ordinary Iraqi.* New York: Grove Press, 2003.

Pope, Jeremy: *TI Source Book 2000 – Confronting Corruption: The Elements of a National Integrity System.* Berlin: Transparency International (TI), 2000.

Sakr, Naomi (ed.): *Arab Media and Political Renewal.* London: IB Tauris, 2007.

Sen, Amartya: *Identity and Violence: The Illusion of Destiny.* London: Penguin Books, 2007.

Sharabi, Hisham: *Neopatriarchy: a Theory of Distorted Change in Arab Society.* Oxford: Oxford University Press, 1988.

Tarabichi, Georges (Jurj Tarabishi): *Min al-nahdah ila al-riddah: Tamazzuqat al-thaqafah al-Arabiyah fi asr al-awlamah* ('From Arab Renaissance to Apostasy – Arab Culture and its Discontents in the Age of Globalisation'). Beirut: Dar al-Saqi, 2000.

Vandewalle, Dirk: *Libya Since Independence: Oil and State Building.* Ithaca/London: Cornell University Press, 1998.

Waters, Malcolm: *Globalization.* London/New York: Routledge, 1995.

Whitaker, Brian: *Unspeakable Love: Gay and Lesbian Life in the Middle East.* London: Saqi Books, 2006.

Index